The
F
Word

Jesse Sheidlower is a senior editor in the Random House Reference Department, where he is chiefly responsible for slang and new words. He has written about language for Harper's, The Atlantic Monthly, Esquire, and other publications, and is a sought-after authority for journalists around the country. He is also a regular commentator on language for National Public Radio. Educated in English linguistics at the University of Chicago and Trinity College, Cambridge University, Mr Sheidlower lives in Manhattan with his wife, his dog, his two razor-clawed cats, and a f#@k of a lot of books.

The

F

Word

Second Edition

Edited by Jesse Sheidlower
Illustrations by Ross MacDonald

faber and faber

First published in the USA by Random House, Inc. in 1995
First published in this Second Edition in the USA by
Random House, Inc. in 1999
First published in the UK in this Second Edition in 1999
by Faber and Faber Limited
3 Queen Square London WC1N 3AU

Printed in England by Mackays of Chatham plc,
Chatham, Kent

This work is based on the *Random House Historical
Dictionary of American Slang*.

A CIP record for this book
is available from the British Library

ISBN 0–571–19730–2

2 4 6 8 10 9 7 5 3 1

'Tis needful that the most immodest word
Be looked upon and learned.

—Shakespeare, *Henry IV, Part II*

Contents

Acknowledgments

For help with citations, Bernard W. Kane was indefatigable in providing buckets of useful suggestions; John A. Simpson generously sent me several citations from the files of the *Oxford English Dictionary*; Fred Shapiro's wizardry with database searches yielded a large number of updatings and important additions to the text; James Lambert, editor of the *Macquarie Book of Slang*, was kind enough to provide extensive citations from Australia and New Zealand in addition to many quotations from often obscure British and American sources; James Rader sent early examples of several terms I had difficulty tracking down.

Anatoly Liberman was kind enough to share his detailed researches into the etymology and bibliography of *fuck.*

H. Bosley Woolf generously sent me a copy of his privately printed pamphlet *The G I's Favorite Four Letter Word,* the earliest published work devoted solely to our word.

For help with certain terms, and for specific editorial advice, I am grateful to Daniel Menaker, Jennifer Dowling, Judy Kaplan, Sarah Burnes, Jeremy Kareken, Charles Levine, Sam Pratt, Alison Biggert, Arnold Zwicky, Tom Dalzell, Barry Popik, William Monahan, Edward Hutchinson, Stephen Berg, Aaron Barnhart, Michele Tepper, and the Old and Young Hats of AFU GmbH.

This editor, and all students of the F-word, owe an enormous debt to Professor Allen Walker Read for his work on the word. Professor Read has made many hugely important contributions to the study of English; he is perhaps best known for his research on *O.K.* But his 1934 article "An Obscenity Symbol" is the pioneering study of the word; without his exhaustive research, we would know far less about this most significant word. His 1974 followup, "An Obscenity Symbol After Four Decades," admirably adds forty years of study to our knowledge.

For assistance and support of various flavors, I would like to thank all my colleagues at Random House.

Jesse Sheidlower

About the F-Word
Introduction

Different kinds of language have been considered incendiary at different times. Several hundred years ago, for example, religious profanity was the most unforgivable type of expression. In more recent times, words for body parts and explicitly sexual vocabulary have been the most shocking: in nineteenth-century America even the word *leg* was considered indecent; the proper substitute was *limb*. Now racial or ethnic epithets are the scourge; one prominent professor told *U.S. News & World Report* in 1994 that if she used *fuck* in class, no one would bat an eye, but that she would never dare to use any racial epithet in any context.

Our Contemporary State of Mind

Today it seems that the taboos against the F-word are weaker than ever. While a few publications still refuse to print *fuck* regardless of the circumstances, the word can be found quite easily in most places. The more literary magazines have printed *fuck* for some time, but now even *Newsweek* has used the uncensored word, and the publication of the Starr Report in the *New York Times* has meant that even that proper paper considers *fuck* fit to print. Even commercial television, though still subject to FCC regulations, is becoming more open in its use. Modern talk shows, with their confrontational attitude, encourage behavior that lends itself readily to this sort of language. For example, on *The Jerry Springer Show* recently a guest used the word *motherfucker*, and rather than bleeping over the whole word, or even the last element, only the -*u*- was apparently bleeped: there was no question at all as to what the word was. In 1994, Phil Donahue uttered the word *cunt* on his talk show (in relating and condemning an employer's insult to a female employee) without any sort of bleep, and without any noticeable reaction from the audience.

The unpredictable nature of live television has allowed the F-word to slip past would-be censors. Kenneth Tynan, then the Director of the National Theatre, was probably the first to manage this, in a 1965 BBC appearance that provoked a huge reaction in England. Similarily the seminal punk band the Sex Pistols in 1976: of the next-day newspaper reaction, the singer Elvis Costello later said, "It was a great morning—just to hear people's blood pressure going up and down over it." The NBC live comedy show "Saturday Night Live" has seen the word used on a number of occasions, perhaps most notably on February 21, 1981. Charles Rocket, playing J.R. Ewing in a sketch based on the TV show "Dallas," said "It's the first time I've ever been shot in my life. I'd like to know who the fuck did it." (Three weeks later, Rocket was fired, along with most of the cast of the slumping show.) And on the same night, the artist then known as Prince sang "Fighting war is such a fucking bore." In 1993, Bono, the lead singer of the rock group U2, used the word during a live broadcast of the Grammy Awards, and a courtside microphone picked up a member of the Chicago Bulls declaring that their victory in the 1998 NBA basketball finals was "fucking unbelievable." And it is becoming more and more acceptable to use *fuck* in social contexts that would have been unthinkable even a generation ago.

Given the current state of the F-word, it may be difficult to believe that the word may not have been *openly* printed in any form in the United States until 1926, when it appeared once, and seemingly without generating any controversy (the word is still included in the book's tenth printing), in Howard Vincent O'Brien's anonymously published *Wine, Women and War,* his diary of the years 1917–19. It is worth noting that he used it in a figurative sense and was explicitly quoting an Australian soldier.

Fuck is found repeatedly in James Joyce's *Ulysses,* first published in book form in 1922 and circulated through clandestine copies in the United States for some time before a court decision in 1933 allowed the book's legal entry. Judge John Woolsey specifically addressed the obscene words in his verdict: "The words which are criticized as dirty are old Saxon words known to almost all men and, I venture, to many women, and are such words as would be naturally and habitually used, I believe, by the types of folk whose life, physical and mental, Joyce is seeking to describe."

It took far longer for D.H. Lawrence's novel *Lady Chatterley's Lover* to be approved by the courts, though when it happened the judge also discussed the dangerous words. Federal Judge Frederick van Pelt Bryan wrote in his decision of July 21, 1959: "Four-letter Anglo-Saxon words are used with some frequency...this language understandably will shock the sensitive minded. Be that as it may...the language which shocks, except in a rare instance or two, is not inconsistent with character, situation or theme." The decision was upheld by an appellate court in 1960. Emboldened by this, the English "published" it by handing it over to the police; the five-day trial produced a not-guilty verdict, and *The Guardian* and *The Observer,* in their coverage, printed "fuck" with no asterisks or dashes.

The language writer Hugh Rawson observes that trials of this sort rarely mention the words at issue. After Lenny Bruce's 1963 obscenity trial in Chicago, Bruce described the prosecutor's commenting, "I don't think I have to tell you the term, I think that you recall it...as a word that started with a 'F' and ended with a 'K' and sounded like 'truck.'" A 1981 trial to force a school board to return a book about Vietnam to the library contained the ruling "that no obscene words should be uttered in court, and that the principal word in question should be referred to simply as 'the word.'"

These juridical qualms existed despite the fact that the first use of *fuck* in an American legal case had occurred back in 1940, in a rape trial in the Arizona Supreme Court:

> When she was in bed asleep the defendant entered her room, grabbed her by the throat...he stood at the head of her bed and when she awoke made this statement to her: "Gonna throw a fuck into you."

The judge regarded this statement as linguistically interesting, but not for the reason one would expect: he immediately went on to note

> that he did not say, "I'm going to" but just "gonna"; that after telling her this he loosened his grip somewhat and kissed her,

and so on, without ever acknowledging that the word *fuck* was, just maybe, more notable than how the rapist pronounced *going to.*

But it was not until the 1950s and '60s that *fuck* was frequently printed in full in mainstream fiction and nonfiction, usually in nonliteral senses. Norman Mailer was persuaded to substitute the invented spelling variant "fug" in his first novel, *The Naked and the Dead,* published to great acclaim in 1948; James Jones was able to use the

xiv

correctly spelled *fuck* in 1951 in *From Here to Eternity,* for which he won the National Book Award (though the reported 258 examples of *fuck* in the manuscript were cut back to a mere 50 in the final book). Many Americans found both of these novels about World War II shocking, despite the fact that their dialogue accurately reflected the way soldiers really spoke.

With the liberating attitudes toward personal freedom that developed in the 1960s and '70s, the use of *fuck* grew still more. Though upholders of mainstream proprieties still largely frowned upon the use of the word, the uninhibited behavior of many of the younger generation forced people to pay attention. Some notable examples of the time include the rise to popularity of the comedian Lenny Bruce, and his many trials for obscenity along the way; the inclusion of *fuck* in a general dictionary, for the first time since 1795; Country Joe leading the throngs at Woodstock in the "fuck cheer" ("Gimme an F!..."); a Federal Court finding that a "Fuck the Draft" sign on a man's jacket represented protected political speech; George Carlin's famous "Seven Dirty Words" comedy routine on the radio that led to the banning of those words (*fuck, shit, cunt, cocksucker, motherfucker, piss,* and *tits*) by the FCC, a ban subsequently upheld by the U.S. Supreme Court; and the inclusion of *fuck,* spelled out in full, in large-circulation general periodicals such as *Harper's, Atlantic,* and *Playboy.*

Despite these often confrontational episodes, it seems that in the movie world, no one tried to have *fuck* uttered on the screen until the country was ready for it. The word's first appearance in mainstream movies was in 1970 (*MASH* and *Myra Breckenridge*), though it had been used earlier in several avant-garde productions.

It took a bit more time for the word to penetrate the august pages of *The New Yorker.* The editorship of Tina

Brown is credited—more usually, faulted—with that journal's frequent use of the word, and though writers did use it frequently under Ms Brown, in fact *fuck* appeared there, spelled in full, more than once during the editorship of her predecessor, the puritanical William Shawn. Calvin Trillin quoted a Nebraska farmer: "Goddam fuckin' Jews!...They destroyed everything I ever worked for!" (March 18, 1985), and Bobbie Ann Mason used the word in a short story: "Maybe you have to find out for yourself. Fuck. You can't learn from the past" (June 3, 1985).

Finally came the remarkable appearance of *fuck*, spelled in full, in the pages of the *New York Times* in 1998. Having committed itself to printing the Starr Report, the *Times* was obligated to include the money passage on page B6 of its issue of September 12: "Ms. Lewinsky said she wanted two things from the President. The first was contrition: He need to 'acknowledge...that he helped fuck up my life.'"

Early Etymological History

Fuck is a word of Germanic origin. It is related to words in several other Germanic languages, such as Dutch, German, and Swedish, that have sexual meanings as well as meanings like 'to strike' or 'to thrust'. Ultimately these words represent a family of loosely related verbs having the structural form f + a short vowel + a stop (a consonant such as k, d, g, or t, in which the flow of air from the mouth is briefly interrupted), often with an l or r somewhere in between. These words have the basic meaning 'to move back and forth', and often the figurative sense 'to cheat'. English examples—all found later than *fuck*— are *fiddle, fidget, flit, flip, flicker,* and *frig.*

The English word was probably borrowed in the fifteenth century, from Low German, Flemish, or Dutch, though the word is found earlier in English than its associates in these languages. *Fuck* is not an Anglo-Saxon word. The relevance of structurally similar words in more distantly related languages (Latin *futuere*, for example), is unlikely. Though the Latin word is vulgar and means 'to copulate', we cannot conclude that it is related to *fuck*, due to complicated linguistic rules that are beyond the scope of this introduction. Other theories attempting to tie the word to more distantly related roots are also uncertain.

Fuck definitely did not originate as an acronym, as some people think. The common examples proposed for this derivation are "For Unlawful [or Found in Unlawful, or Forced Unsolicited, etc.] Carnal Knowledge," abbreviated to *fuck* and allegedly worn on a badge by convicted adulterers, rapists, or prostitutes in Olden Tymes; and "Fornication Under Consent of King," reflecting a belief in the need for royal permission for the sex act itself. Acronyms are rare before the 1930s, and etymologies of this sort—especially for older words—are almost always false. The earliest suggestion of an acronymic etymology for *fuck* appears to be in the 1960s, in the New York underground newspaper the *East Village Other*, on February 15, 1967: "It's not commonly known that the word 'fuck' originated as a medical diagnostic notation on the documents of soldiers in the British Imperial Army. When a soldier reported sick and was found to have V.D., the abbreviation F.U.C.K. was stamped on his documents. It was short for 'Found Under Carnal Knowledge.'" The "king" variant is first found in 1970, in the May issue of *Playboy*: "My friend claims that the word fuck originated in the 15th Century, when a married couple needed permission from the king to procreate. Hence, *F*ornication *U*nder *C*onsent of the *K*ing. I maintain that it's an acronym of a law term used in the 1500s that referred to rape as *F*orced *U*nnatural *C*arnal *K*nowledge."

The most striking recent development has been the popularity of the "pluck yew" story, which conflates the origin of *fuck* with an earlier piece of folklore about the origin of the offensive backhand two-finger gesture. According to the original form of the tale, before the battle of Agincourt in 1415 (later immortalized in Shakespeare's *Henry V*) the French taunted the English longbowmen by waving two fingers at them, saying that those fingers (used to pull back the bowstring) could never defeat the mighty French. After the English longbowmen rather convincingly demonstrated their superiority (10,000 French dead to a mere 29 Brits, in Shakespeare's exaggerated count), the English responded by waving their two fingers back at the French in the now familiar gesture (the usual American version limits it to a single finger). The recent twist has been to use the fact that longbows were traditionally made of yew to claim that the act of drawing back the bowstring was called "plucking yew," and thereby to assert that the victorious English not only waved their fingers at the French but shouted "We can still pluck yew! Pluck yew!" at them. A convenient sound change and a respelling brings us to the familiar phrase "fuck you." This story, totally ludicrous in any version, was popularized on the NPR show *Car Talk,* where it was meant as a joke; many people have taken it seriously, particularly on the Internet.

Despite the importance of the F-word, scholars have yet to discover an example of *fuck* (or any of its Germanic relatives) before the fifteenth century. The lateness of this evidence for the word, whose lineage must reach far back into etymological history, may have more than one explanation. The simplest—and probably the likeliest—is that the word carried a taboo so strong that it was never written down in the Middle Ages. The fact that its earliest known appearance in English, around 1475, is in a cipher lends surprising, though limited, support to this interpretation.

Indeed, there is no shortage of evidence of restrictions on certain forms of speech from the earliest times in England. For instance, one seventh-century law from Kent reads: "If anyone in another's house...shamefully accosts him with insulting words, he is to pay a shilling to him who owns the house."

Since many of the earliest examples of the F-word come from Scottish sources, some scholars have suggested that it is a Norse borrowing, Norse having a much greater influence on the northern and Scottish varieties of English than on southern dialects. But the recently discovered 1528 example—found in that common source of bawdy jokes, a marginal note to a manuscript—and the pre-1500 ciphered example are both from England, proving that *fuck* was not restricted to Scotland in its earliest days. The explanation for the profusion of Scottish examples might be simply that the taboo against the word was less strong in Scotland.

The demand for bawdy humor, however, meant that then as now writers found ways to use certain words even if they were prohibited by social conventions. In Shakespeare, for instance, we find two clear references to *cunt:* in *Twelfth Night* (II.v), Malvolio effectively spells out the word making a pun on *pee* in the process, and in *Hamlet* (III.ii) the prince uses the phrase "country matters" in a manner clearly alluding to *cunt.*

Though Shakespeare never actually uses *fuck* itself, his plays contain several examples of probable puns or references to the word. A Latin grammar lesson in *The Merry Wives of Windsor* (IV.i) gives us the *focative case* (punning on the *vocative case,* used for direct address), followed up immediately with a raft of lewd wordplay, including sexual puns on Latin words and references to various English words for the sexual organs. In *Henry V* (IV.iv) the notoriously bawdy Pistol threatens to "firk" an enemy soldier; though *firk* does have a legitimate sense 'to strike', which is appropriate here, it was used elsewhere in the Elizabethan era as a euphemism for *fuck,* and it is quite likely that Shakespeare had this in mind as well. In several places Shakespeare refers to the French word *foutre,* which is the literal (and also vulgar) equivalent of *fuck;* the most notable is this passage in *Henry V* (III.iv), in which Princess Katherine is having an English lesson:

> KATHERINE Comment appellez-vous les pieds et la robe? [What do you call *le pied* and *la robe*?]
>
> ALICE *De foot,* madame; et *de cown* [a French pronunciation of *gown;* these English words sound like the French words *foutre* 'fuck' and *con* 'cunt'].
>
> KATHERINE *De foot* et *de cown?* O Seigneur Dieu! Ils sont les mots de son mauvais, corruptible, gros, et impudique! [Dear Lord! Those are bad-sounding words, wicked, vulgar, and indecent!]

Shakespeare elsewhere (*2 Henry IV* V.iii) has Pistol say, "A foutra for the world and worldlings base!," and in at least one place (*Merry Wives* II.i) he uses *foot* as a probable pun on *foutre.* As the *Henry V* passage shows, Shakespeare was well aware that this word was vulgar—at least in French—and there is a good possibility that these examples are intended to represent the taboo English word *fuck.*

There is no question that the F-word was considered vulgar in Shakespeare's time; the only question is to what extent. Some notable writers did use it before the twenti-eth century. Aside from the sixteenth-century Scottish examples, it is found in the works of Lord Rochester and Robert Burns, both poets known for their lewd lyrics.

Certainly the word was considered literally unprintable except in obscure, secret, or privately printed publications throughout the nineteenth century. Burns, writing in the late eighteenth century, is probably the latest important author known to use the word before the twentieth, and he uses it only in *Merry Muses of Caledonia,* a bawdy man-uscript intended purely for private circulation. Even Cap-tain Francis Grose—a friend of Burns—in his *Classical Dictionary of the Vulgar Tongue* (1785 and later editions; the word was expunged from the 1811 edition by a differ-ent compiler) felt compelled to spell it *f—k.*

In a striking example of the unfamiliarity of some Vic-torians with bawdy vocabulary, we see that the poet Robert Browning egregiously misunderstood one com-mon word. He encountered the couplet "They talked of his having a Cardinal's hat,/They'd send him as soon an old nun's twat," in a seventeenth-century poem. Erroneously believing from this passage that the word referred to a part of a nun's habit, Browning wrote of "Cowls and twats" in his great poem *Pippa Passes* (1848).

This does not imply that *fuck* was unused, of course. John Farmer and W.E. Henley's monumental *Slang and Its Analogues* (privately printed; the volume with *fuck* appeared in 1893) included the use of *fucking* as both an adjective and adverb, described respectively as "A qualification of extreme contumely" and "a more violent form of *bloody.*" These are labeled "common," despite the fact that this editor has been able to discover hardly any earlier examples of this sense outside Farmer & Henley's dictionary. No doubt this and various other senses were common but unprinted for some time previously. The profusion of senses that appear around World War I is thus more likely to be the result of weakened taboos than of spontaneous word coinage.

For although *fuck* may have been strictly taboo in mainstream usage in the nineteenth century, it was extremely common in the flourishing world of Victorian pornography. Many explicit F-words are found in such sources from the 1860s onwards, often in ways that are scarcely different from the hard-core pornography of the present day.

In two remarkable incidents, *fuck* even found its way into the very proper London *Times* in this allegedly prudish era. Reporting a speech delivered by Attorney General Sir William Harcourt, the *Times* printed on January 13, 1882:

> I saw in a Tory journal the other day a note of alarm, in which they said, "Why, if a tenant-farmer is elected for the North Riding of Yorkshire the farmers will be a political power who will have to be reckoned with." The speaker then said he felt inclined for a bit of fucking. I think that is very likely.

It took the stunned editors four days to run an apology for what must have been a bit of mischief at the typesetter:

> No pains have been spared by the management of this journal to discover the author of a gross outrage committed by the interpolation of a line in the speech of Sir William Harcourt reported in our issue of Monday last. This malicious fabrication was surreptitiously introduced before the paper went to press. The matter is now under legal investigation,

and it is hoped that the perpetrator of the outrage will be brought to punishment.

And later that year, on June 12, 1882, the following advertisement appeared: "Every-day Life in our Public Schools. Sketched by Head Scholars. With a Glossary of Some Words used by Henry Irving in his disquisition upon fucking, which is in Common Use in those Schools."

The F-Word in Dictionaries

The word *fuck*'s first appearance in a dictionary was in John Florio's *Worlde of Words,* an Italian-English dictionary published in 1598—before any monolingual dictionary of English had appeared. It was one of five synonyms given to translate the Italian word *fottere;* the others were *jape, sard, swive,* and *occupy.* The word was first included as a main entry, in its proper alphabetic place, in Stephen Skinner's *Etymologicon Linguae Anglicanae* (1671), an English etymological dictionary written in Latin.

Samuel Johnson's immediate predecessor, Nathan Bailey, listed the word, with a Latin definition, in his 1721 *Universal Etymological English Dictionary.* Bailey's popular 1730 follow-up, the *Dictionarium Britannicum,* contained the curious note that it was "a term used of a goat"; this odd limitation may have been intended to mitigate the inclusion of the word (words inappropriate to humans might be allowable if referring to animals) and not to indicate actual usage. Samuel Johnson excluded it from his great dictionary in 1755, but he made a conscious decision to omit vulgar words, so the absence of it from his dictionary does not indicate the word's rarity. Still, the word's omission provided one of the great dirty-words-in-dictionaries anecdotes: when complimented by a lady for having left out this and other offensive words, Johnson is said to have replied, "No, Madam, I hope I have not daubed my fingers. I find, however, that you have been looking for them."

The last general dictionary of this era to include *fuck* seems to be John Ash's *New and Complete Dictionary of the English Language,* first published in 1775, and still containing the word in its 1795 second edition. Ash—a Baptist minister—called it "a low vulgar word," and defined it as "to perform the act of generation, to have to do with a woman." It is worth noting that Ash also included *cunt* in both editions of his dictionary, also marked as vulgar and defined as "the female pudendum." After Ash, it was to be 170 years until *fuck* again appeared in a general dictionary.

The words *cunt* and *fuck* were kept out of the great *Oxford English Dictionary*—the *F* entries were edited in the 1890s—though by the time the editors made it to *W* in the 1920s, they decided to enter *windfucker* as a name for the kestrel. The slang lexicographer Eric Partridge reported a discussion with C.T. Onions, one of the *OED's* editors, about why the earlier editors had left out *cunt* and *fuck.* Onions: "They considered the two unspeakables to be also unprintable...and although I cannot speak for Craigie, I do myself think them beyond the pale of all decency....I wouldn't have liked my own children to find these words in a volume on my library shelves." Partridge countered by observing that no one would find the words if they didn't already know to look for them, to which Onions grudgingly answered, "Yes, perhaps, perhaps, but I still think the *OED* was right to ban them."

As we have seen, *fuck* has been included in various slang dictionaries since the eighteenth century, but even in the twentieth its presence in such dictionaries has caused problems. Eric Partridge included over a dozen F-words in the first edition of his *Dictionary of Slang and*

Unconventional English, but he spelled the word "f*ck." In spite of this, his compilation, in this and its various later editions, generated protests to the police, school authorities, and libraries; as late as the 1960s special permission was needed to view it in some libraries. In his etymological dictionary *Origins,* published in 1958, Partridge added a second asterisk to make the word a potentially less offensive "f**k."

Other large general dictionaries cannot be seriously faulted for omitting the word, given the tenor of the time. The next major dictionary to blow its chance was *Webster's Third New International Dictionary* in 1961. Groundbreaking in its approach to slang and colloquial language, the *Third* had set a *fuck* entry into type, but the officers of the G. & C. Merriam Co. vetoed it at the last minute. (Mario Pei criticized the dictionary's "residual prudishness" in a review.)

Similarly inhibited was Random House, whose 1966 *Random House Dictionary of the English Language* was the other great dictionary of the 1960s. Jess Stein, the editor-in-chief, told the *New York Times* about a meeting he convened with the company's editorial and sales staff to discuss *cunt* and *fuck:* "When I uttered the words, there was a shuffling of feet, and a wave of embarrassment went through the room. That convinced me the words did not belong in the dictionary, though I'm sure I'll be attacked as a prude for the decision." Stein did not have to wait long to be proved right on the last point: a mere two weeks later, the *Times's* own reviewer wrote, "Unfortunately, a stupid prudery has prevented the inclusion of probably the most widely-used word in the English language. The excuse here, no doubt, is 'good taste'; but in a dictionary of this scope and ambition the omission seems dumb and irresponsible."

Only the previous year, the British *Penguin English Dictionary,* edited by G.N. Garmonsway, had become the first general English dictionary to include *fuck* since Ash's 1795 second edition. In America this honor fell to the 1969 *American Heritage Dictionary*—ironically, given the otherwise conservative approach that dictionary took to language issues.

Fuck and *cunt* finally entered the *OED* in 1972 with the publication of the first volume (A–G) of *A Supplement to the Oxford English Dictionary.* When Robert Burchfield accepted the editorship of the Supplements in 1957, he thought that "the time had not yet come" to include the word, but he eventually changed his mind. In 1968 the delegates of Oxford University Press "approved in principle the inclusion of these two four-letter words." The press' Director explained: "Standards of tolerance have changed and their omission has for many years, and more frequently of late, excited critical comment."

Euphemism: The Phrase "The F-Word" Itself

As one can see from the entry for *eff* in this book, the use of the first letter of *fuck* as a euphemism for the word itself arose by the 1920s at the latest. There are earlier precedents for this dodge. In *H.M.S. Pinafore* (1878) Sir W.S. Gilbert alludes to the use of *damn:*

> Though "Bother it" I may
> Occasionally say,
>   I never use a big, big D.

A fascinating—and much earlier—parallel is found in classical Latin, as David L. Gold has shown in a recent article. In his *Menippeae,* Marcus Terentius Varro (116–27 B.C.) writes *psephistis dicite labdeae.* The sense of the first word in this context is not known, but the next two words are crystal clear: they are an allusion to the Latin idiom *laecasin dicere* 'to tell (someone) to go to hell', which literally means 'to tell (someone) to suck', and is based on *laikazein*, a vulgar Greek verb for 'fellate'. (*Labdeae* is the word for lambda, the Greek letter *L*.) An English translation of the Varro quote, then, would be something like "Tell him to go S himself!"

Of course, all this is not to suggest that the expression "the F-word" is modeled on a Latin phrase—or even on a Gilbert and Sullivan comedy. But the two usages illustrate the same device: the name of the first letter of a vulgar word euphemistically standing for that word.

The expression *four-letter word* is first found in 1897 and was well enough established by the 1930s to be used in Cole Porter's classic lyric "Anything Goes" in 1934: "Good authors, too, who once used better words/Now only use four-letter words/Writing prose/Anything goes." (The related expression *four-letter man* 'man who can be described by a four-letter word' [usually *shit*, but sometimes *goof, bore,* or *dumb*] was common in the 1920s.) With both *eff* and *four-letter word* in use in the 1930s, it would not be too surprising if *the F-word* were used at that time as well. However, the earliest example of which the editor is aware is not until the early 1970s, after the word *fuck* had become common in movies as well as fiction. The evidence suggests that it was then mainly a childish euphemism—another reason to believe that it may have been used earlier, since words such as these are seldom written down.

The use of *the F-word* increased throughout the 1970s and '80s, and eventually the suffix *-word* began to be used freely with the first letter of a word—any word—to be avoided. There are occasional examples from the early 1980s of, for instance, *the L-word* for "lesbian," but this practice did not really peak until the mid- to late-1980s. By this time it was often jocular, as in *the L-word* for "love" or "liberal," or *the T-word* for "taxes," but serious examples were also used: *the N-word* for "nigger." This combining form of *-word*, finally liberated from association with *fuck*, appeared by itself in general dictionaries by the early 1990s.

Selection of Entries

This book contains every sense of *fuck*, and every compound word or phrase of which *fuck* is a part, that the editor believes has ever had currency in English. It does not contain words meaning 'to have sex' or 'to victimize' that are used, often unconsciously, as euphemisms for *fuck*, such as *lay, screw, shaft,* or *do it.* However, it does include euphemisms for *fuck* that directly suggest, in sound and meaning, the word itself: thus the inclusion of *freaking, foul up, mofo,* and others.

While priority has been given to American English, British, Australian, and other sources have occasionally been used.

Preference has been given to words found in actual use, though we did find it necessary to consult other dictionaries or word lists. In many cases, words that are found only in dictionaries are joke words, made up as a lark, and there is no way of gauging their true currency. For example, *snafu* gave rise to a number of other words with the *fu* element; this book includes only *janfu, snefu,* and *tarfu*, and *fubar* and its relations. Certain specialized dictionaries or glossaries of World War II language contain many more examples, but we have no written or spoken evidence of actual use. This suggests that these words were never used seriously, but treated only as jokes.

We have omitted a number of terms for which we have only sparse evidence. Since *fuck* can be used in so many different ways, it is difficult to tell if a term heard only once has any real currency. Some words which are not in this book include *clothesfuck* 'a difficulty in deciding what to wear'; *figure-fucking* 'altering financial documents; "cooking the books"'; *fuckbreak* 'a leave from work taken by a woman in order to get pregnant'; *fuckomania* 'rampant sexual desire'; and *fuck-stain* 'a foolish or offensive person'.

The Entries

The entries in this book are arranged alphabetically, letter by letter. A word may be shown as a main entry more than once, depending on its use as a noun, verb, adjective, adverb, interjection, or infix (a word inserted within another word or set phrase, as *-fucking-*, which forms such other words as *absofuckinglutely*).

Within an entry, numbered senses are ordered by the date of the first citation, as are the lettered subsenses within a numbered sense. This allows the historical development of the senses to be clearly seen.

Phrases using the F-word are listed alphabetically at the end of the main entry. Phrases are preceded by the finger symbol ☞ for clarity.

Cross-references to other words in this volume are given in SMALL CAPITALS. Cross references to phrases are given in *italic* type and specify the main entry word where the phrase may be found.

Certain citations have been placed in square brackets to indicate that the example does not clearly show the use of the word it is meant to illustrate. Examples are the first two citations under *fuck-up*. Brackets are not used in cases where an example is clearly a euphemistic use, as in *rat copulation* for *ratfuck*.

Field labels, such as *Military* or *Black English,* describe the group or subculture of people who use the word (not necessarily those to whom the word applies). The choice of labels was made on the basis of the evidence, and it is not intended to be limiting. The presence of a label should not imply that the word is used exclusively by the designated group, nor that persons using such words have real ties to the group.

The Examples

Each entry in this book is illustrated with a large number of examples of the use of the word in context—quotations from books and magazines, from movies or television, even from speech. These examples, called *citations* (or *cites* for short) by dictionary editors, have several purposes: to demonstrate that a word or sense has actually been in use; to show the length of time it has existed; to show exactly how it has been used; and so forth.

In every case, the first citation given is the earliest one we have been able to find. The last citation is, within reason, the most recent example available. Only a few F-words are truly obsolete and therefore have no recent example. The dates provide important evidence for the use of a word. We may discover that although *fuck around* is recorded only from the early twentieth century, the similar use of *frig* is found in the late eighteenth. Therefore, that sense of *fuck* itself may be just as old but simply unrecorded owing to the vulgarity of the term.

Every example is preceded by its source. Most of the sources may be found in a good research library, though some are from manuscripts or other sources kept in the files of the Random House Reference Division. Examples taken from speech were collected by the editor or by researchers for Random House; the date refers to the year in which the example was actually collected.

The date shown for each citation is the date when we believe the word was actually written or used. In most cases, this will be the same as the publication date. Occasionally, when a book is known to have been written at an earlier date, that date will be given instead, which is why Norman Mailer's novel *The Naked and the Dead* is listed at 1947 instead of its publication date of 1948. When a book or magazine is quoting an earlier source, the word "in" appears after the date: 1528 in *Notes & Queries*.

Jesse Sheidlower
New York

Introduction to the Second Edition

Since the publication of the original edition of *The F-Word*, we have continued to gather evidence of the use and history of *fuck*, and our reading program—an ongoing effort to collect contextual examples of interesting words—has brought to attention many F-words old and new. In addition, many people have written to suggest words or phrases that were left out of the first edition, either intentionally (*zipless fuck,* which we felt at the time was just *fuck* in its usual noun sense with the modifier *zipless,* often found with other words as well), or through ignorance (we had never encountered the common term *genderfuck*). Finally, we made a policy change to include F-words from non-American varieties of English, such as the Irish *feck* and the Australian and British *fuckwit*.

As a result, we have added a number of terms in this edition. These include, in addition to the terms mentioned above, *drug-fucked, force-fuck, fuck-buddy, fuckee[1], fuckerware party, fucksome, fucktruck, fucky, fuck-you* (as noun and adjective), *hate fuck, unfuck,* and others.

Within each entry we have also added certain senses. Most prominently, we decided to split the main sexual definition of *fuck,* verb, 1.a. into two parts. The original definition had been "to copulate or copulate with. Also used in transferred senses." In linguistics, a transferred sense is one whose meaning has been broadened to refer to a wider range of things—in this case, sexual acts other than heterosexual vaginal sex. We have now added a new definition, 1.b., carefully defined to encompass such acts. Some other new definitions include a new sense of *fucked* as an adjective meaning 'exhausted'; the fascinating interjectional use of *fucking,* adverb; and *ratfuck* referring to a busy social party. Certain definitions were rewritten to make them more accurate or to encompass new citations added in the revision process: *eyefuck, fist-fuck, fuckfest,* and others.

Along with these entirely new entries and subentries we have included hundreds of additional examples of the words already entered. Perhaps the most important category is antedatings. In historical lexicography, an antedating is a citation earlier than those previously known for a word or sense. The discovery of antedatings forces us to rethink what we thought we knew about the historical usage and development of language. Some of the antedatings we have discovered are "for fuck's sake" under *fuck,* noun, pushed back from 1961 to 1946; *fuckable,* definition 1 by only a few years but definition 2 by almost a century to 1889; *fuckface,* pushed back from 1961 to 1945; *fuckhead,* 1962 to 1945; *fuck-me,* 1989 to a 1974 David Bowie song; *fuck-up,* verb, definitions 2.a. and 2.b. by a few years; *fuck-you money,* 1986 to 1975; *m.f.,* the euphemistic form of *motherfucker,* 1964 to 1959; and *tit-fuck,* 1986 to 1972.

Two other important categories are interdatings—citations that fill significant gaps in the historical record, showing that a word or phrase was in continued use—and postdatings—citations that come substantially later than the latest previously known example, showing that a word or phrase stayed current longer than thought. We have tried especially hard to find postdatings, and most entries in this second edition now end with citations from the 1990s. Some entries having notable inter- or postdatings are *fricking; frig off,* definition 1; *fuck,* noun, definition 1.b.; "fuck of" under *fuck,* noun; *fuck,* verb, definition 3.b.; "fuck (someone's) mind" under *fuck,* verb; *fuck around,* verb, definition 3; *fuckbag; -fucking-,* infix; *fuck up,* verb, definitions 3.a. and 4.a.; *mindfuck,* definition 1; and *motherfucker,* interjection.

Finally, and most broadly, we have added many citations that serve to flesh out existing entries. Several famous uses of *fuck* have been included, such as the scene in *Catcher in the Rye* where Holden sees a graffito of "fuck you" and muses on his desire to protect his sister Phoebe from seeing such vulgarity; the line from Allen Ginsberg's *Howl* where he has seen "The best minds in my generation destroyed by madness,...who let themselves be fucked in the ass by saintly motorcyclists, and screamed with joy"; the scene in Neil Simon's *Odd Couple* where Felix Unger's initials cause unexpected confusion; the use of *bufu* from the Frank Zappa song "Valley Girl" (instead of just in later dictionaries of Valley Girl talk); and the opening lines of Philip Larkin's "This Be the Verse," the only use of *fuck* to be regularly found in dictionaries of quotations: "They fuck you up, your mum and dad." Most entries now have more examples, so that we have four instead of a mere two citations for *fubar* in the sense 'drunk'; three instead of two for *fuck,* noun, definition 5 'an evil turn of events'; two instead of one for *fuck,* verb, definition 5.b. 'to trifle or interfere with'; two instead of one for *fuck away;* four fully up-to-date examples instead of two outdated ones for *fuckee* 'person who plays recipient role in copulation'; three instead of one for *FYFI;* and more.

The

F

Word

Second Edition

Words

absofuckinglutely *adverb* absolutely. Compare -FUCKING-, *infix*.

1921 *Notes & Queries* (Nov. 19) 415 [refers to WWI]: The soldier's actual speech...was absolutely impregnated with one word which (to use it as a basis for alliteration) the fastidious frown at as "filthy".... Words were split up to admit it: "absolutely" became "abso—lutely." **1945** S.J. Baker *Australian Language* 258: Transconti-bloody-nental, abso-f—g-lutely, inde-bloody-pendent. **1970** Major *Afro-American Slang* 19: *Absofuckinglutely*: without doubt. **1973** Huggett *Body Count* ch. viii: That's right, Carlysle, that's abso-fucking-lutely right. **1985** Bodey *F.N.G.* 224: "Like, don't it seem like the time has gone fast now?" "Abso-fuckin'-lutely." **1987** Pedneau *A.P.B.* 228: "Do I detect some anger?" "Abso-fucking-lutely." **1995** *N.Y. Observer* (Apr. 24) 19: "Remember me? "..." Abso-fucking-lutely."

AMF *interjection* "*a*dios [or *a*loha], *m*other*f*ucker"; good-bye; the finish. *Jocular*.

1963 in Tamony *Motherfucker* 7: "A.M.F.... adios mother fucker,"..."goodbye friend." [**1966** Braly *On the Yard* 120: And that's adios mother fuckers.] **1973**

Layne *Murphy* (unpaged): *A.M.F.* Adios mother fahckers. **1974** North Carolina man, age 22: *A.M.F.* Adios, motherfucker! **1980** D. Cragg *Lexicon Militaris: AMF.* Adios (or Aloha) Motherfucker.

ASAFP *adverb* "*a*s *s*oon *a*s *f*ucking *p*ossible"; immediately.

1985 J. Hughes *Weird Science* (film): I want you out of here ASAFP! **1990** Munro *Slang U.* 23: *A.S.A.F.P.* as soon as possible, or sooner.

ass-fuck *noun*

1. an act of anal copulation.

1940 Del Torto *Graffiti Transcript:* Make date for assfuck. **1941** G. Legman, in Henry *Sex Variants* II 1157: *Ass-fuck*...An act of pedication. **1974** "Linda Lovelace" *Diary* 66: He gave me the best ass-fuck I've ever had. **1975** C. Skinner *Carol's Curious Passion* 60: It was no use talking to Bert. For he was carried away with his ass fuck. **1976** J. Johnson *Oriental Festival* 136: I want to give you a tremendous ass fuck.

2. an instance of cruel victimization.

1977 Schrader *Blue Collar* 14: No way he was gonna take this ass-fuck forever.

ass-fuck *verb* to engage in anal copulation [with].

[*ca***1866** *Romance of Lust* IV 361: We had not as yet...indulged even in bottom-fucking the women.] **1940** Del Torto *Graffiti Transcript:* Want to be assfucked. **1941** G. Legman, in Henry *Sex Variants* II

4

1157: *Ass-fuck*...To pedicate. **1971** Rader *Government Inspected* 105: Get ass-fucked like a bender by a butching lover. **1974–77** Heinemann *Close Quarters* 184: She would...ass-fuck. **1984** Ehrhart *Marking Time* 66: Pam, that old boyfriend of yours— you...even ass-fuck the guy! **1992** Madonna *Sex* (unpaged): That's what ass-fucking is all about. It's the most pleasurable way to get fucked. **1998** *Sick Puppy Comix* (No. 8) (Sydney, Australia) 21: You gotta write about sweet, tender little girlies getting arse-fucked like cheap little whores!

B

Words

beans and motherfuckers, see under MOTHER-
FUCKER.

bearfuck *noun Military.* a confused or chaotic undertaking.

> **1983** K. Miller *Lurp Dog* 92 [refers to Vietnam
> War]: The mission turned out to be another disap-
> pointing bearfuck.

bends and motherfuckers, see under MOTHER-
FUCKER.

BFD *interjection* [*b*ig *f*ucking (or *f*at) *d*eal] so what?
who cares?

> **1971** Dahlskog *Dictionary* 7: *BFD, b*ig *f*at *d*eal, an
> ironic comment meaning "What's so great about
> that?" **1982** Michigan man, age 35: Yeah, well, BFD.
> **1988** J. Brown & C. Coffey *Earth Girls Are Easy* (film):
> "There's a UFO in my pool. A *UFO.*" "BFD." **1988** P.
> Fonda, on *Unauthorized Biography* (Fox-TV): He was
> very angry that I had destroyed his honeymoon—
> *BFD!* **1992** Mowry *Way Past Cool* 12: "I the first,
> 'member?" "BFD!"

BFE *noun* [short for BUMFUCK (or BUMBLEFUCK), EGYPT] *Military & Students.* a very remote place.

1989 P. Munro *U.C.L.A. Slang* 20: Troy...lives out in B.F.E....*Bum Fuck, Egypt.* **1991** Student slang survey: *BFE*—out in the middle of nowhere...Bumblefuck, Egypt. **1997** Student slang survey: Faraway place...*in b.f.e.*

buddy-fuck *verb* Especially *Military.* to deliberately impose upon or betray (a close friend). Hence **buddy-fucker, buddy-fucking.** Compare FUCK-YOUR-BUDDY WEEK.

1966 in Indiana Univ. Folklore Archives *Folk-Speech*: Denotes asking a friend for money. *Buddy-fuck.* **1968** Baker et al. *Col. Undergrad. Slang Survey* 89: *Buddy fucker, play.* Take someone else's date away. *Buddy-fuck.* Take someone else's date away. **1970** College student, age 21: At Fort Gordon [Ga.] last year I kept hearing *buddy-fucker.* It's a guy who turns around and shafts people. **1972** College student, age 25: You *buddy-fuck* a guy like if you start going out with his girl without telling him. *Buddy-fucking* means letting somebody down or ripping them off. **1985** Tate *Bravo Burning* 161: Wash your mouth out...buddyfucker.

BUF *noun* [big ugly (fat) fuck(er)] *U.S. Air Force.* a Boeing B-52 Stratofortress. Also **BUFF.**

1968 Broughton *Thud Ridge* 32: BUF stands for big ugly fellows in polite conversation, but is suitably amplified in [fighter pilot] conversation....The Strategic

Air Command general... issued an edict that the B-52 "Stratofortress" was not to be referred to as a BUF. **1972** in J.C. Pratt *Vietnam Voices* 510: 6 "Bufs" came in and rippled that road. **1972** Bob Hope at U.S. Air Force base in Thailand, on *CBS Evening News* (Dec. 22): This is the home of the B-52s. Also known as BUFFs—big ugly friendly fellows [laughter]. **1981** *Time* (Mar. 16) 8: To air crews the B-52 is known as BUFF, a fairly loving acronym that stands for Big Ugly Fat Fellow. **1985** Boyne & Thompson *Wild Blue* 517: The BUFFs—Big Ugly Fat Fuckers to the crews, Big Ugly Fat Fellows to the press. **1990** Poyer *Gulf* 47: Got a wing of fifty Buffs movin' in.

buffy *noun* [respelling of *BUFE*, for *b*ig *u*gly *f*ucking *e*lephant] *Military.* a large ceramic elephant commonly sold in South Vietnam as a souvenir. *Jocular.*

1973 *N.Y. Post* (Jan. 15) 29: A buffy (rhymes with stuffy) is an enormous, glazed ceramic elephant....The name derives from the acronym b-u-f-e, for bloody useless foul-word elephant. **1980** Cragg *Lexicon Militaris* 55: *Buffie.* From the acronym BUFE, *B*ig *U*gly *F*ucking *E*lephants. *Buffies* were large ceramic elephants produced in vast quantities by South Vietnamese craftsmen for sale to Americans. **1982** J. Cain *Commandos* 343: He took the roll of bills stuffed inside the white, ceramic "buffy" elephant.

bufu *noun* [from *butt-f*ucker] a homosexual man. Also as adjective. [Pronounced "Boo-foo."]

1982 F. Zappa *Valley Girl* (pop. song): Like my English teacher...He's like Mr. Bufu...He like flirts with all the guys in the class. **1982** Pond *Valley Girls' Guide* 50: Any dude who'd wear designer jeans *must* be bu-fu, right? **1986** Eble *Campus Slang* (Oct.) 4: *Mo*—a homosexual or someone who acts like one....Also *Bufu.* **1989** P. Munro *U.C.L.A. Slang* 25: He is so femi-nine, you can tell he's a bufu.

bugfuck *adjective Military.* insane.

1970 Ponicsan *Last Detail* 74: You two bastards are trying to drive me bug-fuck in the head, right? **1971** Mayer *Weary Falcon* 11: If Charles doesn't get you, you stand a fine chance of going bug-fuck. **1973** U.S. Navy veteran, age *ca*28: When you go nuts you go *bugfuck.* **1975** S.P. Smith *American Boys* 130 [refers to *ca*1968]: May dead, Irwin dead, Brady bug-fuck. **1979** J. Morris *War Story* 161: My team would go bugfuck when I came back suggesting that we start bayonet drill. **1983** Ehrhart *Vietnam to Perkasie* 199 [refers to Vietnam War]: I was gettin' bug-fuck sittin' around the CP all the time. **1987** D. Sherman *Main Force* 83 [refers to 1966]: We figured you must be going bug-fuck by now, so I came to give you a ride back to Camp Apache. **1991** Nelson & Gonzales *Bring Noise* 167: Law enforcement officials across the country went bug-fuck.

bugfucker *noun* a man with a ridiculously small penis; (*hence*) a contemptible person.

1973 *Zap Comix* (No. 6) (unpaged): Needle Dick the Bug Fucker. **1977** Sayles *Union Dues* 20: "Hey, Nee-dledick, check anybody's oil lately?" "Needledick the Bug-Fucker!" **1966–80** McAleer & Dickson *Unit Pride*

345: Then that dirty bohemian bug-fucker...puts the screws to us.

bull fuck *noun* cream gravy or custard, fancied to resemble the semen of a bull; (in 1991 quotation) stew thickened with flour.

[**1942** Berrey & Van den Bark *American Thesaurus of Slang* 100: Gravy: *Bull shit, come,...gism.*] **1961** Partridge *Dictionary of Slang & Unconventional English* (ed. 5) 1019: *Bull-fuck.* Custard: Canadian railroad-construction crews: since *ca*1910. **1966–67** in *Dictionary of American Regional English* I 445 [in sense "cream gravy"]. **1981** Spears *Slang & Euphemism* 53: *Bull fuck...*A thick gravy with chunks of meat. **1991** Killingbeck *U.S. Army* 40 [refers to 1953]: "Make a bullfuck."...I watched the stew become thicker. "Soldier, that is what is known as a bullfuck."

BULL FUCK

Bumblefuck *noun* [alteration of BUMFUCK, EGYPT] a very remote place. *Jocular.*

1989 P. Munro *U.C.L.A. Slang* 26: *Bumblefuck*...any faraway little town. **1990** Student slang survey: *Bumblefuck*—a word used to describe a location that is very far away or out in the counter. "I can't believe we drove all the way to Bumblefuck to go to this party." **1991** Spears *Slang & Euphemism* (abridged edition 2) 62: *Bumblefuck*...a primitive and rural place; podunk.

bumfuck *noun* a hateful person; an idiot; wretch.

1979 *Easyriders* (Dec.) 6: A pretty crafty way...to get us bumfucks to read your rag cover to cover. **1981** *Easyriders* (Oct.) 47: Cut loose some of those bumfuck, hardluck losers.

bumfuck *verb* to have anal intercourse with. Hence **bumfucker,** *noun.*

*ca***1866** *Romance of Lust* 269: Bum-fucking his adorable wife. **1967** Mailer *Why We Are in Vietnam*: You...been bum fucking the wrong cunt. **1975** *Ribald* (Sydney, Australia) (May 29) 10: Titles included "Tongue Teacher"; "The bumfuckers"; "The House of the Golden Showers." **1996** *Vertigo* (Sydney, Australia) (No. 3) 12: Anal intercourse: buggery, sodomy, arse-fucking, bum-fucking.

Bumfuck, Egypt *noun Military & Students.* a very remote place. *Jocular.* See also BFE, BUMBLEFUCK.

1972 Sgt. E-6, U.S. Army: They probably sent those records out to Bumfuck, Egypt. **1974** Kingry *Monk & Marines* 31: When they asked...whether he would...volunteer for Vietnam, he said he would volunteer for Bumfuk, Egypt, first! **1983** Eble *Campus Slang* (Nov.) 1: *Bumfuck*—the worst place: We had to park in Bumfuck, Egypt. **1986** J. Cain *Suicide Squad* 20: Together, they'll come up with some place beyond Bumfuck, Egypt, to send my sorry ass.

BUMFUCK, EGYPT

butt-fuck *noun*

1. an act of anal copulation.

1971 Dahlskog *Dictionary* 11: *Butt fuck, v.*...To engage in anal intercourse.—[also] *n.* **1981** *National Lampoon* (Apr.) 39: Let's go to my place for brunch and a buttfuck. **1981** Spears *Slang & Euphemism* 58. **1997** *N.Y. Press* (Aug. 27) 18: "I need a buttfuck *now*!" screamed an overpierced male in fluorescent green Speedos.

2. an instance of victimization; an unfortunate event.

1986 Heinemann *Paco's Story* 128: Iwo Jima was a sloppy, bloody butt-fuck.

butt-fuck *verb*

1. to copulate with anally. Also used figuratively. Hence **butt-fucker,** *noun*.

1962–68 B. Jackson *In the Life* 324: Everybody was "Old Butt-Fucker" to him. **1971** Rader *Meat* 72: I liked to get buttfucked. **1976** J. Vasco *Three-Hole Girl* 186: It hurts so good. Oh, you butt-fuck me so good! **1979** Crews *Blood & Grits* 122: Said if I'd butt-fuck him, he'd take me out there on the train and innerduce me. **1983** Eilert *Self & Country* 272 [refers to 1968]: You're butt-fucking each other then. **1985** Dye *Between the Raindrops* 129: Their...buddy has just been butt-fucked by a B-40 [rocket] or some such nonsense. **1990** Poyer *Gulf* 186: The warriors grab the first missionary...[and] butt-fuck him. **1995** *New York Press* (March 8) 67: Dr. Jack Morin, author of the Buttfucker's Bible, *Anal Pleasure and Health*.

2. to victimize.

1979 *Maledicta* III 55: Males in particular...who have been denied promotion, given low grades...been fired, jilted [etc.]...commonly relate that they have been *screwed, fucked,...butt-fucked*...and so on. **1981** Wambaugh *Glitter Dome* 240: He'll be back to being butt-fucked by those bogus producers. **1982** Del Vecchio *13th Valley* 491: Gettin butt-fucked. **1988** J. Stuart *Die Hard* (film): I'm not the one who just got buttfucked on national TV.

Words

celebrity-fucker *noun* a person, typically a young woman, who engages in promiscuous sexual intercourse with film stars or other celebrities; (*broadly*) a hanger-on among celebrities. Compare STARFUCKER.

1972 J.W. Wells *Come Fly* 43: I think that was her name, the celebrity fucker. **1972** Robert A. Wilson *Playboy's Book of Forbidden Words* s.v. *plaster-casters:* A celebrity-fucker (the word was coined by writer-editor John Wilcock) is a young woman who will fuck anybody as long as he's famous. **1984** New York City man, age 37: Celebrity-fuckers are a distinctively modern phenomenon. **1986** R. Campbell *In La-La Land* 232: I thought he was just a celebrity fucker, you know.

CFM *adjective* [*come fuck me*] (of an article of clothing, especially shoes) intended to invite sexual advances. Also as noun, a sexually provocative item of clothing. Compare FUCK-ME, *adjective*.

1990 P. Munro *Slang U* 56: All her other clothes were preppy, but she had a C.F.M. skirt on. **1998** Personal letter to editor (Aug. 26): Out west, sexy boots worn by ladies are known as CFMs. **1998** *Revised: Svengali,* on Usenet newsgroup alt.tv.x-files.creative:

14

Her legs ...were nicely highlighted by the type of shoes Scully had once jokingly referred to as CFM shoes.

chicken-fucker *noun* a depraved or disgusting fellow.—usually used with *baldheaded*. [The 1984 quotation is euphemistic.]

1953 in Legman *Rationale* 20: Suddenly two bald-headed men enter, and the parrot says, "You two chicken-fuckers come out in the hen-house with me." **1976–79** Duncan & Moore *Green Side Out* 276 [refers to *ca*1960]: All right ya bald-headed chicken fuckers, I want this area policed the fuck up. **1967–80** McAleer & Dickson *Unit Pride* 387 [refers to Korean War]: Heave in the first shovelful...and run like a baldheaded chicken-fucker. **1984** S. Terkel *"Good War"* 397 [refers to WWII]: "I'm gonna have you shot."..."You baldheaded so-and-so, go ahead and shoot."

BALD HEADED CHICKEN-FUCKER

15

clusterfuck *noun*

1. an orgy.

1966 "Petronius" *New York Unexpurgated* 242: Zoothageous Klusterfux. **1967–68** N. von Hoffman *We Are the People Our Parents Warned Us Against* 182: Oh, those big cluster fucks! I can't stand them. **1969** Bartell *Group Sex* 134: One advantage of open versus closed swinging, according to most of our informants, is the possiblity of "three-on-one" or "gang bang" (sometimes called "clusterfuck") activity. **1972** R.A. Wilson *Playboy's Book of Forbidden Words* 69: *Cluster Fuck*—Two men copulating simultaneously with the same woman. **1975** Legman *No Laughing Matter* 754: The cheap hippie "group-grope" and "cluster-fuck." **1977** *National Lampoon* (Aug.) 50: Well, they're usually pretty wrapped up in a cluster-fuck with the photo models.

2. *Military.* a bungled or confused undertaking or situation; mess; (*also*) a disorganized group of individuals.

1969 in B.E. Holley *Vietnam* 143: These are the screwups that the American public rarely hears about. They happen often enough over here that we have a term for them—"cluster-fuck"! **1974** New York City man, age 27: A clusterfuck was a big expression in [the N.Y. National Guard] in 1969. It meant any time people were standing around outside of a regular formation. They'd say, "What the hell is this clusterfuck?" "Break up this clusterfuck." **1982** Del Vecchio *13th Valley* 42: This place looks like a giant clusterfuck. *Ibid.* 137: We gonna get this clusterfuck up in the air? **1983** K. Miller *Lurp Dog* 222 [refers to Vietnam War]: Shame

16

to piss up a clusterfuck target like this. **1985** Dye *Between the Raindrops* 42: The rest is up for grabs. This place is a cluster-fuck. **1986** Thacker *Pawn* 135 [refers to 1970]: What you're going to have is an A number one clusterfuck. **1986** Stinson & Carabatsos *Heartbreak* 146: "What's your assessment of this alert?"..."It's a clusterfuck!...marines should be fighting, not...filling out request forms for equipment they should already have, Sir." **1990** Poyer *Gulf* 141: Yeah, but which one's which? What a clusterfuck.

    3. *Military.* a bungler; idiot.

    *a***1987** Bunch & Cole *Reckoning* 284 [refers to Vietnam War]: He's a clusterfuck.

CLUSTERFUCK

cluster-fuck *verb Military.* to congregate in a disorganized or offensive manner.

    1983 Ehrhart *Vietnam to Perkasie* 162 [refers to 1967]: All those amtracs clusterfuckin' around the CP yesterday—Charlie knew somethin' was up.

cunt-fuck *verb* to engage in heterosexual vaginal sex; (also, of women) to rub the genitals against. Also as noun.

17

1879 *Harlequin Prince Cherrytop* 4: Cunt fuck, front tuck, he shall never once begin it. **1908** *Way of a Man with a Maid* 151: Alice and Connie flew into each others' arms—too excited to rush to the couch, they fell on the soft thick carpet and madly cunt-fucked each other till their feelings were relieved. **1990** *Footlicker* 80: I can't cuntfuck with men. Won't ever again. **1998** *Nubile Treat,* on Usenet newsgroup alt.sex.stories (Oct. 1): It was a first-class cunt-fuck, and they dug it as much as the ass-fuck they'd seen before.

D

Words

deck *noun* ☞ In phrase: **fuck the deck,** *U.S. Marine Corps.* to perform push-ups on command.

    1983 Ehrhart *Vietnam to Perkasie* 32 [refers to 1966]: Fuck the deck, piggy!...Push-ups!

dog *noun* ☞ In phrase: **fuck** [or occasionally **screw** or **finger**] **the dog**

    1. to loaf on the job, especially while pretending to be hard at work; fool around; idle; waste time. [The 1918 and 1919 quotations presumably euphemize this expression.]

    [**1918** in Sullivan *Our Times* V 328: *F.T.D.*: Feeding the dog. The supposed occupation of a soldier who is killing time.] [**1919** Warren *9th Co.* 35: The Engineer's Dictionary...*Walking the dog*—Soldiering on the job. When one is caught at it he is said to have stepped on the puppy's tail.] **1935** J. Conroy *World to Win* 201: One of the first things you gotta learn when you're f—n' the dog...is t' look like you're workin' hard enough t' make yer butt blossom like a rose. Rattle templets, beat with a hammer on a beam, but do *somethin'*. If the boss ketches you f—n' the dog while you're helpin' me, he'll eat *me* up blood raw. **1939** Bessie *Men in Battle* 331: They were "fucking the dog," spending what money they had. **1942** Berrey & Van den Bark *American Thesaurus of Slang* 490: Fuck the dog, *to loaf on the job.*

1948 Guthrie *Born to Win* 19: I'll do all I can to stay alive and argufying, alive and kicking, alive and flurking the dog. **1954** *International Journal of Psycho-Analysis* XXXV 351: This was followed by a four-month period of "funking," "fucking the dog," characterized by drinking, missed hours, tardiness, and "sponging" on mother. **1962** E. Stephens *Blow Negative* 54: Those apes are screwing the dog all day long up there. **1967** W. Crawford *Gresham's War* 125: "And meantime?" "Frick the dog, I reckon." **1967** Kolb *Getting Straight* 70: Until you said that, I thought you'd been screwing the dog on this project. **1977** Sayles *Union Dues* 58: You let me catch you fuckin the dog again, so help me, you'll be some sorry characters. **1978** Alibrandi *Killshot* 146: "You bet our entire stake on this one match?" "You got it, kid. No sense fucking the dog. We came to gamble, remember?" **1984** K. Weaver *Texas Crude* 93: *Fuckin' the dog and sellin' the pups.* Wasting time and loafing on the job. **1986** Stinson & Carabatsos *Heartbreak* 125: You hotshots are "fingering the dog" and you wind up killin' every swinging dick in this platoon.

2. to bungle; blunder.

1962 Killens *Then We Heard the Thunder* 144 [refers to WWII]: Saunders, I don't know what I'm going to do with you...You've gone and fucked the dog again. **1985** Heywood *Taxi Dancer* 34: But he had "screwed the dog by the numbers." He had failed to conserve fuel and he had forgotten about their bombs. **1998** Graydon Carter, in *N.Y. Press* (Oct. 21) 17: I gave you the opportunity of a lifetime and you fucked the dog.

dogfuck *noun* trouble.—used with *the*.

> **1978** Groom *Better Times* 30: We're really in the dogfuck now.

dogfuck *verb* to engage in copulation with a male partner entering from the rear, especially anally.

> **1967–80** Folb *Runnin' Lines* 235: *Dog fuck.* Engage in anal intercourse. **1981** in L. Bangs *Psychotic Reactions* 348: When they were done dogfucking they sprawled back awhile to rest and pant. **1986** in Chapman *New Dictionary of American Slang*: Including how to 69 and dogfuck.

double fuck *noun* an act of intercourse in which two people simultaneously copulate with a third person.

> *ca***1866** *Romance of Lust* 218: Bringing his stiff-standing prick against the root of mine, pressing it well down, he gently shoved forward, and gradually sheathed himself within the well-stretched and capacious orbit of my aunt, who winced a little in pretended pain, but who, by the grip she immediately gave to the double fuck within her, showed how much gratified she was. **1998** *Suzifest '98*, on Usenet newsgroup alt.sex.stories.moderated (Oct. 26): Todd and James were going to give Suzi an old fashioned double-fuck....They would "double-fuck" her from behind...a cock in her pussy, with another stuffed up her ass.

double-fuck *verb*

> **1.** (used as an imprecation or oath); God damn.—an emphatic form of FUCK, *verb*, definition 4a.

1966 Fariña *Been Down So Long* 244: Double-fuck the letter.

2. to engage in a DOUBLE FUCK (with).

1984 B. Baker *Sally's Anal Punishment* 161: His brain buzzed with the ecstatic wonder of double-fucking both women. **1995** *Sydney Star Reporter* (Australia) (Nov. 9) 30 [personal ad]: Seek submissive guy to 30 to be double fucked & abused. **1998** (quotation at DOUBLE FUCK, *noun*).

double-fucking *adjective* see FUCKING, *adjective.*— used for emphasis.

1929 Graves *Good-Bye to All That* 79 [refers to 1917]: The Bandmaster, who was squeamish, reported it as: "Sir, he called me a double-effing c—" **1945** in *Verbatim* (Autumn, 1989) 6: *Double [fucking]*...Embellished or emphatic [form] of *fxxxing.* **1991** Tolkin *Rapture* (film): No double-fuckin' *way* would I stop.

drug-fucked *adjective* Australian. intoxicated by drugs. Compare FUCKED, *adjective,* definition 1.

1991 *Arena* (Sydney) (No. 8) 13: When you're that drug-fucked, a piece of navel lint can have occult significance. **1996** *Catalog* (Summer Extra) 9: Drew Barrymore...the world's wildest drug-fucked child starlet. **1996** *Capital Q Weekly* (Sydney) (Mar. 29) 11: Three hundred drug-fucked and horny gay men. **1997** *Rants* (Sydney) (Oct. 23): Fuck you, yer dumb drug-fucked bitch!

dry fuck *noun*

   1. a simulated act of copulation, usually while fully clothed.

   1938 H. Miller *Tropic of Capricorn* 104: Maybe you'll...get a dry fuck. **1965** Trimble *Sex Words* 68: *Dry Fuck*...The act of two lovers rubbing up against each other while clothed and in public, as while dancing, etc., which results in great excitation and, in some cases, orgasm. **1970** Landy *Underground Dictionary* 71: *Dry Fuck*...*n.* The simulated act of sexual intercourse with clothes on. **1971** B.B. Johnson *Blues for Sister* 101: A professional virgin...The kind that always denied you penetration. A dry fuck.

   2. something that is exceedingly tedious or disappointing.

   1945 in T. Williams *Letters* 177: If only Margo could get something of this quality into "The Project."...It is a dry fuck, really!

dry-fuck *verb* [compare earlier synonym *dry-bob*] to simulate sexual intercourse without penetration; to engage in a DRY FUCK with. Also used figuratively.

   [**1935** in J. O'Hara *Selected Letters* 106: Write something...that will help you get rid of the bitterness you must have stored up against all those patronizing cheap bastards in that dry-fucked excrescence on Sharp Mountain.] *ca***1937** in Atkinson *Dirty Comics* 106: Try to dry-fuck the hostess who is the big shot's sweetie. **1938** "Justinian" *Americana Sexualis* 20: *Dry-Fuck. v.* To rub stomach, thighs, and genitals together in an erotic manner

while dancing. Popular in collegiate circles...U.S.,
1925—. **1954** Himes *Third Generation* 243: Now seeing him in the arms of a sweet young girl she was
scalded with jealousy. "What kind of dryfucking shit
is this?" she screamed. **1958–59** Lipton *Holy Barbar-
ians* 156: As long ago as the twenties dancing was
considered "dry fucking" by the *cognoscenti* who
regarded it as something for sub-teenagers only.
1965 Ward & Kassebaum *Women's Prison* 99: That's
more or less a *bulldagger's*...kick, this dry fucking.
1969 Briley *Traitors* 133: They had had a spell of
intense sessions holding hands in the library and
dry-fucking against the back wall of her sorority.
1970 Landy *Underground Dictionary* 71: *Dry fuck*...Go
through the motions of sexual intercourse without
entering the vagina, usually with clothes on. **1983** E.
Dodge *Dau* 110: They dry-fucked in the pre-dawn
darkness. **1991** Jenkins *Gotta Play Hurt* 37: Heike...
dry-fucked the rear fender.

duck *noun* ☞ In phrase: **fuck the duck,** to loaf; *fuck
the dog* under DOG. See also *fuck a duck* under FUCK,
verb.

1968–77 Herr *Dispatches* 57: I met a man in the
Cav who'd been "fucking the duck" one afternoon,
sound asleep in a huge tent. **1978** Selby *Requiem* 31:
Well let's stop fucking the duck and figure out how
we can pick up the bread. **1979** L. Heinmann, in *Tri-
Quarterly* (Spring) 180 [refers to Vietnam War]: He
was taking one of his famous naps—fucking the
duck, we called it.

dumbfuck *noun* a contemptibly stupid person. Also as adjective.

> **1946–50** J. Jones *From Here to Eternity* 531 [refers to 1941]: Shut you dumb fuck Turniphead you. **1966** in Indiana Univ. Folklore Archives *Folk Speech*: Denoting someone's stupidity. *Dumb fuck.* **1970–71** Rubenstein *City Police* 427: You know why that dumb-fuck sergeant has Smith drive him? **1973** *TULIPQ* (coll. B.K. Dumas): Dingbat; super dumb fuck. **1980** Conroy *Lords of Discipline* 150: I want you to rack that chin into your beady, ugly neck, dumbfuck. *a***1987** Bunch & Cole *Reckonings* 151: Of all the dumb-fuck things to do. **1998** *Sick Puppy Comix* (Sydney, Australia) (No. 8) 18: It's not a demon it's nicotine you dumb fuck!

Dutch fuck *noun* an act of lighting one cigarette from another.

> **1948** Partridge *Dictionary of Slang & Unconventional English* (ed. 3) 1039: *Dutch f**k.* Lighting one cigarette from another. Forces': 1940 +. **1974** New York City man, age 23: A Dutch fuck is when you light someone's cigarette with your own.

Words

eff, also **F,** (a partial euphemism for) FUCK in various senses and parts of speech.

1929 Graves *Good-Bye to All That* 79 [refers to 1917]: The Bandmaster, who was squeamish, reported it as: "Sir, he called me a double-effing c—." **1931** E.E. Cummings *I Sing of Olaf Glad and Big*: I will not kiss your f.ing flag. **1931** J. Hanley *Boy* 252: Tell the effin bosun there's only the crew's stuff here now. **1943, 1944** in *Oxford English Dictionary Supp.* **1945** in Hemingway *Selected Letters* 579: You'll hear I'm a phony, a liar, a coward, maybe even a Man of Honor. Just tell them to Eff off. **1950** Hemingway *Across the River and into the Trees* 78: "Eff Florence," the Colonel said. *Ibid.* 173: You would eff-off, discreetly. **1959** Cochrell *Barren Beaches* 130: They've come closer to solving the recreation problem than anyone else in this effing division. **1961** J.A. Williams *Night Song* 152: "Eff you, man," Yards said. **1961** Ellison *Memos* 43: Turn that effin' thing off before I put a fist through it. **1965** Hardman *Chaplains* 34: An effing chaplain's assistant! **1965** N. Simon *Odd Couple* III: "We're all out of Corn Flakes. F.U." It took me three hours to figure out that F.U. was Felix Ungar. It's not your fault, Felix. It's a rotten combination. **1967** Taggart *Reunion* 189: You effin well know it.

1970 Landy *Underground Dictionary* 76: *F. you*—Fuck you. *Ibid.* 77: *F—ing v.* Fucking; having sexual intercourse. *Ibid.* 78: *F—ing around*... Goofing off. **1973** Overgard *Hero* 61: Where in the effin hell have you been? **1977** *N.Y. Post* (Mar. 18) 37: With the language sensitivity of one who knows what will and will not get on TV he later asked: "Am I being effed around, or not?" He actually said "effed." *a***1984** in Terry *Bloods* 127: What the F was I there for? **1987** *Newsweek* (Mar. 23) 58: Don't F with him. *Ibid.* 63: He says he F'd you up. *Ibid.* 65: Stay the F out of the way. *Ibid.* 73: He said *F* the doctors. **1993** *Washington Post* (Sept. 3) A8: What the f are you doing here?

em-eff, variant of M.F.

eye-fuck *verb* to gaze at lecherously; ogle; (especially *Military*) to stare at, especially with hostility; (*hence, Military*) to look around.

   1916 Cary *Slang of Venery* I 79: *Eye Fuck*—To stare and leer at a woman. **1971** Barnes *Pawns* 69: The DI's have picked out the recruits who don't look sharp, who fall behind in the runs, or are caught "eye-fucking." ("Eye-fucking" is a heinous crime in Marine Corps boot camp. It consists of moving one's eyeballs to the side while standing at attention.) **1972** B. Rodgers *Queens' Vernacular* 77: *Eye fuck* (late '60s)...to stare holes through someone. **1980** M. Baker *Nam* 36: Smokey catches the dude looking at him out of the corner of his eye. He says, "Are you eye-fucking me, boy? I don't want your scuzzy eyes looking at me." **1980** Di Fusco et al. *Tracers* 12: While maggots are at attention, they will not talk, they will not eye-fuck the area, they will listen to me and only me! **1983** Ehrhart *Vietnam to Perkasie* 30 [refers to 1966]: You will not talk. You will not eye-fuck the area. *Ibid.* 32: You eye-fuckin' me, sweetpea? You wanna fuck me, scum? **1988** Norst *Colors* 17: Killer Bee...was...eye-fucking McGavin. **1991** J.T. Ward *Dear Mom* 5 [refers to 1968]: You will stand at attention, eyes forward. I don't want you eyefucking me or the area.

EYE-FUCK

Words

F, variant of EFF.

fan-fucking-tastic *adjective* wonderful; fantastic. Compare -FUCKING-, *infix*, for related forms.

1970 Southern *Blue Movie* 108: Tony was delighted. "Fan-fucking-tastic!" **1971** *National Lampoon* (Aug.) 26: Just groove on those colors! Fan-fucking-tastic! **1976** Schroeder *Shaking It* 78: "Fan-fucking-tastic!" Corso whistles in astonishment. **1977** Bredes *Hard Feelings* 42: He said "Fan-fucking-tastic!" over and over. **1981** Graziano & Corsel *Somebody Down Here* 156: Frankie...is fan-fuckintastic! *a***1988** M. Atwood *Cat's Eye* 298: Fan-fuckin'-tastic.

feck *verb Irish.* (a partial euphemism, in various senses, parts of speech, and derived forms, for) FUCK.

1989 H. Leonard *Out After Dark:* I went on clinging to the wall until old Fanning made feck-off gestures of great savagery. **1993** D. Purcell *Falling for a Dancer:* "Fecker," said Hazel passionately. "That's all he is, a fecker. I can't stand the sight of him." **1995** P. Boland *Tales from a City Farmyard:* Some little fecker of a kid pinched the bum off me. **1998** M. McDonagh *Beauty Queen of Leenane* (play): Feck!

fed up *adjective* ☞ In phrase: **fed up, fucked up, and far from home,** *Military.* disgusted, helpless, and far from one's home. Compare *fucked [up] and far from home* under FUCK, *verb.*

1936 Partridge *Dictionary of Slang & Unconventional English* 269: In the [First World War], a military [catch phrase] ran, *fed up, f**ked up, and far from home.* **1977** Caputo *Rumor of War* 93 [refers to 1965]: The Marines are all in the same state of mind as I, "fed-up, fucked-up, and far from home." **1979–81** C. Buckley *To Bamboola* 207: "Fucked up, fed up, and far away from home," he snorted. **1984** Partridge *Dictionary of Slang & Unconventional English* (ed. 8) 383: *Fed-up, fucked up, and far from home*...still being used by the WWI Tommies' soldier-grandsons, 1970s.

ferk *verb* (a partial euphemism for) FUCK in various senses and parts of speech. *Jocular.*

*ca***1929** *Collection of Sea Songs* 43: Perkin you're shirkin your ferkin. **1946–51** J. Jones *From Here to Eternity* ch. xxi [refers to *ca*1940]: Ah, what's the difference? They all the ferkin same. Five cents of one, a nickel of the other. **1965** in Legman *New Limerick* 4: He jerked 'em, and ferked 'em.

fiddlefuck *verb* to play or fiddle about; FUCK AROUND.—usually used with *around.* Also (in 1974 quotation) as noun. [The 1954 quotation represents a different meaning.]

1954 Legman *Limerick* 387: *Fiddle-fucking*: Sub-axillary (copulation) (New Jersey, 1939). **1974** R. Stone *Dog Soldiers* 321: Some of you birds think I'm down here to play fiddle fuck around. **1973–77** J. Jones *Whistle* 506 [refers to WWII]: It was strange, all right, and he didn't fiddlefuck around. **1979** Hurling *Boomers* 84: I'm not going to fiddle-fuck around 'til those pricks come out of the office. **1985** Dye *Between the Raindrops* 192: Can't fiddle-fuck around on the perimeter.

☞ In phrase: **be fiddlefucked,** to be damned.

1976 Atlee *Domino* 52: This is Korea's nuclear reactor one…and I'll be fiddle-fucked if I understand why it hasn't fallen down yet.

fiddlefucking *adjective* see under FUCKING, *adjective*

1970–74 P. Roth *My Life* 19: I guaranfuckingtee you gentlemen, not one swingin' dick will be leavin' this fiddlefuckin' area to so much as chew on a nanny goat's tittie.

fiddler's fuck *noun* a damn; ☞ in phrase: **not make a fiddler's fuck,** not make any difference. [The 1932 quotation is euphemistic.]

1932 Nelson *Prison Days & Nights* 25: We could all rot to death, and they wouldn't give a fiddler's so-and-so for us. **1961** Selby *Room* 187: They ain't worth a fiddlers fuck. **1973** W. Crawford *Stryker* 91: I don't give a fiddler's fuck about jurisdictional disputes, ace. **1976** Atlee *Domino* 175: A shamed patriot…ain't worth a fiddler's fuck. **1978** Selby *Requiem* 183: Why

fiddler's fuck *continued*

didn't make a fiddler's fuck. **1979** G. Wolff *Duke of Deception* 236: I didn't care a fiddler's fuck where my father was. **1984** Caunitz *Police Plaza* 22: I don't give a fiddler's fuck what the Forensic boys like.

fiddly-fuck *noun* see FIDDLER'S FUCK.

1973 New York City man, age 25: Do you think I give a fiddly-fuck?

☞ In phrase: **play fiddly-fuck,** to fool around.

1964–66 R. Stone *Hall of Mirrors* 305: I didn't come out to play fiddly fuck.

fifteen fucker *noun Army.* punishment under Article 15 of the Army Code of Conduct.

1981–89 R. Atkinson *Long Gray Line* 295: Each of them was reprimanded, fined $300, and given an Article 15—an administrative punishment known within the ranks as a fifteen Fucker—"for conduct totally unbecoming an officer."

FIGMO *interjection & adjective Military.* ["*fuck it, got my orders,*" with variations] (used as an expression of contempt or dismissal). Also **FUIGMO.** Compare FUJIGMO. *Jocular.*

1962 F. Harvey *Strike Command* 101: Everybody in the Air Force is familiar with the expression a man about to ship out to some new duty station gives those about him who have some insane notion that they'll get some useful work out of him. It is

"FIGMO!"...the expression which...[he] delivers at his new duty station...is FIGMO spelled backward, or OMGIF! **1968** J.D. Houston *Between Battles* 212: Once he knows [he is scheduled to rotate], he goes FUIGMO—fuck u, I got my orders. At the PX he buys a FUIGMO button. **1969** Moskos *Enlisted Man* 144: Rather, the attitude is typically, "I've done my time, let the others do theirs." Or, as put in the soldier's vernacular, he is waiting to make the final entry on his "FIGMO" chart—fuck it, got my orders (to return to the United States). **1969** *Current Slang I & II* 32: *Figmo*..."forget it, I've got my orders."—Air Force Academy cadets. **1983** Groen & Groen *Huey* 102 [refers to 1971]: Roger and John were among the few remaining...who were not figmo (fuck it, got my orders). *Ibid.* 105: You're figmo...I'll send them.

fingerfuck *noun* an act of masturbation of the vagina or anus.

[**1884** *Randiana* 31: The easy transition from a kiss to a feel, from a feel to a finger frig, and eventually by a more natural sequence to a gentle insertion of the jock.] **1970** Landy *Underground Dictionary* 77: *Finger fuck...n.* Stimulation of the female sex organs with the finger. **1978** J. Webb *Fields of Fire* 228: This bastard wants to kill me for a damn finger-fuck.

fingerfuck *verb* to masturbate the vagina or anus [of].

*a***1793** R. Burns *Merry Muses* 29: She m—s like reek thro' a' the week,/But finger f—s on Sunday, O. *ca***1866** *Romance of Lust* 197: Anything but fingerfucking. *a***1890–91** Farmer & Henley *Slang & Its Analogues* II 398: *Finger-fucking*...masturbation (said of

33

women only). **1916** Cary *Slang of Venery* I 84: *Finger fucking*—to induce a sexual spasm in a woman by digitation. **1921** in Cray *Erotic Muse* 195: There she saw her lovin' boy/finger-fucking Nellie Bly. **1945–48** *Marianas Collection* (unpaged): I started finger fucking myself. **1964** in H. Huncke *Huncke's Journal* 4: Licking—eating—jerking off and finger fucking. **1968** P. Roth *Portnoy's Complaint* 143: She wants you to finger-fuck her *shikse* cunt till she faints. **1970** Byrne *Memories* 157: I get tired of finger-fucking Wanda Farney all the time. **1970** Cain *Blueschild Baby* 53: Boy and girl flirting in hall shadowkiss and finger fuck. **1971** Dahlskog *Dictionary* 23: *Fingerfuck, v. Vulgar.* To arouse (someone) sexually by vaginal or rectal stimulation with the finger. **1976** J. Johnson *Oriental Festival* 139: I'm gonna...slip my finger inside your hot ass....Maybe I should give you a little finger fucking. **1983** *Playboy* (Aug.) 88: He claims that he is obsessed with sex, that he has done it with animals, that he's finger-fucked his cat. **1996** *Village Voice* (N.Y.C.) (Apr. 23) 74: Then he finger-fucks her on a roller coaster.

fist fuck *verb* Especially *Homosexuals.* to insert the hand into the rectum or vagina for sexual stimulation. Also as noun.

*a***1972** B. Rodgers *Queens' Vernacular* 81: *Fist fuck.* The extended process of inserting a fist to the elbow anally. **1978** R. Price *Ladies' Man* 224: That guy's into getting fist fucked...right up the ass. Right up to the elbow. Can you believe that? **1984** H. Gould *Cocktail* 91: He liked to put on mesh stockings...and get fistfucked. **1995** *New Statesman* (Aug. 4) 41: Each month's curse earned her a beating on the bedpost, a fistfuck for failure, exposure on the platform at the march past. **1995** *Village Voice* (N.Y.C.) (Dec. 12) 31: For a grand finale she got fistfucked by a ring-wearing "gypsy" lady while deep-throating a 13-inch dick.

fist-fucker *noun*

1. a man or boy who is a frequent masturbator.— used contemptuously.

1962 Killens *Then We Heard the Thunder* 168 [refers to WWII]: Corporal Solly, you old-fashioned fist-fucker, why don't you come out of that orderly room and get some air in your ass sometimes? **1974** E. Thompson *Tattoo* 111: I feel plumb sorry for you poor Wichita fistfuckers...got nothin to fuck there but their fists. **1984** Sample *Racehoss* 266 [refers to 1960s]: Nelly Nuthin, Proud Walker, Bow Wow, and fistfucker were...dunces.

2. *Homosexuals.* a practitioner of FIST-FUCKING, definition 2.

*a***1972** B. Rodgers *Queens' Vernacular* 81: *Fist fuckers*...those who practice fist fucking. **1973** *Oui* (July) 73: Fist fuckers of America: Their clenched-fist gestures are often an internal expression. **1985** J. Dillinger *Adrenaline* 213: How about *Fistfucker Beach?* **1993** *Folio* (Oct. 15) 57: The organizers [of a gay-rights march in Washington, D.C.] didn't want the Fist Fuckers of America marching down Pennsylvania Avenue.

3. a despicable or contemptible fellow.

1977 in H.S. Thompson *Shark Hunt* 602: If that treacherous fist-fucker ever comes back to life, he'll wish we'd had the good sense to nail him up on a frozen telephone pole.

fist-fucking *noun*

1. male masturbation.

*a***1890–91** Farmer & Henley *Slang & Its Analogues* II 402: *Fist-fucking*...masturbation. **1916** Cary *Slang of Venery* I 85: *Fist fucking*—masturbation.

2. Especially *Homosexuals.* insertion of the hand into the rectum or vagina for sexual stimulation.

*a***1972** (quotation at FIST-FUCKER, 2). **1973** *Oui* (July) 75: We spent some time discussing fist fucking ("it can be dangerous"). **1981** *Film Comment* (May) 21: Oriental beheadings and Occidental gay fistfuckings. **1984** *Body Double* (film): No animal acts, no fist-fucking, and absolutely no coming in my face. **1989** Chapple & Talbot *Burning Desires* 260: Videos that did not stop at fist-fucking. **1992** *Whole Earth Review* (June 22) 94: "Is 'perineal massage' really fist fucking?"..."Of course."...A hand going inside my pussy is...exciting.

flak *verb Military Aviation.* (a jocular euphemism for) FUCK. Also as noun.

1961 Forbes *Goodbye to Some* 120 [refers to WWII]: The 38's will get the flak out of there. **1963** E.M. Miller *Exile* 57: "Flak you, fellows," he said as the door slammed.

flying *adjective*

☞ In phrases:

☞ **flying fuck,** a damn; the least bit.—usually used in negative, with *give.* Also in euphemistic variants.

[*a***1850** (see quotation at FUCK, *noun,* definition 1a).] **1946–51** J. Jones *From Here to Eternity* [refers to 1941]: I don't give a flyin' fuck. **1953** Brossard *Bold Saboteurs* 30: They did not give a flying hoot. **1956** H. Ellison *Deadly Streets* 190: Tony didn't give a flying damn. **1967** in H. Ellison *Sex Misspelled* 154: I...don't give a flying *shit* what time you were behind your desk. **1973** R.M. Brown *Rubyfruit Jungle* 67: I don't give a flying fuck what you do. **1974** Strasburger *Rounding Third* 12: Who gives a flying fuck, Junior? **1980** Conroy *Lords of Discipline* 297: He wouldn't have given a flying crap about this city. **1984** Ehrhart *Marking Time* 19: Most...weren't worth a flying fuck. **1985** Finkelman *Head Office* (film): He doesn't give a flying shit about Steadman's position. **1995** E. White *Skinned Alive* 9: He didn't give a flying fuck about the Crowd. **1997** A. Proulx, in *New Yorker* (Oct. 13) 79: And I don't give a flyin fuck.

☞ **[go] take a flying fuck,** get away! go to hell! Also in euphemistic and elaborated variants.

1926 Nason *Chevrons* 73 [refers to 1918]: Me, I'd tell 'em to take a flyin' fling at the moon. **1929–30** Dos Passos *42nd Parallel* 271: I hadn't the nerve/to...tell/them all to go take a flying/Rimbaud/at the moon. **1932** Miller & Burnett *Scarface* (film): "They said you could take a flyin' —" "That's enough of that!" **1934** W. Saroyan, in North *New Masses* 93: I didn't obey my mother or my teachers and I told the whole world to take a flying you-know-what. **1935** J. Conroy *World to Win* 64: Go take a flyin' jump at a gallopin' goose for all o' me. **1936** Kingsley *Dead End* 706: Well, go take a flyin' jump at ta moon! **1938** in J. O'Hara *Selected Letters* 140: I say go take a flying fuck at a galloping r—ster. **1939** Appel *Power-House* 165: If this's the *Hamilton Dectective Agency* it can take a flyin' trip to the moon. **1941** Brackett & Wilder *Ball of Fire* (film): Tell the D.A. to take a flyin' jump for himself. **1944** Stiles *Big Bird* 105: You can take a flying one at a rolling one. **1949** Bezzerides *Thieves' Market* 122: He can go take a flying frig at himself. **1949** Pirosh *Battleground* (film) [refers to WWII]: Tell him to take a flyin' leap at a rollin' doughnut. **1952** Himes *Stone* 238: How would you like to take a flying frig at yourself? **1961** Brosnan *Pennant Race* 48: Brosnan, you take a flying leap at my —. **1962** Killens *Then We Heard the Thunder* 415: And you and your colored problems can take a flying frig at the moon. **1966** "T. Pendleton" *Iron Orchard* 40: You take a flyin' bite at my ass! **1968** Swarthout *Loveland* 169: "Go take a flying jump at a rolling doughnut!" I hollered. **1968** Vonnegut *Slaughterhouse-Five* 147 [ref. to WWII]: Go take a flying fuck at a rolling doughnut....Go take a flying fuck at the moon. **1971** Cameron *First Blood* 119: Why don't you go take a flying fuck at a rolling doughnut? **1972** N.Y.U. student: Go take a flying fuck for yourself. **1972** R.A. Wilson *Playboy's Book of Forbidden Words* 107: Take a flying Philadelphia fuck in [*sic*] a rolling doughnut. **1972** *Rowan & Martin's Laugh-In* (NBC-

TV): I told him to go take a flying leap. **1979** Hurling *Boomers* 13: I...just told him to take a flyin' fuck at a rollin' doughnut. **1979** McGivern *Soldiers* 185 [refers to WWII]: Why don't you take a flying fuck at a rolling doughnut? **1966–80** McAleer & Dickson *Unit Pride* 117: Go take a flyin' fuck at a rollin' doughnut. *Ibid.* 408: You go take a flyin' fuck at the moon. **1983** S. King *Christine* 296: Tell him to take a flying fuck at a rolling doughnut. **1985** Briskin *Too Much* 264: Tell 'em to go take a flying fuck. *a***1986** in *New Dictionary of American Slang*: Go take a flying frig. **1988** DeLillo *Libra* 93: Take a flying fuck at the moon.

FNG *noun* [*f*ucking *n*ew *g*uy] Especially *Military*. a person who is a newly arrived member, especially of a combat unit. [Most quotations refer to the Vietnam War.]

1966 *N.Y. Times Magazine* (Oct. 30) 104: F.N.G. designates a "foolish new guy." **1966** Shepard *Doom Pussy* 217: Major Nails says several FNGs believe it. **1972** T. O'Brien *Combat Zone* 73: Look, FNG, I don't want to scare you. **1980** M. Baker *Nam* 54: Who the hell was I? This rather quiet, slightly older FNG. **1983** Van Devanter & Morgan *Before Morning* 80: "And what's an FNG?" "What else?...A Fucking New Guy." **1983** Groen & Groen *Huey* 7: Rather than look like FNGs, fucking new guys, including officers, suffered their anxieties quietly. **1985** J. McDonough *Platoon Leader* 65: Despite...his disdain for new guys ("FNGs" he would mutter under his breath),...he was the most respected member of the platoon. **1995** *Newsweek* (May 8) 8: *FNG:* F—ing New Guy; the latest crew hire.

FO *noun & verb* Especially *Military.* See under FUCK-OFF, *noun & verb.*

1945 *American Speech* (Dec.) 262: *F.O.,* to avoid work. **1948** *N.Y. Folklore Quarterly* (Spring) 20. **1957** E. Brown *Locust Fire* 14a [refers to WWII]: I'm an R.O., you F.O. **1974** Strasburger *Rounding Third* 132: F.O., Carter. **1978** Student slang survey: [Go away and stop bothering me] *F.O., get off my case.* **1983** Groen & Groen *Huey* 98: "Just CA for a few months and then FO." Cover your ass and then fuck off.

force-fuck *verb* Especially *Politics.* to rape. Also figurative.

1972 B. Rodgers *Queens' Vernacular* 90: *Force-fuck*...to rape a man's anus. **1976** T. Teal trans. *Suzanne Brogger's Deliver Us from Love* 122: All the women who copulate to keep peace in the house are the victims of rape. All our grandmothers who just "let it happen" were essentially force-fucked all their lives. **1987** *Nation* (May 30) 722: MacKinnon's bluster is stunning....Since women are presumed "force-fucked," sexuality is presented in the light of Marx's theory of work. **1992** Pete Hamill, in *Playboy* (Jan. 1993) 138: According to Dworkin, all women are "force-fucked," either directly through the crime of rape or by the male power of mass media, by male economic power or by the male version of the law.

forget *verb* Originally *Black English.* to hell with; damn; FUCK, *verb,* definition 4a.

1969 *Elementary English* XLVI 495: F'get you,

honky! **1983** *Reader's Digest Success with Words* 85: Black English...*forget it* = "emphatic phrase expressing negation, denial, refutation." **1980–89** Cheshire *Home Boy* 105: Forget you, shit-for-brains. **1990** *Simpsons* (Fox-TV): Forget you, pal! Thanks for nothin'! **1995** (see quotation at FUCK-YOU MONEY).

fork *verb* to hell with; damn; FUCK, *verb*, definition 4a.

   1954–60 Wentworth & Flexner *Dictionary of American Slang*: *Fork You*...Euphemism for *fuck you*. **1972** B. Rodgers *Queens' Vernacular* 88: *Camp:* "Fork you, Rose, we're doing it *my* way!"

fouled-up *adjective* Originally *Navy & U.S. Marine Corps.* confused, chaotic, or disorganized; (*broadly*) mistaken; (*also*) stupid or worthless. [Frequently regarded as a euphemism for FUCKED UP.]

   1942 *Leatherneck* (Nov.) 145: *Fouled Up*—mixed up, confused. **1942** *Yank* (Nov. 11) 4: Navy [slang]... *Foul,* or *foul up*—Trouble or being in trouble or to get someone in trouble. Thus, if a sailor gets all fouled up with a skirt, he's got babe trouble. **1943** *Saturday Evening Post* (Mar. 20) 86: Those knuckleheads are all fouled up. **1944** Kendall *Service Slang* 23: *All fouled up*...messed up. **1945** in *California Folk Quarterly* V (1946) 390: *Fouled up like an ensign's sea bag* is the commonest [U.S. Navy simile]. **1940–46** McPeak *Navy Slang Manuscript:* You're as fouled up as a man overboard in dry dock...as a mess-cook drawing small stores...as a marine at fire drill. **1947** J.C. Higgins *Railroaded* (film): Somebody's all fouled up! **1948** Manone & Vandervoort *Trumpet* 157: Aw, I don't want to go out to ol' Cali-fouled up-ornia and mess with those square people out there. **1949** Grayson & Andrews *I Married a Communist* (film): We're trying to get some sense into a fouled-up situation while there's still time. **1956** Boatner *Military Customs* 125: *Fire Call*. A confused situation or formation. "All fouled up like a fire Call." **1960** Simak *Worlds* 43: It was all just this side of crazy, anyhow. No matter how fouled up it was, Steen seemed satisfied. **1964** Rhodes *Chosen Few* 57: I've been in this fouled-up place for almost four years straight now and I don't think I can or want to get used to it. **1967** W. Crawford *Gresham's War* 7 [refers to Korean War]: I called him Goat, for fouled-up like Hogan's goat, which he was. **1968** W.C. Anderson *Gooney Bird* 124: The whole thing is insanity. More fouled up than an Ethiopian fire drill. **1967–69** Foster & Stoddard *Pops* 1: I've always wanted to write down what I know about the times in New Orleans. Some of the books are fouled up on it and some of the guys weren't telling the truth. **1977** R.S. Parker *Effective Decisions* 2: Some cynics might say, "It's all society's fault. That's the real reason our lives are all fouled up." **1981** Ehrlichman *Witness* 21: Wooley earned a reputation for running the most fouled-up ticket and credential operation in modern Republican history.

foul-up *noun*

1. Originally *Navy & U.S. Marine Corps.* a blunder leading to a state of confusion or inefficiency; (*also*) a state of confusion brought about by ineptitude or inefficiency; (*also*) a mechanical malfunction. [Frequently regarded as a euphemism for FUCK-UP, definition 1.]

1943 in Sherrod *Tarawa* 82: Orders...never came because of the radio foul-up. **1944** *Newsweek* (Feb. 7) 61: *Janfu:* Joint Army-Navy foul-up. *Jaafu:* Joint Anglo-American foul-up. **1945** J. Bryan *Carrier* 139: There's been a foul-up. **1958** Hailey & Castle *Runway* 109: There's a foul-up on the phones in the press room. **1959** Fuller *Marines at Work* 143: "That's the history of the rock, doll," she was told. "Always a foul-up somewhere." **1971** Dibner *Trouble with Heroes* 44: The foul-up was especially galling to this bunch because ten days earlier the landing had been smooth and undetected. **1986** F. Walton *Once Were Eagles* 8: There he ran into a bureaucratic foulup: he couldn't get back into the Marine Corps.

2. Especially *Military.* a bungler or misfit. [Frequently regarded as a euphemism for FUCK-UP, definition 2.]

1945 in M. Chennault *Up Sun!* 136: I know what you foulups were up to. **1954–60** Wentworth & Flexner *Dictionary of American Slang: Foulup*...A person who makes frequent blunders. **1964** Pearl *Stockade* 70: I should have known better than to trust that foul-up Larkin. **1965** Linakis *In Spring* 293: These foul-ups are kids mostly. **1966** Derrig *Pride of Berets* 144: Even if he is a short-timer we can't afford even one foul-up in the outfit. **1987** D. da Cruz *Boot* 49: You're the worst bunch of foul-ups it's ever been my misfortune to have inflicted on me.

foul up *verb*

    1. Originally *Navy & U.S. Marine Corps.* to bring into confusion; mix up; confound; botch; ruin;

☞ in phrase: **foul up the detail,** *Military.* to bungle. Now *colloquial.* [Frequently regarded as a euphemism for FUCK UP, definition 1.]

    1942 (quotation at FOULED-UP). **1943** in Rea *Wings of Gold* 76: I fouled up a navigation quiz completely. **1944** Wakeman *Shore Leave* 21: You know damn well she's in Hartford, making those Pratt-Whitney engines you foul up. **1946** S. Wilson *Voyage to Somewhere* 108: They've just fouled up the mails. I don't doubt she's writing. **1949** Bezzerides *Thieves' Market* 198: She's always fouling us up. **1949** "R. MacDonald" *Moving Target* 82: I'm fouled up. Why should I foul you up? **1952** Uris *Battle Cry* 132 [refers to WWII]: You guys have been fouling up field problems like a Chinese firedrill. **1953** Brackett, Reisch & Breen *Niagara* (film): It'll be all right if I don't foul it up. **1953** Felsen *Street Rod* 83: We'd clobber the first guy that fouled us up by racing or being reckless on the roads. **1955** McGovern *Fräulein* 170: You're in charge here, and I never try to foul you up. **1957** Myrer *Big War* 150 [refers to WWII]: Somebody fouled up the detail, that's for sure. **1958** Plageman *Steel Cocoon* 55: A guy like that is a jinx. He could foul us all up. Don't you see that? *Ibid.* 165: He fouled it up!...We almost had it, just perfect, and he fouled it up! **1958** Cooley *Run for Home* 343: The sonuvabitch nearly fouled up the whole detail. **1966** Rose *The Russians Are Coming!* (film): You're gonna foul up the whole detail! **1966** Christopher *Little People* 179: And you're determined to foul it up if you can. **1971** Capaldi *Art of Deception* 95: He might easily fit both categories and hence foul up the classification again. **1971** Keith *Long Line Rider* 91: He put black pepper behin' 'em to foul up the dogs. **1971** Rowe *Five Years* 402: My screwed-up additions to the map had done some good, even if they hadn't fouled Charlie up completely.

    2. Originally *Navy & U.S. Marine Corps.* to become confused, especially to blunder into or cause trouble; fail through confusion or ineptitude; go wrong or awry. [Frequently regarded as a euphemism for FUCK UP, definition 4.]

    1944 *New Yorker* (May 6) 26: Look how we fouled up on maneuvers. **1946** S. Wilson *Voyage to Somewhere* 197: Pretty soon all the crew will know that to get a transfer, all they have to do is foul up. **1954** E. Hunter *Blackboard Jungle* 27: They'd come to within a term of graduation, and they...didn't want to get thrown out of school for fouling up at this late stage of the game. **1956** M. Wolff *Big Nickelodeon* 243: You fouled up and the old man came and took the kid. **1958** Schwitzgebel *Streetcorner Research* 21: We want to know why kids foul up and why they do the other things they do. **1964** Newhafer *Last Tallyho* 135: If anything fouls up, he wants to be there. **1965** Linakis *In Spring* 292: I don't like to see a G.I. foul up. **1970** Thackrey *Thief* 295: Only my tipsters had fouled up again. **1978** J. Lee *13th Hour* 21: If anything can foul up, it will. **1972–79** T. Wolfe *Right Stuff* 265: Please, dear God, don't let me foul up.

four Fs *noun* a motto for sexual behavior: "find 'em, fool 'em, fuck 'em, and forget 'em." Also variants.

[**1934** Berg *Prison Nurse* 29: No one ever got rich letting suckers keep their dough. My motto is "find them, fool them, and forget them!"] [**1941** Macaulay & Wald *Manpower* (film): You're talkin' to the guy who finds 'em, feeds 'em and forgets 'em.] **1942** in Hollingshead *Elmtown's Youth* 422: The five F's — "find 'em, feed 'em, feel 'em, f— 'em, forget 'em." **1953** Berrey & Van den Bark *American Thesaurus of Slang* (ed. 2) 325: *The four F's,* high-pressure romancing—find 'em, fool 'em, frig 'em, and forget 'em. *a***1961** Partridge *Dictionary of Slang & Unconventional English* (ed. 5) 1096: *Four F method, the.* This is the lower-deck's allusive synonym (C.20) of its sexual motto, *find, feel, f**k and forget,* itself current since *ca*1890. **1965** *Playboy* (Nov.) 67: The Four F's. **1966** Harris & Freeman *Lords* 30: What a sportsman mean when he say weaving the four F's is—you got to find you chick and you got to fool her and you got to frig her and forget her! **1974** Lahr *Hot to Trot* 7: Melish, baby, the Four F's are forever....find 'em. Feel 'em. Fuck 'em. Forget 'em. **1978** Kopp *Innocence* 58: I aspired to the macho four Fs of my generation: find 'em, feel 'em, fuck 'em and forget 'em. [**1978** W. Brown *Tragic Magic* 23: He could find them, fool them, feel them, fuck them, and forget them with exceptional agility.] [**1986** Ciardi *Good Words* 118: *Find 'em, fool 'em, fuck 'em, and forget 'em*....I was first drilled to these orders in WWII and received them as essential GI pitch.]

fox *noun* ☞ In phrase: **hotter than a fresh-fucked fox in a forest fire,** extremely hot (in any sense). *Jocular.*

*ca***1950** in Atkinson *Dirty Comics* 197: Betty! This guy's got me hotter than a fresh fucked fox in a forest fire. **1973** *TULIPQ* (coll. B.K. Dumas): Horny...Hotter than a fresh-fucked fox in a forest fire. **1974** E. Thompson *Tattoo* 264 [refers to 1940s]: It's a bitch down there. Hotter than a fresh fucked fox in a forest fire. **1974** Blount *3 Bricks Shy* 307: I'm hotter than a freshly fucked fox in a forest fire. **1977** S. Gaines *Discotheque* 268: It's hotter in here than a fresh fucked fox in a forest fire. **1980** Ciardi *Browser's Dictionary* 41: Hot as a fresh fucked fox in a forest fire. **1988** Dye *Outrage* 125: Locker room wisdom held churchmen's daughters were "hotter'n a freshly fucked fox in a forest fire."

frap *noun* [formed from FRAPPING] (used as a euphemism for FUCK in various senses and parts of speech).

1992 Eble *Campus Slang* (Fall) 3: What the frap is going on? **1998** *Washington Post* (Apr. 29) D4: "Frap," a way to curse without cursing ("Boy, I really frapped that up."). *Ibid. Off-brand frap*..."a lame girl."

frapping *adjective Military.* (a partial euphemism for) FUCKING, *adjective.*

1968 W.C. Anderson *Gooney Bird* 76: We'll let a whole frapping regiment get away before we'll risk hitting one old lady in sneakers. **1970** *N.Y. Times* (Apr. 19) 1: And finally in desperation: "What's the frappin' altitude?" **1972** W.C. Anderson *Hurricane* 196: And the poor frapping navy! **1973** M. Collins *Carrying the Fire* 334: Yeah, but the frapping thing bombed out again. **1989** Berent *Rolling Thunder* 133: That frapping Dash-K is shooting out our cover by the frapping roots.

freaking *adjective & adverb* (a partial euphemism for) FUCKING, *adjective*.

1928 Bodenheim *Georgie May* 9: Oh yuh cain't catch o-on to thuh freakin' Mistah Stave an' Chain. *Ibid.* 70: Ah hate the hull, freaking pack uh you. **1955** *Harper's* (Mar.) 35: Open the Freaking Door, Joe. **1961** Garrett *Which Ones Are the Enemy* 16: Not freaking likely. **1965** Hardman *Chaplains* 1: A great big freaking disaster! **1972** C. Gaines *Stay Hungry* 152: He's freaking Superman is who he is. **1972–76** Durden *No Bugles, No Drums* 9: It's too freakin' late now. **1978** Wharton *Birdy* 276: It's like my freaking body has some kind of controls all its own. **1972–79** T. Wolfe *Right Stuff* 6: It was a struggle to move twenty feet in this freaking muck. **1982** *Flash* (Dec.) 10: Have you gone freakin' bananas? **1989** U.S. Navy officers, on *Prime News* (CNN-TV) (Jan. 5): "He's got a missile off!" "Freakin' right!" **1998** *Esquire* (Mar.) 148: Enough already with all the theory and dice games and analysts. Let's buy some freakin' stocks.

French fuck *noun* an act of rubbing the penis between a woman's breasts. Compare TIT-FUCK.

1938 "Justinian" *Americana Sexualis* 22: *French Fuck*. n. A form of sexual activity in which the male sits astride the recumbent female and achieves sexual orgasm by rubbing his penis between her breasts, while concomitantly effecting her orgasm by digital stimulation of her vaginal area. Br. & U.S., C. 19-20. **1974** Graduate student: A...French fuck is when you rub your dick between her breasts. It's also called a *muscle fuck*. [Heard in Arkansas, *ca*1970.]

fricking *adjective & adverb* (a partial euphemism for) FUCKING, *adjective*. Also as infix.

    1936 Partridge *Dictionary of Slang & Unconventional English* 982: *Fricking*. A s. euphemism for *f**king*, adj.: C.20 On or ex *frigging*, adj. **1970** in P. Heller *In This Corner* 237: That fricking bum. **1975** Univ. Minn. student: I just finished writing a paper. I'm so frickin' tired. **1976** College student: That's no frickin' reason. **1976** Rosen *Above the Rim* 40: Jesus H. Keerist! What a fricken ball club! **1977** Dowd *Slap Shot* (film): Grab your frickin' gear and get goin'. **1986** *L.A. Law* (NBC-TV): You got a problem with that, you go live in the *frickin'* Soviet Union! **1987** College professor, age *ca*65: In Albany [N.Y., *ca*1934] we used *frickin'* a lot. Certainly more than *friggin'*: "That frickin' son of a bitch!" **1989** *CBS Summer Playhouse* (CBS-TV): Who do you think you are? Attila the Hun? Jack the fricking Ripper? **1989** *21 Jump St.* (Fox-TV): Absofrickin'lutely! We're talking total obliteration. **1998** *Sick Puppy Comix* (Sydney, Australia) (No. 7) 2: Maybe things will change now that I've got this frickin' hi-tech e-mail address.

frig *noun*

    1. an instance of masturbation.

frig *continued*

1786 R. Burns, in Farmer *Merry Songs* IV 282: Defrauds her wi' a frig or dry-bob. *ca***1888–94** in *Oxford English Dictionary Supp.*: I pulled out my prick and with two or three frigs spent in a spasm of pain and pleasure.

2. an act of copulation.

1888 *Stag Party* 62: What is the difference between a flag and a frig? One is bunting, the other is cunting. **1927** *Immortalia* 44: 'Twas a frig to a finish.

3. a damn; FUCK, *noun,* definition 3a.

1954–55 McCarthy *Charmed Life* 66: This is ridiculous....I don't give a frig about Sinnot's heredity. **1968** Myrer *Eagle* 61: Ain't worth a frig.

4. (a partial euphemism for) *the fuck,* definition 1, under FUCK, *noun.*

1944 Kapelner *Lonely Boy Blues* 91: And who the frig is Sam Duncan? **1948** Wolfert *Act of Love* 239: Here the frig we go again. **1964** Howe *Valley of Fire* 98: Leave him the frig alone. **1978** De Christoforo *Grease* 96: And who the frig are you?

frig *verb*

1. [a specialization of the obsolete Standard English sense 'to rub or chafe'] to masturbate.

1598 J. Florio, in Farmer & Henley *Slang & Its Analogues* III 74: *Fricciare*...to frig, to wriggle, to tickle. *ca***1650** in Wardroper *Love & Drollery* 197: And lest her sire should not thrust home/She frigged her father in her mother's womb. **1680** Lord Rochester, in *Oxford English Dictionary Supp.*: Poor pensive lover, in this place, Would Frigg upon his Mothers Face. *ca***1684** in Ashbee *Biblio.* II 333: All the rest pull out their dildoes and frigg in point of honour. *ca***1730** in Burford *Bawdy Verse* 254: *You* know, at fifty-five,/A man can only *frigg* her! **1734** in Legman *No Laughing Matter* III 18: Assembled, and Frigged upon the Test Platter. *ca***1716–46** in Farmer & Henley *Slang & Its Analogues* III 74: So to a House of office...a School-Boy does repair, To...fr— his P— there. **1785** Grose *Vulgar Tongue: To frig.* To be guilty of the crime of self-pollution. **1835** in Valle *Rocks & Shoals* 167: *Question.* Did you ever frig Lt. Burns? *A.* Yes— *Q.* How often? *A.* five or six times. **1865** Capt. E. Sellon *New Epicurean* 13: I frigged and kissed their fragrant cunnies. *ca***1866** *Romance of Lust* 27: Fortunately, I had never frigged myself. **1909** in J. Joyce *Selected Letters* 182: You... frigged me slowly till I came off through your fingers. **1940** Del Torto *Graffiti Transcript:* My finger against his asshole....I pushed it up and began to frig him. **1957** Myrer *Big War* 361 [refers to WWII]: There'll be no friggin' in the riggin'...and no poopin' on the poop-deck. **1970** Peters *Sex Newspapers* 4: I began frigging myself even harder.

2.a. to copulate; (*hence*) to copulate with. [The earliest quotations—variants of the same ribald song—involve word play on the obsolete Standard English sense 'to move about restlessly; wiggle', and suggest that the current sense arose as a euphemism; note that as early as *ca*1650 the word seems to have been regarded as coarse and to be avoided.]

*ca***1610** in Burford *Bawdy Verse* 65: Faine woulde I try how I could frig/Up and downe, up and downe, up and downe,/Fain would I try how I could Caper. *ca***1650** in Wardroper *Love & Drollery* 186: Fain would I go both up and down.../No child is fonder of the gig/Than I to dance a merry jig./Fain would I try how I could —. *ca***1684** in Cary *Sexual Vocabulary* II: You frigg as though you were afraid to hurt. **1865** Capt. E. Sellon *New Epicurean* 19: I had flung her on her back on the hay and was frigging away at her maidenhead. **1888** *Stag Party* 71: Why is the firing of an outhouse like flies frigging? It is arson on a small scale. *ca***1889** E. Field *Boastful Yak*: She would have been frigged, but he reneagued. **1918–19** in Carey *Mlle. from Armentières* II (unpaged): The first Division is having a time,/Frigging the Fraus along the Rhine. **1916–22** Cary *Sexual Vocabulary* I under *copulation*: *Frigging like a mink.* To perform with vigor. *frigging like a rabbit.* To have great capacity. **1922** H.L. Mencken, in Riggio *Dreiser-Mencken Letters* II 463: But frigging, as you must know, is invariably unlawful, save under ecclesiastical permit. **1922** in T.E. Lawrence *The Mint* 155: [It sounded] like a pack of skeletons frigging on a tin roof. **1927** in E. Wilson *Twenties* 413: Story about the fellow whose girl kept on eatin' an apple all the time he was friggin' her. **1927** *Immortalia* 32: The Khan would rather frig than fight. **1930** *Lyra Ebriosa* 12: We'll go over and do some friggin';/Dollar and a half will pay your fee. **1934** in Randolph *Pissing in Snow* 88: She was better frigging than the other girl, so he diddled her twice. **1938** "Justinian" *Americana Sexualis* 23: *Frig* (*Frick*). v. To copulate with....Often used as euphemistic expletive for the phrase "Fuck it!" **1942** McAtee *Supplement to Grant Co.* 4 [refers to 1890s]: *Frig,* v., copulate. **1942** in Legman *Limerick* 18: A young wife.../Preferred frigging to going to mass. **1944** in P. Smith *Letters from Father* 426: He would "frig" her himself. **1969** Jessup *Sailor* 6: Better than you, letting him come up here while I'm at work and frigging from morning til night, probably.

b. (used as an expletive); "screw"; to hell with; (*hence*) to disregard utterly. [Frequently regarded as a partial euphemism for FUCK, *verb*, definition 2a.]

1879 *Pearl* 103: Two prisoners were brought in.... The Sergeant requested orders regarding them. The Major merrily answered: "Oh, take them away and frig them!" **1905** in J. Joyce *Letters* II 104: Cosgrave says it's unfair for you to frig the one idea about love which he had before he met you, and say "You have educated him too much." **1929–35** Farrell *Judgment Day* 629: Phrigg you, Catherine! **1936** Kingsley *Dead End* 691: *Spit.* Frig you! *Drina*...I'll crack you...you talk like that! **1938** O'Hara *Hope of Heaven* 131: Frig dat. **1940** Zinberg *Walk Hard* 133: Aw, frig it, if I hadn't been expecting a fight...it wouldn't of happened. **1946** Gresham *Nightmare Alley* 20: Frig him, the Bible-spouting bastard. **1948** Wolfert *Act of Love* 155: Frig them. *Ibid.* 399: The Navy was still saying, Frig you Joe, I'm okay. **1949** Bezzerides *Thieves' Market* 23: Frig Mom, let her try to stop me. **1953** Manchester *City of Anger* 116: Frig trouble, I always say. Better frig it before it frigs you. **1956** Metalious *Peyton Place* 358: "Frig you," said Kenny hostilely. **1970** Gattzden *Black Vendetta* 102: Let's frig it. **1980** McAleer & Dickson *Unit Pride* 96: Frig 'em all and their mothers too. All but six and leave them for pallbearers.

c. to cheat. [Frequently regarded as a partial euphem-ism for FUCK, *verb,* definition 4a.]

[*ca***1684** in Ashbee *Biblio.* II 339: I'll then invade and bugger all the Gods/And drain the spring of their immortal cods,/Then make them rub their arses till they cry,/You've frigged us out of immortality.] **1928** *American Speech* III (Feb.) 219: *Frig.* To trick, to take advantage of. "They frigged me out of the last bottle of Scotch!" **1935** J. Conroy *World to Win* 209: They'll frig themselves and ever'body else out of a job. **1945** in Perelman *Don't Tread on Me* 60: I don't use a liter-ary agent, but I probably should, because I have been frigged time and again by publishers. **1952** H. Grey *Hoods* 88: He's the kind of guy who talks through both sides of his mouth and whistles "I frig you truly."

3. to trifle or fool about.—used with *with, about,* or *around.* [Frequently regarded as a partial euphemism for FUCK, *verb,* definition 5.]

1785 Grose *Vulgar Tongue: To frig.* ...Frigging is also used figuratively for trifling. **1811** in Howay *New Hazard* 15: Staying jib-boom; loosing and handing sails over; getting boat on the quarter and frigging about all the afternoon. *ca***1900** in *English Dialect Dic-tionary:* I can do nothing while you keep frigging about. **1928** C. McKay *Banjo* 241: Don't think I like frigging round officials. I hate it. **1930** Fredenburgh *Soldiers March!* 151 [refers to 1918]: What the hell do you want, frigging around that echelon? **1933** Masefield *Conway* 211 [refers to 1891]: *Frig about,* to fool around. **1940** Hemingway *For Whom the Bell*

Tolls 272: We do not let the gypsy nor others frig with it. **1946** J.H. Burns *Gallery* 301: Untying his shoelaces and frigging with the buckles on his boots. **1949** Ellson *Tomboy* 127: Do you let any punk in the mob frig around with you? **1952** H. Grey *Hoods* 225: No friggin' around. **1954** Schulberg *On the Waterfront* 11: I worked too hard for what I got to frig around with a cheese-eater. Know what I mean? **1961** A.J. Roth *Shame of Wounds* 34: Now if you was in my gang, we'd fix Nolan for you. He don't frig around with none of us. **1962** Dougherty *Commissioner* 187: You go in there—no friggin' around. **1975** J. Gould *Maine Lingo* 102: *Frig.* A word with four-letter nuance almost everywhere except Maine. Here, it means fiddle around, dawdle, fidget, fuss, fondle idly, putter. A Maine lady of unimpeachable gentility once described her late husband as nervous and ill at ease in public, and said he would sit "*frigging* with his necktie." **1988** M. Bail *Holden's Performance* 113: You can't frig around with nature.

☞ In phrase:

☞ **go frig [yourself]!** get away! go to hell!

1936 Kingsley *Dead End* 726: Ah, go frig! **1951** Sheldon *Troubling of a Star* 20: Tell the bastard to go frig himself.

frigger *noun* (a partial euphemism for) FUCKER, definition 2.

1953 Manchester *City of Anger* 145: That bastard... that no good frigger.

frigging *adjective & adverb* contemptible or despicable; damned; (often used with reduced force for emphasis). Also as infix. [Perhaps originally derived from literal phrases such as *frigging youngster, frigging madman,* etc., used opprobriously; now usually regarded as a partial euphemism for FUCKING.]

*a***1890–93** Farmer & Henley *Slang & Its Analogues* III 74: *Frigging...Adj. and adv.* (vulgar).—An expletive of intensification. Thus *frigging bad*—"bloody" bad; a *frigging idiot*—an absolute fool. **1929–30** Dos Passos *42nd Parallel* 55: If people only realized how friggin' easy it would be. *Ibid.* 89: I told 'em I was a friggin' bookagent to get into the damn town. **1943** in P. Smith *Letters from Father* 332: It was a "friggen" swell party. **1944** Wakeman *Shore Leave* 10: It took me three more weeks to get off that frigging island. **1947** Motley *Knock on Any Door* 194: I'm no friggin' good. **1948** Wolfert *Act of Love* 136: On your feet, you friggin' volunteers. **1949** Bezzerides *Thieves' Market* 3: You're frigging right, Pa. **1947–52** R. Ellison *Invisible Man* 192: A frigging eight-day wonder. **1954** F.I. Gwaltney *Heaven & Hell* 264 [refers to WWII]: That would be oh-friggen-kay with me. **1956** Metalious *Peyton Place* 93: Where's the friggin' bottle? **1957** Mayfield *Hit* 89: "Is he the only one who can drive this friggin' car?" squealed Frank. **1974** Cherry *High Steel* 160: So friggin' what? **1980** J. Carroll *Land of Laughs* 22: I got the friggin' renewal already. **1986** *Newsweek* (Jul. 28) 26: I said, "Give me a break, this ain't no frigging war." **1989** *Tour of Duty* (CBS-TV): There ain't no friggin' justice! **1991** Marcinko & Weisman *Rogue Warrior* 63: I don't frigging believe it. **1992** N. Cohn *Heart of World* 9: Straight off the friggin' boats.

frigging-A *interjection* (a partial euphemism for) FUCKING-A.

1971 Jacobs & Casey *Grease* 13: DANNY. Is that all you ever think about, Sonny? SONNY....Friggin'-A! **1973** W. Crawford *Stryker* 41: You're friggin-A-well right I would have. **1979** McGivern *Soldiers* 139 [refers to WWII]: "So you know what I'm thinking."..."Frigging A." **1984** in Safire *You Could Look It Up* 120: A euphemism from my adolescence, like "Friggin'-A, I'm going."

frig off *verb*

1. to masturbate to orgasm.

1909 in J. Joyce *Selected Letters* 191: Do you frig yourself off first? **1955** "Thirty-Five" *The Argot: Frig up* To mess up (euphemism)....In literal sense, *to frig oneself off,* to masturbate. **1979** *American Speech* LI 22 [refers to *ca*1950]: *Frig* and *frig off.*

2. to go away; go to hell.—used imperatively. [Regarded as a partial euphemism for FUCK OFF, definition 1.]

1961 A.J. Roth *Shame of Wounds* 141: "Go on, frig off," Red's scowl dared him. "See how far you get by yourself." **1965** in *Oxford English Dictionary Supp.*: "Frig off," he said, swinging towards the door.

frig-up *noun* (a partial euphemism for) FUCK-UP, definitions 1 & 2.

1941 S.J. Baker, in *Oxford English Dictionary Supp.*: *Frigg-up,* a confusion, muddle. **1948** I. Shaw *Young*

Lions 542: You're the frig-ups of the Army. **1954** F.I. Gwaltney *Heaven & Hell* 15 [refers to WWII]: Hell no! I ain't no frigup. *Ibid.* 18: They're frigups, sure, but they ain't jailbirds.

frig up *verb*

1. (a partial euphemism for) FUCK UP, definition 1.

1933 in Dos Passos *14th Chronicle* 428: All my plans for work are frigged up for fair, too. **1937** Weidman *I Can Get It for You Wholesale* 60: Something's frigged up around here! [**1942** S.J. Baker *Australian Language* 267: It is common in English for *up* to be added in a verbal sense, thus *mess up, rust up, knock up*, and even for certain nounal forms to emerge....Thus we have...*frigg-up* or *muck-up*, a confusion, a row or argument.] **1954** F.I. Gwaltney *Heaven & Hell* 26: When they frigup [*sic*] here, they ain't no place to send 'em except home in a box. *a***1966** S.J. Baker *Australian Language* (ed. 2) 217: *Frig up*, to mar.

2. (a partial euphemism for) FUCK UP, definition 2a.

1953 Paley *Rumble* 257: The Stompers are saying that only a Digger could frig up like that. *a***1981** in S. King *Bachman* 470: No, I frigged up.

FTA *interjection Army.* "fuck the Army."

1958 "Harde" *Lusty Limericks* 44: Marching Song of the F.T.A. (Fuck The Army). **1963** Doulis *Path* 32: "And what does FTA stand for, Specialist?"... "Sir...excuse me....The initials stand for Fuck the

Army." **1969** *N.Y. Times Magazine* (May 18) 122: Some of the blacks gave the closed-fist militant salute and several soldiers shouted "F.T.A."—initials which recruiting sergeants insist stand for "Fun, Travel, and Adventure" but which most soldiers recognize as a suggestion of what should be done to the Army. **1970** W. Just *Military Men* 67: The slogan is F.T.A., which means Fuck the Army. **1984** Riggan *Free Fire* 109: New helmet covers with none of that FTA stuff written in ballpoint pen on them.

FTL *interjection* "fuck the law."

1992 *New Yorker* (May 18) 28: The graffiti on the walls everywhere said "F.T.L."—I was told that it stood for "Fuck the Law." **1995** H. Rawson *Dictionary of Euphemisms* (rev. ed.) 157: Kids still write "FTL" on walls instead of "Fuck The Law."

FTW *interjection* "fuck the world."

1972 R.A. Wilson *Playboy's Book of Forbidden Words* 113: *F.T.W.* A slogan of Hell's Angels…meaning *fuck the world.* **1980** Hand-lettered sign in student dormitory window: F.T.W.! **1981** *Easyriders* (Oct.) 68: F.T.W. **1995** S. Moore *In the Cut* 111: I saw the letters FTW tattooed crudely on the boy's arm.

FUBAR *adjective* ["fucked up beyond all recognition"; suggested by SNAFU]

1. Originally *Military.* thoroughly botched or confused. Also **fubar'd.** Occasionally as noun. *Jocular.*

1944 *Yank* (Jan. 7) 8: The FUBAR Squadron.… FUBAR? It means "Fouled Up Beyond All Recognition." **1944** *Newsweek* (Feb. 7) 61: Recent additions to the ever-changing lexicon of the armed services: *Fubar.* Fouled up beyond all recognition. **1944** in Tobin *Invasion Journal* 48: The Italian campaign was SNAFU for so long.... SNAFU... means, Situation Normal All Fouled Up—with, of course, an unprintable variation in the most common use....To be FUBAR is much worse. It means Fouled Up Beyond All Recognition. **1952** Uris *Battle Cry* 114: Fubar on the nets and you can louse up an entire landing team. *Ibid.* 300: A full-scale fubar'd mess. **1957** Myrer *Big War* 119: What's to this yarn about you being a fubar character from the word advance? **1972** Davidson *Cut Off* 30 [refers to WWII]: An even stronger superlative was Fubar—Fucked Up Beyond All Recognition. **1982** *Daily Beacon* (univ. newspaper) (Feb. 3) 2: Move it, fubar! **1987** *Daily Beacon* (univ. newspaper) (Apr. 9) 4: I already have a name picked out for my license plate...."FUBAR." figure it out for yourself. [*Hint*]...beyond all repair. **1990** Rukuza *West Coast Turnaround* 196: And the situation? FUBAR.

2. thoroughly intoxicated.

1985 College student: *Fubar* means drunk. Like, "Man, I was fubar last night." **1990** J. Sanders *Cal Poly Slang* 4: *Fubar*—intoxicated beyond all recognition. [*Example:*] I was so *fubar* I couldn't find my date to take her home. **1991** Eble *Campus Slang* (Fall) 2: *Fubar*—very drunk. **1998** *Canberra Times* (Australia) (May 30) A2: Many terms [for drunkenness] are insults—"full as a tick" and the acronym FUBAR, "fouled up beyond all recognition."

FUBB *adjective* [suggested by FUBAR] Originally *Military*. "*f*ucked *up b*eyond *b*elief." *Jocular*.

   1952 *Time* (Aug. 18) 6: Snafu and cummfu are a bit old hat in Washington, along with tarfu ("things are really"), fubar ("beyond all realization"), fubb ("beyond belief"). **1979** Homer *Jargon* 162. **1984** K. Weaver *Texas Crude* 40: *F.U.B.B.*... Fucked Up Beyond Belief.

FUBIO *interjection Military*. "*f*uck *y*ou, *b*ub, *i*t's *o*ver." *Jocular*.

   1946 *American Speech* (Feb.) 72: The final word came after V-J day, FUBIO. Its description of the post-war attitude...meant "F— You, Bub, It's Over."

FUBIS *interjection Army*. ("*f*uck *y*ou, *b*uddy, *I*'m *s*hipping out."). Compare FIGMO.

   1967 Wentworth & Flexner *Dictionary of American Slang* (supplement) 685: *Fubis*...Fuck you, buddy, I'm shipping (out). *Army use since c1960*.

fuck *noun* [see etymology and note at the verb]

   1.a. an act of copulation.

   1680 in *Oxford English Dictionary Supp.*: Thus was I Rook'd of Twelve substantial Fucks. *ca***1684** in *Oxford English Dictionary Supp.*: A little fuck can't stay our appetite. **1763** in J. Atkins *Sex in Literature* IV 154: Then just a few good fucks, and then we die. *a***1850** in Cary *Slang of Venery* I 91: Well mounted on a mettled steed,/Famed for his strength as well as speed,/Corinna and her favorite buck/Are please'd to have a flying f—k. **1860** in Neely *Lincoln Encyclopedia* 155: When Douglas found his chances were scarcely worth a shuck/He bade his Delegates, go

home, to take a little fu—. *ca***1866** *Romance of Lust*
35: I wished to quietly enjoy a fuck. **1867** in Doten
Journals II 949 [in cipher]: Me & my love have had
this far just one hundred good square fucks together.
1879 *Harlequin Prince Cherrytop* 28: Now we can do
no better I'll be bound,/Than to celebrate our joy
with fucks all round. **1879** *Pearl* 127: Oh! What a nice
fuck! **1888** *Stag Party* 42: Adonis...gave her a most
systematical fuck. **1899** *Memoirs of Dolly Morton* 249:
Here goes for the fust fuck. **1923** *Poems, Ballads, &*
Parodies 22: He was working like a son of a bitch/To
get another fuck. **1928** in Read *Lexical Evidence from*
Folk Epigraphy 55: Me and my wife had a fuck. **1934**
"J.M. Hall" *Anecdota* 26: Every time you threw a fuck
into me I put a penny in the bank. **1934** H. Miller
Tropic of Cancer 78: He has absolutely no ambition
except to get a fuck every night. **1938** H. Miller *Tropic*
of Capricorn 104: Into each...one...I throw an imaginary fuck. **1940** *Ramirez v. State* [of Arizona], in
Pacific Reporter, 2d Series 103:461: While she was in
bed asleep the defendant entered her room, grabbed
her by the throat...he stood at the head of her bed
and when she awoke made this statement to her:
"Gonna throw a fuck into you"; that he did not say,
"I'm going to" but just "gonna"; that after telling her
this he loosened his grip somewhat and kissed her....
1947 Willingham *End as a Man* 240: A fuck for a
buck. **1956** in Cheever *Letters* 178: You've just talked
yourself out of a fuck. **1971** *Go Ask Alice* 117: All I
needed was a good fuck. **1990** L.B. Rubin *Erotic Wars*
75: All she wanted was "a good clean fuck." **1997** *GQ*
(March) 166: Good cry, good hug, one last fuck for
old times' sake.

b. copulation.

*ca***1675** in R. Thompson *Unfit for Modest Ears* 49: If guifted Men before now sweare and Rant/(Then surely I for Fuck may Cant). **1687** in Burford *Bawdy Verse* 179: Half ten Guineas spent in Wine and Fuck. *a***1720** in D'Urfey *Pills* VI 266: She'd dance and she'd caper as wild as a Buck,/And told *Tom* the *Tinker,* she would have some —. **1889** Capt. C. Devereaux *Venus in India* 37: He added his initials and "WTBF?" "What does it mean?" I asked. "'Will there be fuck?' of course." **1918** in Carey *Mlle. from Armentières* II (unpaged): The S.O.S. was sure out of luck,/They stayed behind and got all the —. **1938** H. Miller *Tropic of Capricorn* 104: The place is just plastered with cunt and fuck.

c. a person considered as a sexual partner.

1874 in *Oxford English Dictionary Supp.*: I had always held that dear momma was the best fuck in the family. **1879** *Pearl* 211: He's a stunning good fuck. *a***1927** in P. Smith *Letters from Father* 141: What a fuck she was. **1934** "J.M. Hall" *Anecdota* 27: You are a much better fuck than your old mammy here. **1938** "Justinian" *Americana Sexualis* 23: She'd make a good fuck! **1963–64** Kesey *Sometimes a Great Notion* 193: A cigar is just a cigar, but a good woman is a fuck. **1969** Lynch *American Soldier* 163: She was a good fuck. She did everything I told her. **1972** B. Rodgers *Queens' Vernacular* 87: Was Tyrone a good fuck? **1977** N. Wexler *Saturday Night Fever* (film): If you're as good in bed as you are on the dance floor, I bet you're one lousy fuck. **1977** A. Patrick *Beyond Law* 57: One o' the nicest little gals and sweetest little fucks a man could ask for. **1983** Groen & Groen

Huey 122: She's sure a wild fuck. **1993** B. Moore *Lexicon of Cadet Language* 151: *Fuck*...a girlfriend...."Are you off with the fuck tonight?" **1995** *Publication of the Modern Language Association* (May) 379: Nick calls her "the fuck of the century."

2.a. a jot; a goddamn.—usually used in phrases like *not worth a fuck* or *not care a fuck.* [The *ca*1790 quotation, from a satirical poem ("The Discontented Student"), concerns a young man who cannot make love to his wife at night because he is preoccupied with his books, yet conversely cannot concentrate on his studies during the day. Sense seems to demand that the excised phrase in its final line be "a fuck"; no other word is correspondingly vulgar, and only *fuck* makes the pun work.]

*ca***1790** in St. G. Tucker *Poems* 144: Our scholar every night/Thinks of his books; and of his bride by light..../"My wife—a plague!—keeps running in my head/In ev'ry page I read[,] my raging fires/Portray her yielding to my fierce desires."/"G— d— your books!" the testy father said,/"I'd not give — for all you've read." **1879** *Harlequin Prince Cherrytop* 19: For all your threats I don't care a fuck./I'll never leave my princely darling duck. **1917** in E. Wilson *Prelude* 184: An English soldier on the boat: "I down't give a fuck if the bowt goes dahn, it doesn't belong to me!" **1926** Barbusse *Under Fire* 283: He doesn't care a f— for us. **1929** Manning *Fortune* 48 [refers to WWI]: They don't care a fuck 'ow us'ns live. **1931** Dos Passos *Nineteen Nineteen* 200 [refers to 1919]: The bosun said it was the end of civilization and the cook said he didn't give a f—k. **1934** H. Miller *Tropic of*

Cancer 22: Nobody gives a fuck about her except to use her. **1935** T. Wolfe *Death to Morning* 74 [refers to 1917]: I don't give a f— what ya t'ought. **1936** in Oliver *Blues Tradition* 246: When I first met you I thought I fell in good luck,/Now I know you ain't worth a —. **1946** in J. Jones *Reach* 61: It dont mean a *fuck* to me. **1960** Sire *Deathmakers* 44: They don't give a fuck about you. **1965** Reeves *Night Action* 86: It mattered not a fuck. **1969** N.Y.C. man, age *ca*30: Doesn't that pull on your heartstrings? Or don't you give a rusty fuck? **1969–71** Kahn *Boys of Summer* 107: Rocco's a helluva man, but that don't mean a fuck. **1974** R. Carter *16th Round* 53: What makes you think that I give a fuck about you—or the horse you came to town on? **1972–76** Durden *No Bugles, No Drums* 9: Nobody gives two fucks. **1977** Dowd *Slap Shot* (film): It don't make a fuck's bit of difference. **1979** D. Thoreau *City at Bay* 36: Who gives a rusty fuck about some wino? **1995** *New York Review of Books* (June 8) 48: Education nowadays isn't worth a tup-ney fuck. **1998** J. Lahr, in *New Yorker* (Sept. 7) 80: The actor doesn't care a fuck about Shakespeare. The director doesn't care a fuck about Shakespeare. He never really encounters Shakespeare.

b. anything whatsoever.—used in negative.

1970 in *Rolling Stone Interviews* 429: They didn't play fuck. **1971** *National Lampoon* (Dec.) 58: That croaker don't know fuck.

c. (used with *like, as,* or *than* as an emphatic standard of comparison).—also used with *a.*

1938 in Legman *Limerick* 393: The colloquial comparative, "hotter than a Persian fuck." **1976** C.R.

Anderson *Grunts* 61 [refers to 1969]: To them it was still hotter than fuck and rising. **1978** in T. O'Brien *Things They Carried* 171: I'm sure as fuck not *going* anywhere. **1980** Whalen *Takes a Man* 272: "You in pain, man?"..."It stings like a fuck." **1983** Thickett *Outrageously Offensive* 60: It's raining like a fuck outside. **1980–86** in Steffensmeier *Fence* 5: You sure as fuck don't go around telling people: I'm a fence! **1988** "N.W.A." *Fuck tha Police* (rap song): I'm sneaky as fuck when it comes to crime. **1988** P. Duncan *84 Charlie MoPic* (film): He's gonna slow us down like *fuck,* man! *a***1989** in Kisseloff *You Must Remember This* 72: It was no good, that's all, and you suffer like a fuck. **1991** in *RapPages* (Feb. 1992) 67: Lawnge's production is dope as fuck. **1993** J. Watson & K. Dockery *Point Man* 105: Raining like a fuck out, ain't it? **1996** McCumber *Playing off Rail* 336: I sure as fuck hope so.

d. a bit of difference.—used in negative.

1984 Sample *Racehoss* 198 [refers to 1950s]: It don't make a fuck who it is.

3. semen (now *rare*); ☞ in phrase: **full of fuck,** full of sexual desire or (*broadly*) energy. Compare BULL FUCK.

*ca***1866** *Romance of Lust* 390: The cunt full of fuck only excited him the more. *a***1890–93** Farmer & Henley *Slang & Its Analogues* III 80: *Fuck,* subs.... The seminal fluid. *Ibid.* 85: *Like a straw-yard bull, full of fuck and half-starved....*A friendly retort to the question, "How goes it?" *i.e.,* "How are you?" **1916** Cary *Slang of Venery* I 98: *Full of fuck.*—Ready to work. **1938** "Justinian" *Americana Sexualis* 23: *Full of fuck,* amorously potent. **1993** *Farmer's Step-daughter,* on Usenet newsgroup alt.sex.stories: She had thought often about what it would be like to let [him] shoot a full load of his fuck into her face. *Ibid.:* She felt the warm fuck filling her mouth, coating her tongue and draining back toward her throat.

4. a despicable person, usually a man.

[**1788** S. Low *Politician Out-Witted* I ii: Do you call me a foutre, you rascal?] **1927** [Fliesler] *Anecdota* 188: You bloomin' fuck. **1927** in E. Wilson *Twenties* 399: You oughtn'ta be a prizefighter, yuh fuck—yuh ought to be a bootblack! **1933** Ford & Tyler *Young & Evil* 40: Take that fuck McAllen. **1934** H. Roth *Call It Sleep* 414 [refers to *ca*1910]: Yer an at'eist, yuh fuck, he hollers. **1942** in Perelman *Don't Tread on Me* 46: I was that superior fuck who smiled patronizingly and observed..."Recent statistics show that the French have the greatest land army in the world." **1946–50** J. Jones *From Here to Eternity* ch. xxxvi: I told you, you dumb fuck. **1958** T. Berger *Crazy in Berlin* 136: Go on, you fuck, or I'll take ya apart. **1964** in H.S. Thompson *Proud Highway* 473: All these fucks who smile on the TV screen. **1967** Hersey *Algiers Motel* 134: Them fucks took my tape recorder. **1968** J.P. Miller *The Race for Home* 294 [refers to 1930s]: "He said he don't, you dumb fuck," Dawg said. **1970** Byrne *Memories* 117: Come in off of there, you dumb fuck. **1972** B. Harrison *Hospital* 50: I swear I thought that fuck was going to offer me a bribe to save Tessa's life. **1973** Schiano & Burton *Solo* 80: He's the meanest fuck in town. **1973** P. Benchley *Jaws* 191: You lying fuck! **1987** Santiago *Undercover* 63: Don't bother with this fuck. **1991** "Who Am I?" in L.A. Stanley *Rap* 383: He was a big-ass fuck. **1997** W. Allen *Deconstructing Harry* (film): You fucked-up fuck!...Fuck you!

5. an evil turn of events; a cheat of fortune.

1972 Pelfrey *Big V* 9: "Regulars by God." Conscripts by fuck. *a***1984** in Terkel *"Good War"* 306: Know what they did? They made him a lieutenant colonel and me a captain. Ain't that a fuck? **1998** T. Gilliam, in *New Yorker* (May 25) 74: To start pulling things off the soundtrack now is a fuck!

☞ In phrases:

☞ **flying fuck,** see under FLYING.

☞ **for fuck's sake,** for heaven's sake.

1946 D. Brennan *One of Our Bombers* 210: They're coming up to starboard! Weave! For f——sake! **1961** J. Jones *Thin Red Line* 16 [refers to WWII]: Don't *talk* like that!...for fuck's sake. **1964** A. Davidson, in *Worlds of Tomorrow* (Aug.) 11: You space-apes who haven't signed the Declaration, don't hang around picking your toes, for — sake, come on out and *sign* it! **1966** G.M. Williams *Camp* 94: What'll we call you then for fuck's sake? **1966** in *Oxford English Dictionary Supp.* **1976** Schroeder *Shaking It* 20: An inmate kicked irritably at an uncooperative piece of machinery and announced succinctly that "the fuckin fucker's fucked, fer fuck sakes!" **1964–78** J. Carroll *Basketball Diaries* 26: Now he's on tour for fuck's sake. **1997** *Sick Puppy Comix* (Sydney, Australia) (No. 5) 17: The moral of this story is: for fuck's sake don't talk to strange little kids!

☞ **fuck of,** a notable example or quantity of; hell of.

1928 in Read *Lexical Evidence from Folk Epigraphy* 55: This is a fuck of a rain. **1942** H. Miller *Roofs of Paris* 121: It would be a fuck of a lot more interesting. **1970** Thackrey *Thief* 230: Oh, wow! What a fuck of a way for a couple hot-rocks like them to go out. **1973** Flaherty *Fogarty* 26: It was a fuck of a country that could scrimmage for souls. **1977** Bartlett *Finest Kind* 20: I'll have a fuckuva time getting back in. **1978** Truscott *Dress Gray* 219: It's gonna be one fuck of a long two months. **1982** C.R. Anderson *Other War* 171: Thanks a lot, Altizer. Thanks a fuck of a lot. **1985** Bodey *F.N.G.* 114: He's lost a fuckuva lot of blood. **1996** P.F. Hamilton *Reality Dysfunction* 983: The doctors wired your neural nanonics to your liver....It was one fuck of a lot smarter than your brain.

☞ **holy fuck!** (used to express astonishment).

1945 in Shibutani *Company K* 202: Holy fuck! We're gonna freeze our ass off. **1967** Wentworth & Flexner *Dictionary of American Slang* (supp.) 690. **1977** T. Jones *Incredible Voyage* 373: "Holy fuck!" I thought, "I've only got a mile of sea-room." **1983** Ehrhart *Vietnam to Perkasie* 138: "Holy fuck," he muttered. **1989** Zumbro & Walker *Jungletracks* 89: Holy fuck, Lieutenant, kill 'em quick! **1996** *Picture* (Sydney, Australia) (Dec. 4) 3: "Holy fuck!" whispered one. "Jeez!" murmured another.

☞ **like fuck,** like hell. Compare definition 2c, above.

*a***1950** Partridge *Dictionary of Slang & Unconventional English* (ed. 3) 1054: *F*ck! like....*"certainly not!": low: late C. 19-20. **1995** N. Hornby *High Fidelity* 302: Like fuck you are.

fuck *continued*
☞ **the fuck**

1. (used as an expletive); the hell.—also used with *in*. [The phrase *why* or *what the puck* in the 1864 and *a*1903 quotations is precisely synonymous with *why the devil*; the similarity of both the phonetics and the construction may have influenced the development of the present usage of *fuck*.]

[**1864** S. LeFanu, in *Oxford English Dictionary* (ed. 2) under *puck, n.*: And why the puck don't you let her out?] [*a***1903** in *English Dialect Dictionary* under *puck, n.*: What the puck are you doing?] **1934** H. Roth *Call It Sleep* 23 [refers to *ca*1910]: An de nex' time watch out who de fuck yer chas—. **1936** Levin *Old Bunch* 122: Where the f— you think you're trying to horn in?...Who the f— wants to ride in your robber hacks anyway? **1942** H. Miller *Roofs of Paris* 23: I don't know what the fuck to say. **1943** Tregaskis *Invasion Diary* 45: You f—g eight balls get the f— off this Goddamn hill before I rap this rifle-barrel around your neck! **1945** in Shibutani *Company K* 291: Where in the fuck's that truck? **1951** *American Journal of Sociology* XXXVII 138: But what the f—, that's his business. *Ibid.* 140: Sure, they're a bunch of f—ng squares, but who the f— pays the bills? **1959** W. Burroughs *Naked Lunch* 33: How in the fuck should I know? **1962** Mandel *Wax Boom* 273: I might blow my top...if people don't start leaving me the fuck alone! **1963–64** Kesey *Sometimes a Great Notion* 6: He don't even the fuck know! **1968** Schell *Military Half* 185: Abruptly, someone called out, "Where the fuck are we?" **1971** in L. Bangs *Psychotic Reactions* 86: Why'n the fuck d'ya think? **1977** Illinois photographer, age *ca*25: What the flying fuck is he talking about? **1979** *National Lampoon* (Dec.) 59: I go to Medicine Hat, way the holy fuck up in fuckin' Alberta, Canada, man. **1966–80** McAleer & Dickson *Unit Pride* 128: "Did you ever see such a screwy bunch?"..."Guess the fuck I ain't." *a***1987** Bunch & Cole *Reckoning for Kings* 42: "Looks that way." "What the fuck, over." **1990** Bing *Do or Die* 218: What the fuck I want to change for? **1997** *New York* (June 16) 81: It's always those people who get harassed and picked on who flip the fuck out.

2. the hell; like hell.—used as an interjection.

1965 Linakis *In Spring* 50 [refers to WWII]: "They don't keep you locked up."..."The fuck they don't." **1966** Keefe *The Investigating Officer* 184: "This one I happen to remember very well." "The fuck you do." **1970–71** Rubinstein *City Police* 328: "You ain't [arresting] my mother." ..."The fuck I ain't." **1974** G.V. Higgins *Cogan's Trade* 4: The fuck you sell driving lessons to people. **1975** Sepe & Telano *Cop Team* 148: The fuck I am! **1983** P. Dexter *God's Pocket* 65: The fuck I have, you think I'm crazy?

3. daylights; hell.

1971 *Rolling Stone Interviews* 448: I even got another guy out of jail, a spade cat they'd...beat the fuck out of. **1972** College student: There's only one thing left to do—beat the fuck out of you. **1975** College student: I felt like kicking the fuck out of the computer terminal, but I figured it would cost me $2000. **1989** *Life* (July) 27: "This s—, literally, scares the f— outta me."...girl, 15.

☞ **the fuck of it,** the fun of it; the hell of it.

1970 College student: I'd beat him up just for the fuck of it. **1976** Hayden *Voyage* 196: Take a look. Just fer the fuck of it. **1979** Southern man, age 27: I went down there just for the fuck of it. **1985** Bodey *F.N.G.* 174: Doing it...just for the fuck of it. **1990** Bing *Do or Die* 123: Who's gonna die "for the fuck of it"? *a***1995** in *New Yorker* (June 12) 35: You know, just for the fuck of it.

fuck *adjective* describing, depicting, or involving copulation; pornographic; erotic.—used before a noun.

1941 W.C. Williams, in Witemeyer *Williams-Laughlin* 61: You've got to feed 'em the bunk—love and war and all the old fuck stuff. **1942–44** in *American Speech* (Feb. 1946) 33: *F—k Books, n.* Sexy pulp magazines. **1950** in Hemingway *Selected Letters* 694: They start writing those over-detailed fuck scenes. **1966** in Steinbrook *Allies* 70: A boy approached me and asked if I wanted to buy some "f--k pictures." **1966** Fry *Slang Transcript:* Will show fuck movies. **1967** Mailer *Why We Are in Vietnam* 27: Pretending to write a...fuck book in revenge. **1967** Rechy *Numbers* 105: I got some fuck-movies at home. **1969** in Estren *Underground* 11: The State University will never contain any "fuck books." **1975** T. Berger *Sneaky People* 60: He's got a fuck-book there, too. **1975** C. Skinner *Carol's Curious Passion* 23: You mean, I might have a career with Bobby in fuck films? **1976** "N. Ross" *Policeman* 105: Phil liked to hear fuck stories on stakeouts. **1981** *National Lampoon* (Aug.) 68: Let's turn this solemn occasion into a real fuck party. **1984** J.R. Reeves *Mekong* 12: Bullshitting, kidding, telling fuck jokes. **1987** Zeybel *Gunship* 6: I'd watched the live fuck shows in the Angeles night clubs. **1997** *Village Voice* (N.Y.C.) (Oct. 14) 90: A brand new genre of filmmaking, a fuck film that actually had some artistic merit. **1998** *New Yorker* (Apr. 6) 89: A stack of fuck books on one side of the toilet.

fuck *verb* [English form of a widespread Germanic word; compare Middle Dutch *fokken* 'to thrust, copulate with'; dialectal Norwegian *fukka* 'to copulate'; dialectal Swedish *focka* 'to strike, push, copulate'; and *fock* 'penis'; and German *ficken* 'to copulate'; probably borrowed into English in the fifteenth century from Low German, Flemish, or Dutch; part of a group of words in Germanic languages having the basic meaning 'move back and forth', and the common figurative meaning 'to cheat'; see Introduction for a fuller discussion; the recent forms *fug, fugg* are printed euphemisms and do not represent pronunciation.]

1.a. to engage in heterosexual intercourse involving the penetration of the penis into the vagina [with]. Hence **fucking,** *noun.* [The date of the initial citation, from a poem attacking the Carmelite Friars of Ely (a town in Cambridgeshire), may be as early as 1450–75. The poem is written in a garbled mixture of English and Latin, and several English words have pseudo-Latin endings. In the manuscript, the English words in this passage, from *fuccant* (the -*ant* is pseudo-Latin) to *heli* (i.e. Ely) are written in a cipher in which each letter is replaced with the one following it in the alphabet; the original form of the passage is "gxddbov xxkxx3t pf ifmk." The cipher suggests that the word was considered taboo even at that time (the word *swive*, a now archaic vulgarity for sex, was also in cipher). It translates as "They (the monks) are not in heaven/because they fuck the wives of Ely." For asterisks in 1848 and 1854 quotations, see note at FUCKING, *adjective*.]

*a*1500 in *Verbatim* (May 1977) 1: Non sunt in celi/quia fuccant uuiuys of heli. *ca*1500 in W. Dunbar *Poems* 40: He clappit fast, he kist, he chukkit...Yit be his feiris he wald haif fukkit. **1528** in *Notes & Queries* ccxxviii (N.S.) (Mar. 1993) 29: O d fuckin Abbot. **1535–36** in D. Lindsay *Works* I 103: Ay fukkand lyke ane furious Fornicatour. *ca*1550 in D. Lindsay *Satyre* 88: Bischops ar blist howbeit that thay be waryit/For thay may fuck thair fill and be unmaryit. *a*1568 in Farmer & Henley *Slang & Its Analogues* III 80: Allace! said sche, my awin sweit thing,/Your courtly fukking garis me fling. **1598** J. Florio, in *Oxford English Dictionary Supp.*: *Fottere*, to iape, to sard, to fucke, to swive, to occupy. *ca*1610 in Burford *Bawdy Verse* 63: She's a damn'd lascivious Bitch/And fucks for half-a-crown. *ca*1650 in Wardroper *Love & Drollery* 187: Had ever maiden that good luck.../O 'twould invite a maid to —. **1683** in Farmer & Henley *Slang & Its Analogues* III 80: From St. James's to the Land of Thule,/There's not a whore who f—s so like a mule. **1730** N. Bailey *Dictionary: To Fuck*...a term used of a goat; also *subagitare foeminam*. **1760** in I. McCormick *Secret Sexualities* 109: He asked me, if I never got any girls, or if I never f—ed 'em. **1766** in Eliason *Tarheel Talk* 185: As to the flesh tho', I cannot say I have occasion for any violent longings, as I have reduced

F—n almost to a regular matrimonial system. **1775** J. Ash *New and Complete Dictionary*: *Fuck* (*v.t. a low vulgar word*) To perform the act of generation, to have to do with a woman. **1778** in Connor *Songbag* 24: He often times fuck't the old whore in the Night. **1785** Grose *Vulgar Tongue: To f—k.* To copulate. *ca***1800** in Holloway & Black *Later Ballads* 223: Jenny cries nay, I won't F—k for a shilling. **1845** in A. Johnson *Papers* I 218: In other words...he was "Chewing drinking & *fucking* his way to the legislature." **1848** [G. Thompson] *House Breaker* 42: I was going to **** that same little *blowen,* in Boy Jack's *crib.* **1849** Doten *Journals* I 40: There are plenty of girls in Talcahuano and the principal business carried on is—F—ing. **1854** in *American Speech* IX (1934) 271: [According to the actor David Garrick,] when it was asked what was the greatest pleasure, Johnson answered *******. **1864** in Rable *Civil Wars* 161: Have you any sisters? If you have I should like to fuck them. That was my business before I came into the service, and now I am fucking for Uncle Sam. **1865** in M. Hodes *White Women, Black Men* 142: Did he say he fucked the young gal? **1865** Capt. E. Sellon *New Epicurean* 14: I don't see why I am not to be fucked as well as her! **1867** in Doten *Journals* II 949 [in cipher]: The best fucking on the face of the earth. **1877** in Stallard *Glittering Misery* 146: Didn't you — that girl yourself? **1879** *Harlequin Prince Cherrytop* 5: Flat on my back he stretched me in the sun,/Fucked me three times, and paid for every one! **1882** *Boudoir* 226: She f—d me as dry as a stick, last night. **1887** Stanislaus de Rhodes *Autobiography of a Flea* 141: "In fact, I want to fuck you, my darling." Bella saw the huge projection give a flip up. "How nasty you are!—What words you use." **1888** *Stag Party* 219: Sodom...was the worst place for wild fucking of all descriptions... (barring Chicago). **1916** M. Cowley, in Jay *Burke-Cowley Correspondence* 22: He drinks, fucks, swears,...is popular with girls. **1918** in Carey *Mlle. from Armentières* II (unpaged): Over the top with the best of luck,/The first over there is the first to —. **1938** in J. O'Hara *Selected Letters* 134: Oh, and Mrs. — — —, who wanted everybody to get drunk and start fucking. **1940** in T. Williams *Letters* 11: I am taking free conga lessons...and fucking every night. **1947** in Cheever *Letters* 125: I want to write short stories like I want to fuck a chicken. **1964–66** R. Stone *Hall of Mirrors* 194: Is she fuckin' other people? **1966** Fariña *Been Down So Long* 105: I wasn't making love to her, I was FUCKING her. The difference is kind, not goddamned degree. **1967** Jim Morrison, "The Doors," *The End* (rock song): "Father?" "Yes, son." "I want to kill you. Mother? I want to fuck you." **1973** E. Jong *Fear of Flying* 33: Silent Bennett was my healer. A physician for my head and a psychoanalyst for my cunt. He fucked and fucked in ear-splitting silence. **1982** R.M. Brown *Southern Discomfort* 195: Great ladies don't even admit fucking with their husbands. **1985** E. Leonard *Glitz* 88: Iris was fucking *some*body. *a***1990** E. Currie *Dope & Trouble* 205: You know, they fucked, and everything. **1993** L. Phair *Flower* (pop. song): Every time I see your face...I want to fuck you like a dog....I'll fuck you till your dick turns blue.

b. to make a sexual thrust into; rub against in a sexual way; engage in intercourse other than heterosexual genital intercourse [with].

*ca***1684** in Ashbee *Biblio.* II 337: Then arse they fuck, and bugger one another. **1829** *New South Wales State Archives* (Oct. 5) (T 143), in *Gay Perspectives* 34: I slept in the middle and the Prisoner kept putting his arms & legs over me & he said on different occasions "Fox I should like to fuck you" and added "you may do the same to me whenever you like." **1879** *Pearl* 203: Can't you just fuck her in the bum? **1908** *Way of a Man with a Maid* 139: She felt Connie's cunt against hers and the exciting friction again commencing. Connie was evidently very much worked up, and she confessed afterwards that the consciousness that she was fucking Molly's mother in Molly's presence sent her to fever heat. **1909** in J. Joyce *Selected Letters* 184: I feel mad to...fuck between your...bubbies. **1923** *Poems, Ballads & Parodies* 47: A bull dog fucked him in the ear. **1955–56** A. Ginsberg *Howl* I: Who let themselves be fucked in the ass by saintly motorcyclists, and screamed with joy. **1968** P. Roth *Portnoy's Complaint* 145: They have a whore in there, kid, who fucks the curtain with her bare twat. **1976** J. Vasco *Three-Hole Girl* 164: Stick your tongue in my pussy hole, Lisa, fuck my pussy with your mouth! **1994** "G. Indiana" *Rent Boy* 23: Back in his own country guys only get fucked when they're real little and when they grow up they're supposed to, you know, do the fucking, and it's considered unmanly for a guy in his twenties like Mohammed to get off on getting fucked.

c. (in various similes and proverbs). See also FOUR Fs.

*ca***1677** in Rochester *Complete Poems* 137: My heart would never doubt,/...To wish those eyes fucked out. **1884** *Randiana* 28: He had thrown her down...and had fucked her heart out in a shorter space of time than it takes me to write it. **1916–22** Cary *Sexual Vocabulary* I under *copulation*: *Fucking like a mink.* To copulate frequently. [**1928** Benét *John Brown's Body* 99: The whole troop grumbled and wondered, aching/For fighting, fleeing or fornicating/Or anything else except this bored waiting.] **1932** Longstreet *Nell Kimball* 15: He...never did anyone a favor, fucked like a mink. **1941** R.P. Smith *So It Doesn't Whistle* 102: Dutch would say: "The —ing you get ain't worth the —ing you get." **1942** McAtee *Supplement to Grant Co.* 6 [refers to 1890s]: *Mink", "fuck like a,* phr., with the senses of enthusiastically, enduringly, intensively. **1952** in Legman *Dirty Joke* 284: I'm going to fuck you till your ears fly off. **1964** Peacock *Drill & Die* 140: He'd fuck a snake if someone would hold its head. **1965** Linakis *In Spring* 60: The fellow said the fraulein's name was Gertie and she fucked like a mink. **1970** W.C. Woods *Killing Zone* 112: I wish you were here too, so I could fuck your brains out. **1971** S. Stevens *Way Uptown* 241: And 'fore you could fuck a duck they were into the whole white-guilt thing. **1972** in *Penthouse* (Jan. 1973) 116: Emily is fucking like a minx. **1974** Univ. Tenn. student: I'd like to fuck her eyes out. **1974** G.V. Higgins *Cogan's Trade* 14: I would've fucked a snake, I could've got somebody [to] hold it for me. **1975** Wambaugh *Choirboys* 248: You don't look big enough to fight, fuck or run a footrace. **1976** Kalamazoo, Mich., man, age 29: My father used to say, "Now you're ready to fight, fuck, or run a footrace." It meant all ready to go. **1976** Hayden *Voyage* 663:

Make or break. Fuck or fall back. **1976** Braly *False Starts* 204: I thought I should have been able to fuck a bear trap if someone had glued a little hair on it. **1978** Alibrandi *Killshot* 235: These kids today don't know whether to fuck, fight or hold the light. **1979** College student: He was mad enough to fuck a duck. **1980** in *Penthouse* (Jan. 1981) 26: By that time she was so hot that she would have fucked a rock pile if she thought there was a snake in it. **1980** Di Fusco et al. *Tracers* 35: Sounds like...two skeletons fuckin' on a footlocker. **1983** Ehrhart *Vietnam to Perkasie* 14: While every...hippie in Trenton fucked her eyeballs out. **1986** Chapman *New Dictionary of American Slang: Fuck like a bunny*...To copulate readily and vigorously. **1988** C. Roberts & C. Sasser *Walking Dead* 143: Everybody said you'd fuck a snake if somebody held its head. **1988** P. Duncan *84 Charlie MoPic* (film): Quick, like a bunny fucks! *Ibid.* You two make more noise than two skeletons fucking on a tin roof.

d. (used as an interjection to express dismay, disbelief, resignation, surprise, etc.; often used with *it,* occasionally elaborated); shit; hell. Compare definition 4a, below.

1929 Manning *Fortune* 160 [refers to WWI]: A man...uttered under his breath a monosyllabic curse. "Fuck." **1933** in H. Miller *Letters to Emil* 131: Fuck it! I'm starting off bad with my colors. **1934** "J.M. Hall" *Anecdota* 146: "Oh, fuck!" he cried in disgust. **1934** in J. O'Hara *Selected Letters* 93: My message to the world is Fuck it! **1935** in Oliver *Blues Tradition* 231: Whee...tell 'em about me! Fuck it! **1938** "Justinian" *Americana Sexualis* 23: Fuck a dead horse! **1943** in Morriss *South Pacific Diary* 196: I welcome the day when people say "fuck!" in polite and mixed company. **1945** in Shibutani *Company K* 301: Fuck, we're gonna be in the army for another year anyway. **1959** Kerouac *Dr. Sax* 40: Ah fuckit, Zagg—helmets is helmets. **1962** in B. Jackson *In the Life* 157: I'm no gambler because if I tried to gamble, fuck, I'd lose my goddamned drawers. **1964–66** R. Stone *Hall of Mirrors* 51: Fuck no, I ain't stoppin' you. **1973** P. Benchley *Jaws* 194: "Fuck!" he said, and he threw the full can into the wastebasket. **1980** Garrison *Snakedoctor* 186: Well, fuck-a-doodle-doo! **1981** Stiehm *Bring Men & Women* 263: One woman officer...told of stopping an activity because a frustrated woman had said, "Oh, fuck." **1982** West Virginia woman, age *ca*27: Well, fuck a snake! Look who's here! **1985** E. Leonard *Glitz* 207: I thought, fuck, the guy's a natural. **1987** Chinnery *Life on Line* 208: Brian...said, "Oh, f***." Then he died. **1990** L.B. Rubin *Erotic Wars* 180: Fuck it, why not? **1996** A. Pacino *Looking for Richard* (film): Fuck!

2.a. to harm irreparably; finish; victimize. Hence **fucking,** *noun.*

*ca***1775** *Frisky Songster* 37: Hey ho! the wind did blow, down they fell,/Breeches and petticoat into the well./O, says the breeches, I shall be duck'd./Aye, says the petticoat I shall be f—k'd. /O, how my old grannum will grumble and grunt,/When she's got ne'er a petticoat to cover her c—t. **1929** Hemingway *A Farewell to Arms* 206 [refers to WWI]: "It's all —ed," I said. **1929** in Fitzgerald *Correspondence* 226: Now you make them read the word cooked (+ fucked would be as bad) *one dozen times.*

1931 Dos Passos *Nineteen Nineteen* 7 [refers to *ca*1914]: I guess I'm f—d for fair then. **1934** H. Miller *Tropic of Cancer* 48: We'll take his lousy review and we'll fuck him good and proper....The magazine'll be finished. **1935** L. Zukofsky, in Ahearn *Pound/Zukofsky* 160: Time fucks it. **1937** Binns *Laurels Are Cut Down* 200 [refers to 1920]: We did all their fighting. Now that we've quit, they're —ed. **1938–39** Dos Passos *Young Man* 257: Less said everything was the matter, American Miners was f—d to hell and back, the boys in Slade County was f—d and now here was this christbitten hellbound party line f—g them proper. **1941** in Hemingway *Selected Letters* 532: We are fucked in this war as of the first day. **1947** Mailer *Naked & Dead* 10: Even *they* can't fug me this time. **1958** Schwitzgebel *Streetcorner Research* 50: If a kid went and fucked up, you just don't go out and give him a fuckin'. **1967** Mailer *Why We Are in Vietnam* 111: He, Rusty, is fucked unless he gets that bear. **1970** M. Thomas *Total Beast* 137: He was fucking old Sunshine with that knife! **1970** Byrne *Memories* 90: The snowdrifts and slush made darting and dodging impossible. I was, in short, fucked. **1972** Jenkins *Semi-Tough* 159: We got too many ways to fuck 'em. **1984** Wallace & Gates *Close Encounters* 155 [refers to 1968]: I drew a breath and continued, man to man. "Vietnam fucked you, Mr. President, and so, I'm afraid, you fucked the country." **1984** K. Weaver *Texas Crude* 3: I got you faded, fucked, and laughed at. **1989** S. Lee *Do the Right Thing* (film): I oughta fuck you just for that.

   b. to botch; bungle; FUCK UP, definition 1.—also used with *it*.

1969 L. Sanders *Anderson Tapes* 43: It might fuck the whole thing. **1973** Karlin, Paquet & Rottman *Free Fire Zone* 108: Pellegrini, you fucked it again. *Ibid.* 110: Them niggers fucked the roof—built this house so *fast*. **1972–79** T. Wolfe *Right Stuff* 243: Oh, it was obvious...that Grissom had just *fucked it*...that was all.

3.a. to cheat; victimize; deceive; betray. Compare synonyms *screw* and FRIG. Hence **fucking,** noun. [At the 1866 quotation, there is a note by the notary public following "fucked" that reads: "Before putting down the word as used by the witness, I requested him to reflect upon the language he attributed to Mr Baker, and not to impute to him an outrage upon all that was decent. The witness reitterated [*sic*] it, and said that it was the word used by Mr Baker."]

1866 in Berlin et al. *Black Military Experience* 789: Mr Baker replied that deponent would be *fucked* out of his money by Mr Brown. **1927** [Fliesler] *Anecdota* 76: It looks like you've fucked yourself out of a seat. **1932** in H. Miller *Letters to Emil* 114: But they fucked me all right. Fucked me good and proper. **1934** H. Miller *Tropic of Cancer* 49: One by one I've fucked myself out of all these free meals which I had planned so carefully. **1935** in E.E. Cummings *Letters* 136: "Fuck" has been changed to "trick" in new [*New English Weekly*] today arriving with editor's comments. **1942** Berrey & Van den Bark *American Thesaurus of Slang* 312: Cheat; defraud...*fuck (out of)*. **1945** in D. Levin *From Battlefield* 56: He has been fucked again and again by the Corps. **1951** in *Inter-*

national Journal of Psycho-Analysis XXV (1954) 39: To "get fucked" is to be made a "sucker." **1954** Yablonsky *Violent Gang* 75: Although I hang with them for protection, I fuck everybody. They try to burn me, I get my blade, I'll get 'em all but good. **1959** W. Burroughs *Naked Lunch* 179: You're trying to fuck me out of my commission! **1960** Sire *Deathmakers* 44: They're out to fuck you. The whole fucking world. So fuck them first. **1961** Baldwin *Another Country* 77: We been fucked for fair. **1965** in J. Mills *On Edge* 8: You thought you were going to get laid, and what you really got was fucked. **1969** Whittemore *Cop!* 27: So it's the Puerto Ricans that fuck the Puerto Ricans. They sell their own people the worst shit. **1972** Halberstam *Best & Brightest* 66 [refers to 1961]: Carl Kaysen...brought in the news that the Soviets had resumed atmospheric [nuclear] testing. The President's reaction was simple and basic and reflected due frustrations of that year. "Fucked again," he said. **1978** Strieber *Wolfen* 201: But he ain't gonna fuck me. He must think I'm some kind of schoolboy. **1979–82** Gwin *Overboard* 195: As Mick tried to teach me, "Top dog fucks the bottom dog. That's the law of the jungle." **1983–86** G.C. Wilson *Supercarrier* 67: "Being in the Russian military is like being in a chicken coop," Belenko would say in his lectures. "You know you're going to be fucked, you just don't know when."

b. (in variations implying especially cruel deception or brutalization).

1945 in Shibutani *Company K* 115: We'd get fucked out of Saturday afternoon though....In this place they always fuck you in the ass when they get a chance.

1965 in H.S. Thompson *Shark Hunt* 114: We read/a newspaper and saw where just about everybody/ had been fucked in the face/or some other orifice or opening.../by the time the Chronicle went to press. **1974** R. Carter *16th Round* 257: The cops knew that they were fucking me with a dry dick. **1977** Torres *Q & A* 75: You got ten big ones....We will fuck Reilly in the ass. **1978** R. Price *Ladies' Man* 106: Me? I went to [college]. I got fucked up the ass...I dropped out of school with six months to go. **1983** D. Mamet *Glengarry Glen Ross* 36: When they *build* your business...fuck them up the ass. **1997** *New Yorker* (Sept. 8) 37: Gil didn't understand how much firepower Steve had....Steve is going to fuck Gil so hard his eardrums will pop.

c. to exploit to one's own benefit.

1985 M. Baker *Cops* 282: I'm going to stay here, but I'm going to fuck the job to death. They're not going to get anything out of me.

4.a. (used as an imprecation or oath); God damn; to hell with; curse.

[**1905** *Independent* (Mar. 2) 486: "D—n you, Jack, I'm all right," is being gradually adopted by the lords of the forecastle and quarter deck alike in place of the old time motto of generous consideration that was world famous, "Remember Your Shipmates."] *ca***1915** in Brophy & Partridge *Long Trail* 229: Dieu et mon droit./F— you, Jack, I'm all right. **1916** in Gammage *Broken Years* 126: Goodbye and — you! **1916–18** in *Notes & Queries* (Nov. 19, 1921) 417: — you, Jack, I'm in the lifeboat. **1918** in E. Wilson *Prelude* 213: I've often seen a couple o' chaps bringin' back a wounded prisoner and they get tired of leadin' 'im and one of 'em says: "Aw, fuck 'im, Jock! Let's do 'im in," and they shoot 'im and leave 'im there. **1914–21** J. Joyce *Ulysses* 603 [refers to 1904]: God fuck old Bennett. **1922** E.E. Cummings *Enormous Room:* F— it, I don't want it. **1924** in Hemingway *Selected Letters* 113: I have lost the fine thrill enjoyed by Benj. Franklin when entering Philadelphia with a roll under each arm. Fuck Literature. **1926** Barbusse *Under Fire* 27: Ah, f— it! *Ibid.* 110: F— them. **1929** in E. O'Neill *Letters* 341: But I am forgetting our old watchword of the Revolution— F—k 'em all! **1931** Dos Passos *Nineteen Nineteen* 249 [refers to WWI]: Hey sojer your tunic's unbuttoned (f—k you buddy). **1934** H. Roth *Call It Sleep* 420 [refers to ca1910]: Yu crummy bastard....Fuck yiz! **1934** H. Miller *Tropic of Cancer* 280: He was for eating a sandwich. "Fuck that!" I said. **1935** McCoy *They Shoot Horses* 37: "F— you," Gloria said. **1942** Tregaskis *Guadalcanal Diary* (Sept. 1): "F— you, Mac," he said, indulging in the marines' favorite word. **1943** in Morriss *South Pacific Diary* 72: So cheer up lads—fuck 'em all. **1947** Mailer *Naked & Dead* 169 [refers to WWII]: I'm fugged if I'm going to tote a box all the way back. **1949** Van Praag *Day Without End* 215: "Orders be fucked!" he muttered. **1946–51** J.D. Salinger *Catcher in the Rye* 201: Somebody'd written "Fuck you" on the wall. It drove me damn near crazy. I thought how Phoebe and all the other little kids would see it, and how they'd wonder what the hell it meant....I kept wanting to kill whoever'd written it. **1952** Bellow *Augie March* 397: Oh, fuck Oliver! **1961** Peacock *Valhalla* 425 [refers to 1953]: Eat the apple and fuck the Corps in '54! **1965** Linakis *In Spring* 206:

"Are you?" "Fucked if I know." **1967** Yablonsky *Hippie Trip* 206: I said fuck this shit and moved over here. **1974** 2Lt, U.S. Army, age 24: A big expression is "Fuck 'im if he can't take a joke." It means you don't care what the fuck happens to the guy. **1978** Maupin *Tales of the City* 70: Fuck you very much. **1983** Ehrhart *Vietnam to Perkasie* 55 [refers to 1967]: Fuckin' ARVN got better equipment than we do. Eat the apple and fuck the Corps. **1976–84** Ettinger *Doughboy* 8 [refers to 1918]: Fuck you. If you got any sisters, fuck them too. **1985** J. Dillinger *Adrenaline* 102: He drew a few stares in his...Bermudas and...sport shirt. Fuck 'em if they couldn't take a joke. **1990** P. Munro *Slang U.* 85: Fuck you! I did not go out with Dave last night! **1990** in N. George *Buppies, B-Boys* 143: Robin made saying "Fuck you" an art form. **1994** *Esquire* (Feb.) 80: Fuck 'em if they can't take a joke. **1995** *CA v. Simpson* (Court-TV) (Sept. 6): Fuck the rules. We'll make them up later.

b. (in stronger, more vivid, or more elaborate curses).

1940 Del Torto *Graffiti Transcript:* Fuck you where you breathe. **1958** *Stack A Lee* 1: So fuck Billy the Lion in his motherfucking ass. **1962** Mandel *Wax Boom* 72 [refers to WWII]: I fuck you all where you breathe. **1967** Rechy *Numbers* 68: Fuck you in the ears, muscle-ladies. **1968** Gover *JC* 164: As for the board [of directors], fuck it with a sixpenny nail. **1969** N.Y.C. man, age *ca*45: When we were kids we'd say, "Fuck 'em all, big and small, right up to the nostrils!" **1970** Conaway *Big Easy* 94: *"Chinga su madre!"* "Fuck you in the heart," he rejoined. **1970–71** Higgins

The Friends of Eddie Coyle 92: Fuck you, lady,...*and the horse you rode in on.* **1971** Selby *Room* 134: You're a rotten lousy son of a bitch and I fuck you where you eat, and your mother too. **1973** Scorsese & Martin *Mean Streets* (film): I fuck you where you breathe! I don't give two shits for you! **1975** S.P. Smith *American Boys* 309: Fuck you in your mouth, Red! **1972–76** Durden *No Bugles, No Drums* 78: Fuck you...'n' the horse you rode in on. **1977** Bunker *Animal Factory* 117: If she's been a jiveass bitch, fuck her in her ass. **1978** Truscott *Dress Gray* 370: Yeah? Well, fuck them and their marching orders. **1979** *National Lampoon* (Dec.) 17: Fuck you in the eye. **1980** Gould *Fort Apache* 51: Fuck them and the horse they rode in on....Fuck 'em all, big and small. **1979–82** Gwin *Overboard* 185: Fuck you in the mouth, kiddo. This job is mine. **1983** S. Wright *Meditations* 297: Fuck you in the ear. **1984** Caunitz *Police Plaza* 254: Fuck 'em where they breathe. **1984** Sample *Racehoss* 217 [refers to *ca*1960]: Fuck all ya'll rat dead in the ass! **1987** N. Bell *Cold Sweat* 11: So fuck you both in the heart. **1993** G. Lee *Honor & Duty* 130: Fuck you in the ear. **1995** A. Ginsberg, in *Nation* (Nov. 27) 669: Fuck you in the face. **1996** D. Gilbert, in *Harper's* (July) 72: "Man, you're hopeless."..."Fuck your teeth." **1997** *Village Voice* (N.Y.C.) (Apr. 22) 53: Fuck my gums!

c. to cease or abandon, especially suddenly; ditch.

1925 *Englische Studien* LX 279 [refers to WWI]: *Fuck it*...meant much the same as *chuck it*, "put a sock in it"—stop talking; or even "clear out." **1965–70** J. Carroll, in *Paris Review* (No. 50) 103: No solution is coming so I fuck it and start to yell. **1973** R. Roth *Sand in Wind* 150: I got the idea to fuck everything and head for California. **1979** Charyn *7th Babe* 174: Hell...Carl, why don't we fuck baseball camp and stay right here? **1980** L. Fleischer & C. Gore *Fame* 158: Coco's temper snapped. "Look, I'm not 'my dear,'" she exploded. "You can fuck 'my dear'!" **1984** W. Henderson *Elvis* 8: For two cents I'd fuck this job! Two goddamn cents —. **1990** G. Lee *China Boy* 92: Le's fuck dis shit an leave da sucka be.

5.a. to trifle, toy, meddle, or interfere; fool; play; (*hence*) to harass, tease, or provoke; mess.—used with *with*. [Both Chandler quotations are euphemistic; compare FUCK AROUND, definition 2 and FRIG, *verb,* definition 3.]

1938 R. Chandler *Big Sleep* ch. 26: Don't fuss with me, little man. **1940** R. Chandler *Farewell, My Lovely* 5: I'm feelin' good...I wouldn't want anybody to fuss with me. **1946** in Shibutani *Company K* 391: The Boochies won't fuck with him because they don't want to catch shit. **1948** in Hemingway *Selected Letters* 644 [refers to *ca*1915]: I learned early to walk very dangerous so people would leave you alone; think the phrase in our part of the country was not fuck with you. Don't fuck with me, Jack, you say in a toneless voice. **1953** M. Harris *Southpaw* 239: Do Not F— With Me. **1962** Killens *Then We Heard the Thunder* 221 [refers to WWII]: Why do you fuck with me so much, man? There are millions of other people in the Army. **1965** C. Brown *Manchild in the Promised Land* 189: It was practically a twenty-four-hour-a-day job trying to get some money to get some stuff to keep the [heroin] habit from fucking with you. *Ibid.*: If you fuck wit that rent money, I'm gon kill you. **1968**

Tauber *Sunshine Soldiers* 169: No one fucks with chow. You eat when you're supposed to. **1968** Gover *JC* 100: Can't rezist fuckin with him jes one more time. **1970** Thackrey *Thief* 209: Took the carburetor off and soaked it in solvent and put it back on. fiddled and fucked with it. And finally it seemed to be okay again running good. **1968–71** Cole & Black *Checking* 113: I...turn around and scream, "Don't fuck with my mind!" *Ibid.* 198: Stay the fuck away.... And if you think I'm fucking with you, try me. **1971** *Playboy* (June) 216: I don't like anyone fucking with my head while I'm doing [a movie]. **1977** Bunker *Animal Factory* 46: "Tony tells me you're good at law." "I used to fuck with it. No more." **1977** L. Jordan *Hype* 230: Them people are fuckin' with us, man! **1981** Crowe *Fast Times* 92: They're just fuckin' with us! **1990** Bing *Do or Die* 122: 'Cause he fucked with my food...took one of my French fries. **1997** *TV Guide* (May 18) 48: "Don't f--- with the Babe!" is her bold-face battle cry throughout her book. **1998** *New Yorker* (March 16) 34: You don't say no to the Mafia, you don't challenge the Mafia, you generally don't fuck with the Mafia.

b. to trifle or interfere with; fool; lie to.

1989 S. Lee *Do the Right Thing* (film): Look, don't fuck me, awright? **1991–95** Sack *Co. C* 185: "You're *fuckin'* me, XO," Burns erupted. "You said it's a *T-55* and it's plainly a *Bradley*!...You're lying to *me*!"

☞ In phrases:
☞ **fuck a duck**

1. get out! go to hell!—used with *go*.

[**1785** Grose *Vulgar Tongue: Duck f-ck-r*. The man

89

who has the care of the poultry on board a ship of war.] [**1932** *American Speech* VII (June) 332: *Go milk a duck*—"mind your own business."] **1933** in H. Miller *Letters to Emil* 133: Tell her to go fuck a duck! **1946** Gresham *Nightmare Alley* 47: Go frig a rubber duck. **1953–55** Kantor *Andersonville* 183: Aw, go fuck a duck. [**1958** Chandler *Playback* 168: Why don't you go kiss a duck?] **1965** Beech *Make War in Madness* 67: Go fuck a duck, Otis. **1967–72** Weesner *Car Thief* 258: I don't give a shit, they can go fuck a duck. **1973** *TULIPQ* (coll. B.K. Dumas): You mother, go fuck a duck. **1977** in Partridge *Dictionary of Catch Phrases* (ed. 2) 104: *Go fuck a duck!* "Get lost!" "Beat it!" Current, 1920s (in US), now virtually dead. *a***1990** Poyer *Gulf* 389: Bernard gave him a go-to-hell sneer....He could fuck a duck.

2. to engage in indiscriminate sexual promiscuity.—used with *will* or *would*.

*a***1930** in Legman *No Laughing Matter* 177: Fuck-a-duck films. **1951** Thacher *Captain* 40: Hambley, as the saying goes, would frake a drake. **1972** *National Lampoon* (Apr.) 34: You can get anything from an ugly chick....Really foul, but they'll fuck a duck.

3. (used as an interjection to express anger or astonishment).

1934 H. Miller *Tropic of Cancer* 36: Well, fuck a duck! I congratulate him just the same. **1954–60** Wentworth & Flexner *Dictionary of American Slang*. **1972–76** Durden *No Bugles, No Drums* 234: I looked at Ski. He looked away. Lord fuck a duck. **1976** Hayden *Voyage* 420: Well, now, fuck a duck, whaddaya know about that? **1977** Bredes *Hard Feelings* 250: Operation Rollaway!...Fuck a *duck!* **1990** P. Munro *Slang U.* 85: *Fuck a duck!*...Damn! **1998** College student: This whole Monica Lewinsky thing. Well, fuck a duck. It gives people something to live for.

4. (see 1971, 1979 quotations at definition 1c, above).

☞ **fucked [up] and far from home,** in a hopeless situation. See also *fed up, fucked up, and far from home* under FED UP.

1936 Partridge *Dictionary of Slang & Unconventional English* 305: *F*cked and far from home.* In the depths of misery, physical and mental: a military [catch phrase]: 1915. **1950** Partridge *Dictionary of Slang & Unconventional English* (ed. 3) 1054: *F*cked-up and far from home*...dates from 1899. **1972** R.A. Wilson *Playboy's Book of Forbidden Words* 117: When the IRS was through auditing my return, I was fucked and far from home.

☞ **fucked by the fickle finger of fate,** thwarted or victimized by bad fortune. *Jocular.*

1944–46 in *American Speech* XXII 56: *Flucked by the flickle flinger of flate.* Doomed by Army snafu. **1957** E. Brown *Locust Fire* 93 [refers to 1944]: The fickle finger would foul you sure in the end. It would goose you over the edge. Fouled by the fickle finger of fate. **1968** D. Stahl *Hokey* 220: I was being totally and fatally fucked by the fickle finger of fate. **1972** R.A. Wilson *Playboy's Book of Forbidden Words* 104: *Fucked by the fuckle* [sic] *finger of fate,* (said by those whose plans are thwarted). **1976** in Partridge *Dictio-*

fuck *continued*

nary of Slang & Unconventional English (ed. 8) 433:
Fucked by the fickle finger of fate...Current in U.S.
(student) circles at least several years earlier [than
WWII]. *a***1986** Chapman *New Dictionary of American
Slang:* Fucked by the fickle finger of fate.

FUCKED BY THE FICKLE FINGER OF FATE

☞ **fuck 'em all but six,** Especially *Military.* to hell
with them all. Also in elaborated and euphemistic
variants.

1916–17 in *Tennessee Folklore Society Bulletin* XXI
(1955) 100 [bowdlerized]: Cuss 'em all, cuss 'em
all,/Cuss 'em all but six! **1932** Nicholson & Robinson
Sailor Beware! 22: "All but six." "And you can use
them for pallbearers." **1931–34** Adamic *Dynamite* 393
[refers to *ca*1925]: The motto in a factory where I
once worked was: "To hell with 'em all but six; save
them for pallbearers!" **1950** Stuart *Objector* 216:
"Screw the Army, the whole God-damned Army." "All
but six....They'll need pallbearers." **1952** Uris *Battle
Cry* [refers to 1942]: "Fugg you guys and save six for

pallbearers," Levin shouted. **1920–54** Randolph *Bawdy Elements* 120: Oh, fuck 'em all but six, and save them for pall-bearers. **1960** MacCuish *Do Not Go Gentle* 116 [refers to 1941]: Screw all but six and save them for pallbearers. **1972–76** Durden *No Bugles, No Drums* 7: Dumb bastards. Fuck 'em all but eight. Leave six for pallbearers and two to beat the drums. **1987** *National Lampoon* (June) 14: How about the famous Army saying "Fuck all of them but six and save *them* for pallbearers."

☞ **fuck me!** (used to express anger or astonishment); I'll be damned!—also in elaborated variants.

1929 Manning *Fortune* 126 [refers to WWI]: "Well, you can fuck me!" exclaimed the astonished Martlow. **1943** G. Biddle *Artist at War* 77: Teddy's run of literary allusions is a pleasant relief after the too concentrated diet of "fuck me's" and "fuck you's" of the G.I.'s. **1944** L. Glassop *We Were the Rats* 194: and — me if he doesn't get stook into it with grenades. **1944–57** Atwell *Private* 64 [refers to WWII]: F— me, I'm not hangin' around here! **1958** Talsman *Gaudy Image* 197: Well, fuck me double...if it isn't Aphrodite Schultz in person. **1957–62** Higginbotham *U.S. Marine Corps Folklore* 24: Fuck me dead! **1970** Wakefield *Going All the Way* 296: Fuck me in the teeth. What a fuckin piece of luck. **1973** Hirschfeld *Victors* 32: Fuck me blind! That hole ain't half done. **1977** Bredes *Hard Feelings* 293: I'm just trying to talk myself out of being scared shitless because, fuck me, I have to go down there. **1984** K. Weaver *Texas Crude* 28: Fuck me naked! Fuck me a-runnin'! **1985** Dye *Between the Raindrops* 315: Well, fuck me blind. OK, Lieutenant. Got the picture right here. **1988** D.

Waters *Heathers* (film): Fuck me gently with a chainsaw! **1993** G. Lee *Honor & Duty* 330: Well, fuck me to tears!...It's really Joe Schmoe the ragman. **1995** Junot Díaz, in *New Yorker* (Jan. 19, 1996) 78: I hop the fence, feeling stupid when I sprawl on the...grass. Nice one, somebody calls out. Fuck me, I say. **1997** Student slang survey: If something goes wrong, you say, "Well, fuck me up the goat's ass."

☞ **fuck (someone's) mind,** to astonish, intimidate, or befuddle (someone). Compare MIND-FUCK, *noun & verb*.

1966 Goldstein *One in Seven* 113: Mind-fucking is taking advantage of a student who is high on pot—and thus susceptible to suggestion. For instance: "You tell someone who's inhaled pot for a while that he's been holding his breath for twenty minutes, and he's liable to believe you. It really fucks his mind!" **1968** Gover *JC* 137: Hey that sure would fuck some minds, huh. **1970** Landy *Underground Dictionary* 84: *Fuck someone's mind...v.* To persuade forcefully without regard for the feelings of those being persuaded. *a***1974** in *Adolescence* XIII (1978) 467: [Solitary confinement] fucks your mind, you keep saying you want to go home. **1998** *New Times* (L.A.) (Oct. 29): You can fuck my body, baby, but please don't fuck my mind.

☞ **fuck the deck,** see under DECK.

☞ **fuck the dog,** see under DOG.

☞ **fuck the duck,** see under DUCK.

☞ **fuck wise,** to act or speak like a know-it-all.

1979 Gram *Boulevard Nights* 49: "Don't fuck wise!" shot back Chuco.

☞ **get fucked!** go to hell!

*a***1950** Partridge *Dictionary of Slang & Unconventional English* (ed. 3) 1054: *F*cked!, go and get....*mid C.19-20. **1966** Shepard *Doom Pussy* 151: We told him to go ahead and ask. And he did. And *we* say, "Get f—." **1968** L.J. Davis *Whence All Had Fled* 218: "Get fucked," he said. **1986** Dye & Stone *Platoon* 16: Tell that dipshit to get fucked. *a***1990** Westcott *Half a Klick* 125: Tell him ta get fucked with a mule's dick, I don't care.

☞ **go fuck [yourself],** go to hell! get out! be damned! Also variants with other objects, especially **go fuck your mother.** [*Go fuck your mother* is generally perceived as the most offensive and provocative curse in English.]

1879 *Pearl* 210: He'd been told,/To bloody well bugger himself. **1897** in Cary *Sexual Vocabulary* II under *fuck*: Go, and f..k yourself....Get out of my cart and go and f..k yourself. [**1905** W.S. Kelly *Lariats* 273: If yer don't like 'em, go and puke yourselfs.] **1920** in Dos Passos *14th Chronicle* 306: As for an intellectual class it can go f— itself. **1922** T.E. Lawrence *The Mint* 99: "Go and fuck rattlesnakes," retorted Garner. **1926** Barbusse *Under Fire* 243: Go and f— yourself. **1929** D. Marquis, in Legman *No Laughing Matter* 149: Go fuck thy suffering self. **1931** Dos Passos *Nineteen Nineteen* 150 [refers to WWI]: Joe got sore and told him to go f— himself. **1932** Hemingway *Winner* 152: F— yourself. F— your mother. F— your sister. **1933** in H. Miller *Letters to Emil* 126: Tell her to go fuck herself. **1938** R. Chandler *Big Sleep* 60: Go — yourself. **1942** in D. Schwartz *Journals* 88: "Then go fuck yourself!" said May, hanging up, enraged. **1947** Mailer *Naked & Dead* 12: Go fug yourself. **1951** *African Studies* X 32: "Copulate with your mother!" Normally no insult could be more frightful. **1955** Sack *Here to Shimbashi* 92: Sometimes they toss cigarettes to the MP's on patrol, and sometimes they have been known to shout, "Hey, GI — your mother!" in English. **1959** New York City schoolboy, age 13: Aw, go fuck your mother in bed, you little prick! **1961** J. Baldwin *Another Country* 34: Drop dead, get lost, go fuck yourself. **1961** Granat *Important Thing* 80 [refers to WWII]: You just go f—. **1967** Mailer *Why We Are in Vietnam* 94: Go fuck, D.J.'s got his purchase on the big thing. **1969** in Girodias *New Olympia Reader* 68: She [was] screaming, "Go fuck your mother." [**1976** C. Amuzie, in *Journal of Black Studies* VI 416: Among the Igbos, one could hear male and very old female adults cursing [in Igbo] as follows: "fuck your mother," "fuck your sister," "may a dog fuck your mother." These curses are perceived by the Igbos as among the worst.] **1976** J. Harrison *Farmer* 28: Oh go fuck yourself. **1973–77** J. Jones *Whistle* 320 [refers to WWII]: "Appreciate it." "Go fuck." **1977** *Maledicta* (Summer) 12: Go fuck yourself with a rubber weenie. **1980** E. Morgan *Surgeon* 195: "Leah," screamed the little girl. "Go fuck your cat, fuck your mother." [**1985** J.M.G. Brown *Rice Paddy Grunt* 122: The gook tells him, "*Du Mau, Du Mau*" (to fuck his mother, in Vietnamese).]

fuck *interjection*

   1. see under FUCK, *verb,* definition 1c.

   2. [reduction of *fucked,* past participle of fuck, *verb,* definition 4] damned [if].

   1978 Maupin *Tales of the City* 18: Fuck if I know. **1983** Ehrhart *Vietnam to Perkasie* 143: Fuck if I'm stickin' around. **1984** Ehrhart *Marking Time* 123: Fuck if I know. **1998** *Daily Variety* (Apr. 23) A45: When was the moment we broke out? Fuck if I know, even I have a hard time dissecting that one.

   3. see *the fuck,* definition 2, under FUCK, *noun.*

   1983 S. King *Christine* 147: "Turn out your pockets, Buddy."..."Fuck I will." **1996** McCumber *Playing off Rail* 272: "I don't do that to you." "Fuck you don't."

fuckable *adjective*

   1. sexually desirable.

   1889 Capt. C. Devereaux *Venus in India* 110: The poor man had at last outwitted his careful wife and obtained the much-longed-for fuckable cunt. *a***1890–93** Farmer & Henley *Slang & Its Analogues* III 80: *Fuckable*...Desirable. **1938** "Justinian" *Americana Sexualis* 23: *Fuckable,* sexually desirable (of a female). **1974** Lahr *Hot to Trot* 15: "I'd like to dip my wick into that." "Fuckable." **1973–77** J. Jones *Whistle* 233: She was...eminently fuckable. **1986** R. Campbell *In La-La Land* 3: Showing how brave, how manly, how fuckable he was. **1997** *GQ* (Sept.) 258: Anne-Marie...is a blow-up doll—highly fuckable for her lack of will and personality.

2. sexually available.

1889 Capt. C. Devereaux *Venus in India* 142: I should never at any time object to so great a pleasure as having my prick and my balls handled by a very pretty girl, whom I knew to be fuckable. **1972** B. Rodgers *Queens' Vernacular* 25: *Available* open for sexual consideration.... Syn[onyms]: *catchable; fuckable;* [etc.]. **1977** College student: What you do is, you just come right out and ask her, "How fuckable are you?"

fuckaholic *noun* [FUCK, *verb,* definition 1a + *-aholic*] a person who compulsively engages in promiscuous sexual intercourse. *Jocular.*

1981 Jenkins *Baja Okla.* 246: He's just a fuckaholic, is all he is. **1989** Southern man: I'm getting to be a fuckaholic. **1989** Chapple & Talbot *Burning Desires* 294: Both were serious fuckaholics.

FUCKAHOLIC

fuck-all *noun*

1. absolutely nothing; FUCK, *noun,* definitions 2a

& b; (in negative constructions) anything at all; the least bit.—also as adjective.

1918 Noyes *Slang Manuscript* (unpaged): *Fuck-all.*—(1) nothing. "There's not a fuck-all to do this afternoon." **1919** *Athenaeum* (Aug. 1) 695: There is a very queer phrase denoting "nothing"—"— all!" No record of war slang is complete without it. **1929** Manning *Fortune* 130 [refers to 1916]: We all go over the top knowing sweet fuck-all of what we are supposed to be doing. **1939** Bessie *Men in Battle* 133: Nobody's seen fuck-all of 'em. **1941** in Legman *Limerick* 35: The cube of its weight.../Was four fifths of five eighths of fuck-all. *ca***1944** in A. Hopkins *Front & Rear* 54: The officers they know fuck all. *ca***1950** in Cray *Erotic Muse* 116: There was fuck-all else to do. **1961** Hemingway *Islands in the Stream* 400: But I am not going to put Willie and Ara and Henry into one of those burp-gun massacres in the mangroves for fuck-all nothing. **1965** Linakis *In Spring* 74: Didn't mean fuck-all to the ones that busted you. **1967** Kornbluth *New Underground* 91: The *Daily Mirror* carried thirteen thousand inches of advertising—and fuck-all to read. **1976** College student: That ain't worth fuck-all. **1976** Atlee *Domino* 160: They would have fuckall chance against us. **1978** Truscott *Dress Gray* 45: Said the supe...didn't know fuckall. **1979** in L. Bangs *Psychotic Reactions* 283: What have we got! Fuckall! **1995** R. Williamson, folk singer, in concert in N.Y.C.: Shut up, Dad, you don't know fuck-all! **1997** *Harper's* (Feb.) 68: I taught you nothing. I taught you fuck-all. **1997** A. Proulx, in *New Yorker* (Oct. 13) 83: But fuck-all has worked the way I wanted.

2. hell (as an expletive).

    1938 in Hemingway *Selected Letters* 466: It's been a fuckall of a six weeks. Nobody's got any social standing at all now who hasn't swum the Ebro at least once. **1958** Cooley *Run for Home* 138 [refers to 1920s]: Who the fuck-all does he think he is?

    3. a damn; a fuck.

    1958 Cooley *Run for Home* 20 [refers to 1920s]: I don't give a fuck-all what you think!

fuck-all *adverb* utterly; at all; absolutely.

    1961 Forbes *Goodbye to Some* 169 [refers to WWII]: Nothin'. Absolutely fuckall nothin'. **1961** Hemingway *Islands in the Stream* 336: I feel fuck-all discouraged about things sometimes. **1991** O. Stone & Z. Sklar *JFK* (film): Don't matter fuck-all. **1992** J. Wolcott, in *Vanity Fair* (Sept.) 301: The flatulent influence of Foucault on sex, about which Foucault...knew fuck-all nothing.

fuck-all *interjection* see FUCK, *interjection,* definition 1.

    1918 Noyes *Slang Manuscript* (unpaged): *Fuck-all*...(2) Also used as an expression of disgust. "Oh fuck-all!" **1966** Reynolds & McClure *Freewheelin Frank* 29: FUCK ALL! I GOT THE CLAP.

fuckaround *noun* contemptuous treatment; a disappointing situation—sometimes used with *play*.

    1965 in H.S. Thompson *Proud Highway* 509: My good time badass fuckaround is going out of style.

1970 in H.S. Thompson *Great Shark Hunt* 101: Well, to hell with it. You don't need publicity and I sure as hell don't need this kind of fuckaround. **1972** in H.S. Thompson *Great Shark Hunt* 123: A gig that was a... fuckaround from start to finish. **1980** Conroy *Lords of Discipline* 394: This is the last night we're going to play fuck-around with that bunch. **1984–87** Ferrandino *Firefight* 39: I'll teach you to play fuck around with me. **1996** McCumber *Playing off Rail* 245: Just another fuckaround, waiting all night for no action.

fuck around *verb*

1. to engage in promiscuous sexual intercourse.

1931 in H. Miller *Letters to Emil* 76: I fucked around with this one and that. **1942** H. Miller *Roofs of Paris* 201: Does she know that you've been fucking around with her father? **1951** *American Journal of Sociology* XXXVII 138: Eddie f—s around too much; he's gonna kill himself or else get killed by some broad. And he's got a nice wife too. **1969** Crumley *One to Count Cadence* 100: Yes, I know my wife is fucking around. **1978** Schrader *Hardcore* 39: Your daughter was an absolutely clean girl, she never had rebellious or impure thoughts, she didn't fuck around. **1989** Sorkin *A Few Good Men* 36: Don't fuck around with this one, Danny.

2. to play or fool around; trifle; mess. Compare FRIG, *verb,* definition 3. [*Fuck about* in 1922, 1929 quotations is the usual British English form; compare synonym *muck about*. The 1938 quotation is euphemistic.]

[**1922** T.E. Lawrence *The Mint* 49: I wasn't going to fuck about for those toffee-nosed buggers.] [**1929** Manning *Fortune* 17 [refers to WWI]: They kept 'em fuckin' about the camp, while they sent us over the bloody top.] **1931** in H. Miller *Letters to Emil* 76: "My dear," she says. "I just couldn't stay away from you. I'm sick of all this fucking around." *ca***1933** in Sevareid *Wild Dream* 39: What's the difference between a mountain goat and a soda jerk?...The soda jerk mucks around the fountain. **1935** T. Wolfe *Death to Morning* 73 [refers to 1917]: What are ya doin' here ya f— little bastards!—who told ya t'come f— round duh hangah? *Ibid.* 74: Don't f—aroun' wit' me, ya little p—. **1936** Dos Passos *Big Money* 313: If you f—k around it'll cost you more. **1938** R. Chandler *Big Sleep* 66: So all you did was not report a murder that happened last night and then spend today foxing around so that this kid of Geiger's could commit a second murder this evening. **1942** H. Miller *Roofs of Paris* 260: And here I am fucking around trying to get her to buy a camera. *ca***1944** in A. Hopkins *Front & Rear* 55: They fuck around but they never work. **1947** Mailer *Naked & Dead* 539: We're gonna move out in half an hour, so don't be fuggin' around. **1950** G. Legman, in *Neurotica* (Autumn) 13: I could stop fugging around writing pulp. **1952** Kerouac *Visions of Cody* 220: I stayed out all night and fucked around. **1954** Weingarten *American Dictionary of Slang* 141: *Stop f—g around.* Common in the street language. **1955** Yablonsky *Violent Gang* 48: We don't fuck around—man, when you want to whip one on, just call....Our boys are always ready. **1971** Torres *Sting like a Bee* 34: He's just fucking around....He'll be O.K.

1978 *N.Y. Post* (Dec. 9) 13: I won't shoot to kill, but I'll shoot them so they know not to fuck around with me no more. **1981** T.C. Boyle *Water Music* 67: A sandstorm is nothin' to fuck around with. **1995** W. Monahan, in *N.Y. Press* (Apr. 26) 18: Brompton Cocktail[:] Heroin, Morphine, Cocaine, Gin....There's definitely no fucking around with a Brompton Cocktail.

3. to cheat or treat with contempt; make trouble for.

[*a***1900** in *English Dialect Dictionary* under *frig*: They are not going to frig me about.] **1944** L. Glassop *We Were the Rats* 69: "It's the way they — you around ....They — you around."..."You're in the army, aren't you? You're being — around by experts." **1960** Pollini *Night* 29: Why you fucking me around? **1970** A. Young *Snakes* 144: Big a juicehead as he is, he gon fuck me round over some gauge. **1970** E. Thompson *Garden of Sand* 328: Don't try to fuck me around, old man. **1970** T. Wolfe *Radical Chic* 125: They ripped off the white man and blew his mind and fucked him around like nobody has *ever* done it. **1973** W. Crawford *Stryker* 68: Don't try fucking me around. **1977** Bunker *Animal Factory* 105: "Would he kill somebody over that?" "Oh yeah...quick if he thought the guy was deliberately fuckin' him around." **1992** A. McGahan *Praise* 72: I don't think you'd fuck me around or anything, or have other women.

4. to astonish; bring up short.

1978 W. Brown *Tragic Magic* 139: *Sands of Iwo Jima.* That's the one that really fucked me around.

fuckass *noun* a despicable or contemptible person.

    *ca***1960** Partridge *Dictionary of Slang & Unconventional English* (ed. 5) 1099: *F*ck-arse.* A low term of contempt: C.20. **1968** Cuomo *Thieves* 219: LaSala was really a slob, old fuck-ass everybody called him. **1969** R. Hugo *Good Luck* 40 [refers to WWII]: Fuck-ass...shithead...cunteyed bastard. **1987** Kalamazoo, Mich., man, age 40: Whoever wrote that fuck-ass's script knew just what he was doing.

fuckass *adjective* contemptible.—used before a noun.

    1961 J. Jones *Thin Red Line* 30 [refers to WWII]: Any man'd leave it layin around's a fuckass soldier anyway. **1979** College student: I hate that fuckass course.

fuckathon *noun* [FUCK + mar*athon*] a prolonged period of orgiastic sexual activity. *Jocular.*

    1968 in *Rolling Stone Interviews* 58: If you were at a fuck-a-thon, you'd have to know when a good fuck went down to know what's happening. **1972** *Anthropological Linguistics* (Mar.) 102: *Fuckathon* (*n.*): Refers to an extended period of sexual activity in which a large number of persons participate. **1973** *Ribald* (Sydney, Australia) (May 18) 7: We are giving our services free for the night....She's calling it a fuckathon. **1982** Del Vecchio *13th Valley* 336: How could he confess to him that he'd been on a fuckathon? **1991** Jenkins *Gotta Play Hurt* 295: We'll have an old fashioned fuck-a-thon.

fuck away *verb* to squander or idle away; "piss away."

1975 S.P. Smith *American Boys* 171: The others...
fucked their bread away on booze. **1979** C. Keller
Subway Orgy 158: The money he would receive from
the kidnapping would be gone soon. He would spend
it on broads, booze, and just fuck it away in general.

fuckbag *noun* a disgusting person; "asshole"; etc.

1972 U.S. Air Force A 1/c Taiwan, age 20: I would-
n't go out with that fuckbag if she was the last
woman on earth....Listen here, fuckbag. **1977** College student: Hi, fuckbag! **1998** *Re: Wrestling*, on
Usenet newsgroup rec.sport.pro-wrestling (Nov. 3):
What a fuckbag. If this guy was my dad, I'd open my
wrists with a rusty can opener.

fuck book *noun* see under FUCK, *adjective.*

fuck box *noun* the vagina or vulva.

1976 J. Vasco *Three-Hole Girl* 158: She felt it building in her fuck box as she watched Tad's swollen
purple dong head. **1998** *A Swinger's Story*, on Usenet
newsgroup alt.sex.swingers (Oct. 24): Peggy reached
down and grabbed her fuck box with one hand and
her breast with the other.

fuckboy *noun* a catamite; (*hence*) a man who is victimized by superiors. Also (euphemistic) **screw-
boy.**

1954 F.I. Gwaltney *Heaven & Hell* 233 [refers to
WWII]: Grimes loves the army and the army's using
him for a screw-boy. **1971** J. Blake *Joint* 67 [refers to

1954]: They were known as pussyboys, galboys, fuckboys, and all had taken girls' names like Betty, Fifi, Dotty, etc., and were universally referred to as "she" and "her." **1974** R. Carter *16th Round* 76: A goddamned faggot, a fuckboy. **1973–76** J. Allen *Assault* 124: One or two slip through who aren't so obvious. There's a lot of them we call undercover fuck boys. **1994** in *Esquire* (Jan. 1995) 91: [In prison] Once you've become somebody's fuck-boy, you stay a fuck-boy, and your new "man" will use you any way he wants.

fuckbrain *noun* see FUCKHEAD. Hence **fuckbrained,** *adjective.*

1970 Whitmore *Memphis-Nam-Sweden* 35: Not at all like the lazy fuckbrain before him. *a***1981** Spears *Slang & Euphemism* 149: *Fuck-brained.* stupid. **1986** N. Jimenez *River's Edge* (film): You pot-head fuckbrain! **1994** *New Statesman* (Dec. 16) S1: You fuckbrained little parasite.

fuck-buddy *noun* Especially *Homosexuals.* a sexual partner; (*specifically*) a friend with whom one engages in casual sex.

[**1972** B. Rodgers *Queens' Vernacular* 184: *Fucking buddies* two who are not lovers cruising together for threesomes, *etc.*] **1983** in E. White *Burning Library* 150: Even the word *lover* is too rude for all the gradations of commitment and intimacy; one friend uses an ascending scale of Trick, Number, Fuck Buddy, Lover, and Husband. **1992** in *Gay Perspectives* 161:

Andrew has a few friends with whom he has sex, but this is no "fuck buddy" circle. **1995** "Pansy Division" *Fuck Buddy* [rock song]: Fuck buddy..../Someday I'll find a guy/Who means something more/But that's not what/This relationship is for. **1995** R. Athey, in *Village Voice* (N.Y.C.) (Feb. 14) 32: I try role-playing and maintaining a fuck-buddy relationship with my butch stud Cuban daddy. **1996** *Guardian* (London) (Mar. 26) T6: Young lesbians...know themselves and they will announce that they are father, mother, butch, femme, fuck-buddy, boy, girl, top, bottom or any mixture that they choose. **1996** *SF Weekly* (Nov. 13): Paul Ramana Das Silbet, not his wife/fuck-buddy Marilena, seems to be the real brains...behind this operation. **1997** *Village Voice* (N.Y.C.) (Apr. 22) 123: Fuck buddies—friends who fuck—usually don't date prior to becoming fuck buddies.

fucked *adjective*

1. completely exhausted.

*a***1950** Partridge *Dictionary of Slang & Unconventional English* (ed. 3) 1054: *F*cked*, adj. Extremely weary; (utterly) exhausted; late C. 19-20. **1977** H. Garner *Monkey Grip* 216: I only want to crash, right now. I'm absolutely fucked.

2. see FUCKED UP, definition 2a.

1965–66 in Maurer *Language of the Underworld* 301: *Fucked* or *fucked up*. Stoned. **1970** Landy *Underground Dictionary* 84: *Fucked*...under the influence of a drug. **1972** Smith & Gay *Don't Try It* 202: *Fucked up*. High on heroin (sometimes other drugs): "He was so fucked up he couldn't even drive a car."...Also *fucked around, fucked over,* and just plain *fucked*. **1973**

TULIPQ (coll. B.K. Dumas): Drunk...fucked to the max. **1976** in L. Bangs *Psychotic Reactions* 195: You're probably so fucked that it doesn't...hurt yet. **1990** P. Munro *Slang U.* 85: *Fucked*...drunk...under the influence of drugs.

3. lacking in sanity or good sense; crazy.

1970 Landy *Underground Dictionary* 84: *Fucked*... messed up; confused. **1975** in L. Bangs *Psychotic Reactions* 180: You're allll [*sic*] fucked....I can do anything I want. **1978** B. Johnson *What's Happenin'* 64: "He don't care what he says as long as people notice him." "He's fucked, man." *Ibid.* 167: You guys are fucked. You don't even know what you talkin' about. **1981** C. Nelson *Picked Bullets Up* 31: Babich looked at me through jaundiced eyes. "Kurt, you're fucked." **1985** B.E. Ellis *Less than Zero* 100: Girls are fucked. Especially this girl. **1990** *National Lampoon* (Apr.) 97: They're fucked in the head.

4. exceedingly bad or offensive; rotten; awful.

1971 in L. Bangs *Psychotic Reactions* 86: Some cat... made a really fucked album. **1973** *TULIPQ* (coll. B.K. Dumas): I had a fucked time last night.... That exam was really fucked. **1975** S.P. Smith *American Boys* 58: Morgan [was] yelling at the top of his lungs about how fucked everything was while Padgett...egged him on. **1976** Schroeder *Shaking It* 121: I mean, like, the last stanza's completely fucked, man! **1978** Maupin *Tales of the City* 92: Your karma is *really* fucked! **1980** Conroy *Lords of Discipline* 311: We're living in fucked times. **1985** J. Dillinger *Adrenaline* 115: "Want to know something

fucked?"..."How fucked?" "We're outa gas." **1985**
O'Bannon *Return of Living Dead* (film): first, I got a
really fucked headache; then my stomach started
cramping up. **1990** P. Munro *Slang U*. 85: *Fucked*...
unfair. **1986–91** Hamper *Rivethead* 161: Squeezing
rivets is fucked! **1997** Nunez *Ulee's Gold* (film):
Everyone's life you've ever touched is fucked. You
know that, Ulee?

fucked duck *noun* a person doomed to die; "dead
duck."

1939 Bessie *Men in Battle* 133: If France don't
come in now, we're fucked ducks. *Mucho malo....
Mucho fuckin' malo.* **1968** Spradley *Owe Yourself a
Drunk* 30: I had twenty-three bucks when booked.
Now they tell me I've got $3.30. I guess I'm a fucked
duck—I've got twenty days hanging.

fucked off *adjective* angry; "pissed off."

1940–45 in M. Page *Kiss Me Goodnight* 80: Because
I'm fucked off, fucked off, fucked off as can be....
Fucked off lads are we. **1971** Dahlskog *Dictionary* 25:
Fucked off...Angry; irritated; tee'd off. **1973** N.Y. college student: *Fucked off* means the same as *pissed
off*. **1974** Social worker, age 26: I've heard a few people say, "He was really fucked off," when they meant
"pissed off." This was in the past couple of years.
1977 College student: I'm really fucked off! **1997**
Scotland on Sunday (April 6) 7: Paul is deeply fucked-
off with a certain type of Welsh nationalist...attitude.
1998 *SF Weekly* (Jan. 7): Hatred, revenge, and viola-
tion are...strangely heartbreaking and entirely con-
vincing. Clearly, Reid Paley has every right to be
fucked off with the world.

fucked out *adjective* exhausted from excessive copulation; (*hence*) utterly exhausted.

    *ca*1866 *Romance of Lust* 443: Poor Mr. Nixon was evidently fucked out. **1879** *Harlequin Prince Cherrytop* 29: Changed from the gorgeous king to a buffoon,/Be weak-kneed, cunt-struck, fucked-out Pantaloon. **1884** *Randiana* 71: The inward and spiritual grace so necessary to please the ladies is now almost dormant in my fucked-out nature. **1934** H. Miller *Tropic of Cancer* 225: It is…the dry, fucked-out aspect of things which makes this crazy civilization look like a crater. **1942** H. Miller *Roofs of Paris* 259: She's as drunk as we're fucked out. **1945** in Hemingway *Selected Letters* 605: Suffer like a bastard when don't write, or just before, and feel empty and fucked out afterwards. **1950** in Inman *Diary* 1480: I guess…Billy was just plain fucked out, the way he looked. **1966** Susann *Valley of Dolls* 121: And what should an ingenue look like? A fucked-out redhead with big tits. **1967** Schmidt *Lexicon of Sex* 42: Sexually exhausted; fucked out. **1969** Girodias *New Olympia Reader* 91: By Christ, you tired old bag, you're asleep. Fucked out. **1973** R. Roth *Sand in Wind* 239: The ones he had seen didn't have the fucked-out eyes of American prostitutes, and so many other American women. **1975** R.P. Davis *Pilot* 144: They called her the "fucked-out, boozy bitch" or the "FOBB." **1977** Sayles *Union Dues* 144: It's a Monday, they're all fucked-out from the weekend. **1978** *National Lampoon* (Oct.) 26: Gertrude was so fucked out that she never wanted to do it with anyone again. **1981** Hathaway *World of Hurt* 162: Must've got so fucked out in two days, you had to come back to rest up. **1994** "Gary Indiana"

Rent Boy 25: A great-looking dude who's so fucked out he needs a half-hour blow job just to get semi-hard. **1995** *3 on 1* (pornographic story on Usenet newsgroup alt.sex.stories): We were all tired and totally fucked out and rested a while before I showered and left a totally satisfied man.

fucked over *adjective*

1. see FUCKED UP, definition 2a.

1972 (quotation at FUCKED, definition 1). **1973** College student: *Fucked over* can mean very, very drunk. Like I've heard guys say, "I was *fucked over* last night. Man, I wasn't worth a dime." **1979** College student paper: [Drunk:] queezy, fucked over, stewed, zonked.

2. see FUCKED, definition 4.

1978 Wharton *Birdy* 197: You know,...this is really a fucked-over situation. **1983** S. King *Christine* 257: You look like a sleepwalker. You look absolutely fucked over.

fucked up *adjective*

1. Especially *Military.* ruined or spoiled, especially through incompetence or stupidity; botched; chaotic; in difficulty; (*broadly*) messed up. Also (especially *Military*) in fanciful similes.

1939 Bessie *Men in Battle* 133 [refers to 1937]: The detail's all fucked-up. **1942** (quotation at SNEFU). **1942** in Morriss *South Pacific Diary* 44: The trouble with the Army is it isn't fucked up enough—somebody is always trying to go 'em one better. **1943** in H. Samuelson *Love, War* 200: You've never seen such a fucked-up mess in your life. **1954–60** Wentworth & Flexner *Dictionary of American Slang: Fucked-up...in* trouble. **1961** Forbes *Goodbye to Some* 173 [refers to WWII]: Their balance is all fucked up too....They can't stay right side up. **1962** G. Ross *Last Campaign* 36: I never heard of such a fucked-up mess. *Ibid.* 293: The boxes are busted open, see. And the [machine gun] belts are all fucked up with snow. **1963** Doulis *Path* 108: Man, there ain't *ever* been such a fucked-up operation! **1964** H. Rhodes *Chosen Few* 118 [refers to *ca*1950]: It don't make sense t'get fucked up on a humble. **1972** Pearce *Pier Head Jump* 49: They're as fucked up as a Mongolian fire and lifeboat drill. **1972–76** Durden *No Bugles, No Drums* 1: Right off I knew things were gonna be fucked up as a picnic in a free-fire zone. **1976** Atlee *Domino* 53: My company has a reputation for quality, but we've been fucked up here like Hogan's goat. **1987** Kent *Phrase Book* 156: As fucked up as a Chinese fire drill. **1997** Student slang survey: *More fucked up than a soup sandwich in a rainstorm*...extremely unusual.

2.a. heavily intoxicated by liquor or drugs.

*ca***1944** in Hopkins *Front & Rear* 179: There was old Uncle Ned, he was fair fucked up. **1965** in H.S. Thompson *Hell's Angels* 185: We'll smoke up some weed, get all fucked up, feel no fuckin pain. *ca***1969** Rabe *Hummel* 44: Ohhh, you know how much beer I hadda drink to get fucked up on three-two beer? **1970** A. Young *Snakes* 40: Man, I was fuhhhhhked-up! **1973** *Oui* (Apr.) 108: God, but I'd love some cocaine....I got so gloriously fucked up the other night. **1973** R. Roth *Sand in Wind* 148: I was timing myself on every glass. I was getting fucked up but not as fucked up as I wanted to be. **1977** Patrick *Beyond Law* 144: Either you can sit around here gettin' fucked up and feelin' sorry for yourself, or you can straighten up and solve this God damn case. **1978** Fisher & Rubin *Special Teachers* 31: He was fucked up on weed. **1979** Hiler *Monkey Mountain* 109: "Eddy!... You fucked up?"..."No, he's not fucked up....He's just crazy." **1967–80** Folb *Runnin' Lines* 238: *Fucked up.* Excessively *high.* **1985** D. Steel *Secrets* 48: Sandy's not fucked up again, is she? *a***1997** G. Sykes *8 Ball Chicks* 87: Janet's always so fucked up on sherm [PCP].

b. thoroughly confused; mentally or emotionally ill; crazy. Also (especially *Military*) in fanciful similes.

1945 in Dundes & Pagter *Urban Folklore* 108: The returning soldier is apt to find his opinion different from those of his civilian associates. One should call upon his reserve of etiquette and correct his acquaintances with such remarks as "I believe you have made a mistake" or "I am afraid you are in error on that." Do NOT say "Brother, you're really f—d up!" **1945** J. Bassett *War Journal* 7: It's no good to keep going, it's all fucked up, it's crazy. **1946–50** J. Jones *From Here to Eternity* 537: I've even seen a couple of them that clean lost their head and had to actually be carried out finally they got so fucked up. **1961** Peacock *Valhalla* 385: If he didn't see Chebe-san he would be more fucked up than Hogan's goat. **1965** Linakis *In Spring* 214: I would even go so far as to say that you're all fucked up from the war, as they do say. **1967** Rechy *Numbers* 138: It happened long ago, when I was fucked up! **1968** H. Ellison *Deadly Streets* 103: He wasn't a bad kid, just fucked-up. **1970** in Estren *Underground* 155: Wow, man, what kind of fucked up trip are *you* on? **1970** Terkel *Hard Times* 136: It's the textbooks that are fucked up. **1973** G.C. Scott, in *Penthouse* (May) 61: Fucked-up kids live in fantasy worlds anyway. **1972–76** Durden *No Bugles, No Drums* 31: You're fucked up like a Filipino fire drill. **1976** A. Walker *Meridian* 178: I know white folks are evil and fucked up. **1978** in Fierstein *Torch Song Trilogy* 52: And here you are, more fucked up than ever. **1984** J. McCorkle *Cheer Leader* 162: You're crazy, Jo, fucked up. **1989** "Capt. X" & Dodson *Unfriendly Skies* 115: "Aw, hell" said one of the pilots, "now I'm all fucked up here." **1992** in *Harper's* (Jan. 1993) 23 [cartoon]: You're too fucked up—Next patient, please.

c. deeply troubled or upset; distraught.

1948 in Hemingway *Selected Letters* 648: I was all fucked up when I wrote it and threw away about 100,000 words which was better than most of what I left in. **1951** *American Journal of Sociology* LI 421 [refers to WWII]: We learn of soldier attitudes to authority by noting the sympathy for those who are not successful in adjusting but are "f—ed up."...It may connote inability or inefficiency. **1962** Riccio & Slocum *All the Way Down* 68: I ain't hooked. I only use it when I feel all fucked up. **1970–71** Rubinstein *City Police* 404: He's so fucked up about it he's thinkin' of quittin'. **1966–80** McAleer & Dickson *Unit Pride* 115: I was gonna change it myself but I was too fucked up at the time. **1983** P. Dexter *God's Pocket*

158: I got to have this funeral on time....Jeanie's all fucked up over this. **1998** Phila. drug addict, on *All Things Considered* (National Public Radio) (Mar. 4): I felt real fucked up because I didn't want to hit [i.e., inject] her.

3. contemptible; worthless; miserable; (*hence*) damned; FUCKING.

1945 in Shibutani *Company K* 124: I never been in such a fucked up place in my life. *ca***1960** in Abrahams *Down in Jungle* 130: He throwed me a stale glass of water and flung me a fucked-up piece of meat. **1963** J. Ross *Dead Are Mine* 269: And you won't worry about Felix and all the other Felixes in the whole fucked-up Army. **1970** *Playboy* (Sept.) 278: I've met a lot of politicians, and politicians are fucked up everywhere, and they fuck us up because we allow them to. **1974** V.E. Smith *Jones Men* 103: Shit!...This is fucked up. **1982** D.A. Harper *Good Company* 76: A half gallon of that old fucked-up wine. **1980–89** Cheshire *Home Boy* 105: They'd go for your ankles and sink their fucked-up teeth right into you. **1990** "Ice Cube" *Who's the Mack?* (rap song): Rolling in a fucked-up Lincoln...[with a] leopard interior. **1994** in C. Long *Love Awaits* 95: That good-look'n, clean-look'n girl can have some good look'n, fucked up shit [*sc.* venereal disease].

4. utterly fatigued; FUCKED, definition 1.

1979 Gram *Boulevard Nights* 93: I'm tired man. Fuckin' fucked up. **1998** Poker player in N.Y.C.: I've gotta go home, I'm so tired....I'm too fucked up to play any more.

fuckee[1] (used in pidgin English, or the imitation thereof, in various constructions referring to sexual intercourse). Often **fuckee-suckee.**

1867–92 Capt. E. Sellon *Ups & Downs of Life* 47: For make fuckee business, sahib, that girl who is splashing the other one would be too much good. **1963** in H.S. Thompson *Proud Highway* 379: The filthy whore in the laundry said we can go out to the *"campo"* (country) and fuckee-fuckee. If I ever hear that phrase again I am going to break teeth. **1975** *Ribald* (Sydney, Australia) (Nov. 13) 7: Newcomers visiting *Ribald*'s offices often get all bug-eyed about the fuckee-suckee pix lying around the place. **1987** Kubrick et al. *Full Metal Jacket* (film): Do you want number one fuckee? **1998** J. Stewart *Naked Pictures of Famous People:* Their father [was]...shacked up in some Backwater Indonesian Fuckee Suckee bar.

fuckee[2] *noun*

1. a person who plays the recipient role in copulation. *Jocular.*

*ca***1938** in Barkley *Sex Cartoons* 118: The fuckee does a handstand while the fucker simply drops it in. **1975** N.Y.C. man, age 27: And who was the fuckee in this transaction? **1995** *Village Voice* (N.Y.C.) (Feb. 14) 38: Early flashes of fiery pain in the fuckee as well as surprise soft bendings of the fucker make ass-fucking in any position a [complex] negotiation. **1995** *Village Voice* (N.Y.C.) (Nov. 28) 73: Vidal also wants to make quite sure we understand that in his many sexual exploits he's always been the fucker, never the fuckee.

2. the victim of malicious treatment. *Jocular.*

1971 S/Sgt., U.S. Army, Fort Campbell, Kentucky: I am one big ugly fucker and I am always on the lookout for fuckees! You *don't* want to be one of them! **1980** W. Sherman *Times Square* 23: You're either the fuckee, the fucker, or you're not in any kind of business. **1983** R.C. Mason *Chickenhawk* 158 [refers to 1960s]: The Fuckee's Hymn. **1986** Merkin *Zombie Jamboree* 44: They'd rather be fuckers than fuckees. **1986** College instructor: I do recall hearing "He is the fuck*er* and you is the fuck*ee*" sometime in the '70s. **1991** *Inside Media* (Dec. 18) 1: Lee Wolfman, in speaking of back-end cash blending, often referred to BMC [a marketing company] as the "fucker" and to its clients as the "fuckees." **1996** *N.Y. Observer* (Jan. 8) 4: Behold the...smug shifting the blame from society's fuckers to its fuckees. **1996** *Village Voice* (N.Y.C.) (May 14) ("Choices") 1: Belzer's politics rise off his don't-fuck-with-me stand. Most of the time, identifying with potential fuckees, he sprays a democratic vitriol that's bracing in stand-up.

fuck-else *noun* nothing else.

1978 Groom *Better Times* 33: You mean you got fuck-else to worry about than something happened sixty years ago?

fucker *noun*

1. a person, usually a man, who copulates, especially promiscuously.

1598 J. Florio, in *Oxford English Dictionary Supp.*: *Fottitore,* a iaper, a sarder, a swiver, a fucker, an occupier. *ca***1866** *Romance of Lust* 275: She grew madly lewd, called me her own dear delightful fucker. **1882** *Boudoir* 239: Such a prince of f—kers as he is. **1889** Capt. C. Devereaux *Venus in India* 124: I have known so many instances of girls marrying against their wills...yet become quite happy women simply and solely because their husbands turned out to be first-class fuckers. **1928** D.H. Lawrence *Lady Chatterley's Lover* ch. xviii: I'm not just my lady's fucker, after all. *ca***1938** (quotation at FUCKEE). **1973** *TULIPQ* (coll. B.K. Dumas): I'm a fucker, a fighter and a wild-bull rider! **1995** (two quotations at FUCKEE).

2. a person, especially a man, who is despicable, wretched, formidable, etc.; bastard; (*loosely*) a person; fellow.

*a***1890–93** Farmer & Henley *Slang & Its Analogues* III 80: *Fucker*...a term of endearment, admiration, derision, etc. **1918** in *Englische Studien* LX (1926) 277: We had a sergeant-major/Who never saw a Hun,/And when the Huns came over/You could see the fucker run. **1914–21** J. Joyce *Ulysses* 600 [refers to 1904]: I'll wring the bastard fucker's bleeding blasted fucking windpipe! **1926** *Englische Studien* LX 279 [refers to WWI]: The noun *fucker*...the very old term of derision, as well as pity (cp. "that poor blighter!")...was used in the sense of "bloke," "rotter," "blighter," or "bastard," a word which decorated the speech of overseas men and Americans. **1927** *Immortalia* 159: The dirty old fucker. **1929** Manning *Fortune* 146 [refers to WWI]: Laugh, you silly fuckers! *Ibid.* 150: I'd rather kill some other fucker first. *Ibid.* 208: If any o' us poor fuckers did it, we'd be for th' electric chair. **1945** in Shibutani *Company K* 197: Them fuckers piss me off. **1945** in D. Levin *From Battlefield* 52: Hey, you old fucker!...How long you been out here? **1949** Van Praag *Day Without End* 168: Make your shots count!...Kill the lousy stinking fuckers! **1959** Morrill *Dark Sea Running* 11: We carry high-octane gas that burns. If I catch any of you fuckers smoking forward of the messroom doors, I'll crack your nobs. **1960** Sire *Deathmakers* 43: You're a mean fucker, Chico. **1961** McMurtry *Horseman, Pass By* 142: "I used to ride them bulls when I was a young fucker," he said. **1961–64** Barthelme *Come Back, Dr. Caligari* 43: Oh that poor fucker Eric. **1965–70** J. Carroll, in *Paris Review* (No. 50) 107: Her mother [was a] dumb, New Jersey, housewife fucker. **1969–71** Kahn *Boys of Summer* 96: Gonna get them fuckers....Teach them fuckers to mess with me. **1972** Hannah *Geronimo Rex* 96: Monroe, you dopey fucker. **1975** Brownmiller *Against Our Will* 364: I hate that fucker more today than I did when it happened to me. **1981** Gilliland *Rosinante* 117: The fucker is going to set himself up as *king*. **1989** M. Norman *These Good Men* 115: I love my son; I love that little fucker. **1992** G. Wolff *Day at Beach* 127: Only thing to keep the fuckers out.

3.a. an annoying or hateful thing; (*hence*) a difficult task.

1945 in Shibutani *Company K* 155: I don't think I could walk a mile with this fucker on. **1947** Mailer *Naked & Dead* 10 [refers to WWII]: Let's stop shuffling the fuggers and start playing. **1958** Berger *Crazy in Berlin* 186: If you are that close to the end, you can put the fucker aside for fifteen minutes and write me a letter to the wife. **1968** Myrer *Eagle* 695: And the fucker better work, I'm telling you! **1973** *Penthouse* (May) 62: Oh my God, I've got to come back tomorrow and do this fucker again. **1976** in Mack *Real Life* (unpaged): Sixteen out of 178 of us got in! It's a *fucker* isn't it! **1980** in *Penthouse* (Jan. 1981) 173: He wanted me to wear this schoolgirl rig and shoes—and shine the fuckers first. **1981–85** S. King *It* 30: Just give me the fucker. **1987** Blankenship *Blood Stripe* 68: Took me five years to earn that fucker. **1992** G. Wolff *Day at Beach* 180: You fucking get the fucker up, Dad.

b. a splendid or wretched example.

1980 Kotzwinkle *Jack* 156: She'll burn up the competition....It's one fucker of an engine.

fuckerware party *noun* [FUCK + (*Tupp*)*erware party*] Especially *Homosexuals*. a gathering of women for the group use of sexual toys.

1985 *Hustler* (Nov.): She joins Erica Boyer, Beverly Bliss and Barbie Dahl in a "fuckerware" party. As the girls try on lingerie and sample lotions, body paints and sex toys, the party breaks out in a rash of dueling dildos. **1986** *Playboy* (Nov.) 25: The authors attend a fundamentalist sex seminar..., a fuckerware party and other events. **1990** S. Bright *Susie Sexpert's Lesbian Sex World* 47: How many of you have attended a home sex toy presentation with a group of friends? They're called fuckerware parties in the business. **1998** T. Dalzell *Slang of Sin* 177: *Fuckerware party*...a women's party where sex toys are displayed and sold.

fuckery *noun* [FUCK + treach*ery*] treachery.

    1978 S. King *Stand* 461: That was an act of pure human fuckery. **1994** *Village Voice* (Nov. 1) 69: Taking on the genre's most seismic vocalist was arrogant fuckery to begin with.

fuckface *noun* an ugly or contemptible person.—usually used abusively in direct address.

    1945 in *Verbatim* (Autumn, 1989) 6: *Fxxxface*...1. A fool, a joker, one not held in high regard or likable....2. Greeting, form of address, semi-humorously or strongly contemptuous. **1961** J. Jones *Thin Red Line* 39 [refers to WWII]: All right, fuckface! Where's that fucking platoon roster...? **1967** W. Crawford *Gresham's War* 139: Hey, frickface. **1968** J.P. Miller *Race for Home* 294 [refers to 1930s]: "Tell what happened to 'im, fuckface," Dawg said. **1968** Mares *Marine Machine* 5: You come down here with this blade to cut me, fuckface? *Try it!* **1971** T. Mayer *Weary Falcon* 126: I tried giving it to the fuck faces whole, but then they sell it. **1977** College student: You'll get some fuckface writin' about ballads. **1983** W. Walker *Dime to Dance* 55: Why don't you mind your own business, fuckface? **1995** *Jerry Springer Show* (syndicated TV series): F—ckface! [vowel bleeped out].

fuckfaced *adjective* having an ugly or miserable face; despicable. [The 1940 quotation is euphemistic.]

    1940 Hemingway *For Whom the Bell Tolls* 369: Muck my grandfather and muck this whole treacherous muck-faced mucking country. **1973** W. Crawford

Gunship Commander 24: You fuckfaced animal. Either do something with that or put it away. **1978** *Penthouse* (Apr.) 130: Gradually people file down for breakfast. Totally bleary-eyed and fuck-faced.

fuckfest *noun* an occasion, period, or portrayal of unrestrained or orgiastic sexual activity.

1976 Lee *Ninth Man* 183: They had simply engineered themselves a good old-fashioned fuckfest. **1992** Rudner & Bergman *Peter's Friends* (film): I hardly think my three-year-old marriage is the same as your two-week-old fuckfest. **1996** *Village Voice* (N.Y.C.) (April 30): Mom was speaking of childhood slumber parties, not all-night saffron-scented fuckfests. **1997** *SF Weekly* (April 2): The black-and-white existential fuckfest *Sex Garage* (1972), which brilliantly evokes both Kenneth Anger's bike fetish and the car-sex crazies of *Crash* in a sequence where a bored biker graphically attacks the exhaust pipe of his Harley. **1998** *Playboy* (Apr.) 66: In the Seventies, life was a real fuckfest for me. I worked at a bar...and women in their early 20s used to wait around to see who I would go home with.

fuckhead *noun* a stupid or contemptible person. Hence **fuckheaded,** *adjective*.

1945 in *Verbatim* (Autumn, 1989) 6: *Fxxxhead*...A cheese head, an easily confused or misled individual. **1962** in Rosset *Evergreen Reader* 467: Manager merchant banker professional fuckhead. **1964** in Bruce *Essential Lenny* 97: I mean, it's the fault of the motion pictures, that have made the Southerner "a shit kickuh, a dumb fuckhead." **1965** Linakis *In Spring* 348 [refers to WWII]: Go ahead fuck-head. You'll do me a favor. **1964–66** R. Stone *Hall of Mirrors* 116: You simple-minded fuckhead. **1969** Jessup *Sailor* 389: You're nothing but a dumb fuckhead sailor. **1970** Quammen *Walk the Line* 149: Boss action, fuckhead. **1971** T. Mayer *Weary Falcon* 121: Shut up, you fuckheaded slope. **1980** Kotzwinkle *Jack* 56: How ya doin', fuckhead. **1984** Hammel *Root* 244: Come on fuckhead, get your ass out of the way! **1996** *Picture* (Sydney, Australia) (Dec. 4) 59: I'd say your brother is indeed a fuckhead.

fuckhole *noun*

   1. the vagina.

   *ca***1890–93** Farmer & Henley *Slang & Its Analogues* III 80: *Fuck-hole*...The female *pudendum.* **1916** Cary *Slang of Venery* I 97: *Fuck hole*—The vagina. **1934** "J.M. Hall" *Anecdota* 23: First you muck up me fuck hole. **1959** in Cray *Erotic Muse* 73: At the fuck-hole of Kathusalem. **1975** *Ribald* (Sydney, Australia) (May 29) 15: Her gaping, hot fuck-hole readying itself for the prick. **1976** J. Vasco *Three-Hole Girl* 152: Cherry's fuck hole opened to her probing tongue. **1989** *Maledicta* X 58: Flabby cunt...*fuck-hole.* **1998** *Weekly's Literary Supplement* (Stern Publishing) (May 8) 22: The females in Miller's *Tropics* weren't mostly depersonalized fuckholes.

   2. a despicable person.

   *a***1981** in S. King *Bachman* 621: Goddam...fuckhole! **1985** J. Dillinger *Adrenaline* 54: Unlock my cuffs, fuckhole. *Ibid.* 215: Hey, fuckhole. **1996** *Rivera Live* (CNBC) (Jan. 30) (transcript): Steps towards him kind of spits at him and calls him a "fuck hole."

fuck-in *noun* (among hippies) a love-in that includes public copulation. Usually *jocular.*

1967–68 N. von Hoffman *We Are the People Our Parents Warned Us Against* 211: That was when we had a fuck-in at the White House. **1968** in Estren *Underground* 17: Grand Opening of the Great International Fuck-In and Orgy-Riot. **1971** Le Guin *Lathe of Heaven* 69: And there were the riots, and the fuck-ins, and the Doomsday Band and the Vigilantes. **1971** *Playboy* (Apr.) 184: If you want to get rid of dormitory rules, you have a fuck-in.

fucking *noun* see at FUCK, *verb,* definitions 1a, 2a, 3a.

fucking *adjective* contemptible or despicable; goddamned; (often used with reduced force for emphasis). [Perhaps originally taken from opprobrious literal phrases such as *fucking whore* or *fucking bitch* (as in the 1882 and 1917–20 quotations, and ambiguous 1888 quotation below). *Fucking* is probably the word intended in the 1857 quotation: the number of asterisks is correct for the length of the word, and any word less vulgar would only be partly omitted (compare representation of *bitch* in the same quotation); compare the identical use of asterisks in clearer contexts from the same era in the 1848 and 1854 quotations at FUCK, *verb,* definition 1a.]

1857 *Suppressed Book about Slavery* 211: The Dr...

applied the lash. The Woman writhed under each stroke, and cried, "O Lord!"...The Doctor... thus addressed her (the congregation must pardon me for repeating his words). "Hush, you ******* b—h, will you take the name of the Lord in Vain on the Sabbath day?" [**1882** *Boudoir* 160: Hurray, hurray, she's a maid no more,/But a f—g wife for evermore!] **1888** *Stag Party* [unpaged]: Now this gives us another fucking scene, leastways it is not exactly a fucking scene, though it came near being one. It shows you Joseph and Potiphar's wife. *a***1890—93** Farmer & Henley *Slang & Its Analogues* III 80: *Fucking...Adj.* (common).—A qualification of extreme contumely. **1915** E. Pound, in Materer *Pound/Lewis* 18: God damn the fucking lot of 'em. **1915** in P. Adam-Smith *ANZACS* 168: You fucking xt I've only just got the f...g thing off the other f...g table you b..t..d. **1918** in [O'Brien] *Wine, Women & War* 205 [diary entry for Sept. 26]: Hi, Tommy, 'ere's one o' yer fuckin' English hofficers wants t' be saluted. **1917—20** Dreiser *Newspaper Days* 233 [refers to 1893]: A large, Irish policeman...[said] "She's a Goddamned drunken, fucking old whore, that's what she is." *Ibid.* 276: I'm living...with a Goddamned fucking whore. **1914—21** J. Joyce *Ulysses* 595: I'll wring the neck of any bugger says a word against my fucking king. *Ibid.* 600: I'll do him in, so help me fucking Christ! **1921** *Notes & Queries* (Nov. 19) 415 [refers to WWI]: [*Fucking*] was used adjectivally to qualify almost every noun in the soldier's vocabulary. **1923** McAlmon *Companion Volume* 51: What in fucking hell do youse think this is, a sunday school picnic, or a tea party? **1927** *Immortalia* 124: He's a fucking son-of-a-bitch. **1928** in Read *Lexical Evidence from Folk Epigraphy* 54: You god Dam fucken fool.

1929–30 Dos Passos *42nd Parallel* 77: Jack, it was a fucking shame. **1934** H. Roth *Call It Sleep* 231 [refers to *ca*1910]: Didja ever see dat new tawch boinin' troo a goider er a flange er any fuck'n hunka iron? **1935** T. Wolfe *Of Time & the River* 598: I'll kick duh f—kin' s—t outa duh f—kin' lot of yuh, yuh f—kin' bastards, you. **1937** Hemingway *To Have & Have Not* 225: A man alone ain't got no bloody fucking chance. **1938** in Oliver *Blues Tradition* 170: I...don't deny my fuckin' name. **1939** T. Sturgeon, in *First Flight* 88: He took his lips from hers, buried his face in her hair and said clearly: "I hate your — guts." And that "—" was the most perfectly enunciated present participle of a four-letter verb I have ever heard. **1942** Algren *Morning* 39: Dey ain't a book in da f— place. **1943** Wakeman *Shore Leave* 184: "The f—ing island," Crewson corrected. **1948** Cozzens *Guard of Honor* 561: Said why the f— holy hell didn't they get a boat from Lake Armstrong. **1951** Morris *China Station* 129: You're a fucking liar. **1953–55** Kantor *Andersonville* 224: What?—with this fucking pistol of yours? **1955** O'Hara *Ten North Frederick* 365: I think you're a fucking hypocrite. **1960** in A. Sexton *Letters* 97: My (fucking) book comes out March 1st in case you've forgotten. **1964** Faust *Steagle* 105: I can't ever get a fuckin break. **1972** Captain John W. Young on lunar surface, in *Newsweek* (May 1) 24: "I haven't eaten this much citrus fruit in twenty years," he snorted. "And I'll tell you one thing: in another twelve f— days, I ain't ever eating any more." **1992** *Newsweek* (Nov. 23) 32: We're going to blow up your f— building. **1995** *New Yorker* (July 17) 50: I'm not your fucking scribe! I write what's meaningful to me!

fucking *adverb* **1.** exceedingly; damned; (often used with reduced force for emphasis).

*a***1890–93** Farmer & Henley *Slang & Its Analogues* III 80: *Fucking... Adv.* (common) Intensive and expletive; a more violent form of *bloody*. **1918** in E. Wilson *Prelude* 210: The situation is fucking serious! **1918** E. Pound, in J. Joyce *Letters* II 424: The world is too fucking with us. **1929** Manning *Fortune* 6 [refers to WWI]: They can say what they bloody well like....but we're a fuckin' fine mob. **1933** Ford & Tyler *Young & Evil* 31: It's too fucking cold to be running around trying to raise fifty dollars. **1934** in H. Miller *Letters to Emil* 153: I'm getting fucking critical of people. *Ibid.* 156: Maybe I'll get...fucking famous one day. **1942** H. Miller *Roofs of Paris* 250: I'm so fucking mad now that I don't care what she does. **1947** Mailer *Naked & Dead* 10: Pretty fuggin funny. **1956** Chamales *Never So Few* 510: You're asking too fucking much of me. **1963** Hayden *Wanderer* 126: You're pretty fucking dumb, kid, you know that. **1964** in A. Sexton *Letters* 254: It's too fucking hard to write. **1969–71** Kahn *Boys of Summer* 312: "Well, how did you get to play it like that?" "I worked, that's fucking how." **1973** R. Roth *Sand in Wind* 83: STOP! FUCKING STOP! **1977** Caron *Go-Boy* 152: I'll be fucking seeing you later. **1979** Gutcheon *New Girls* 12: "You're very fucking rude, Lisa," said Jenny. **1993** *New Yorker* (Jan. 11) 78: I'm getting out of here, you fucking crazy.

2. (used as an emphatic interjection to indicate hesitation, uncertainty, or the like); "um"; "er."

1989 P. Munro *U.C.L.A. Slang* 41: *Fucking*...3. um (word used when hesitating or unsure how to continue)...[example:] And then after that, let's see,

fucking...I went to the movies, and.... *a***1990** Currie
Dope & Trouble 202: No!... (Laughs.) Fucking—they
gave me this...ugly old...stationery. **1991** P. Munro
U.C.L.A. Slang II 42: Fuckin', give me a call and
maybe, fuckin', we can work something out. **1995** N.
Hornby *High Fidelity* 315: And fucking...when's it all
going to fucking stop? [Ellipsis in orig.] **1998** Graduate student: So, fuckin', he tells me to get the paper
in on time, or else.

-fucking- *infix* (used for emphasis in the middle of a
word or set phrase). See also ABSOFUCKINGLUTELY,
FAN-FUCKING-TASTIC, GUARANFUCKINGTEE.

1921 *Notes & Queries* (Nov. 19) 415 [refers to
WWI]: Words were split up to admit [*fucking*]:
"absolutely" became "abso—lutely," and Armentières
became Armen—teers." "Bloody"...quite lapsed as
being too polite and inexpressive. **1939** (quotation at
FUCKED DUCK). **1945** in *Verbatim* (Autumn, 1989) 5:
Twenty-fxxxing-four faces to feed. Blame it on your
anti-fxxx'n-aircraft units, mate. **1952** in Russ *Last
Parallel* 13: Reveille goes tomorrow at four o'fuckin'
clock. **1962** E. Sagarin *Anatomy of Dirty Words* 148:
Irrefuckinsponsible, imfuckinpossible, unfuckincon-
scious,...unfuckinsociable. **1965** C. Brown *Manchild
in the Promised Land* 86: I wondered if he thought he
was Jesus or some fucking body like that. **1966** Fariña *Been Down So Long* 84: He gets himself infuck-
ingvolved. **1968** Mares *Marine Machine* xii:
Outfucking-standing, Private Smith! **1968** Gover *JC*
158: That's the ee-fuckin-*end* of it. **1971** *Playboy*
(Mar.) 189: Unfucking-believable! **1971** Sonzski

Punch Goes Judy 19: Tele-*fucking*-phone for you. **1972** Pearce *Pier Head Jump* 6: It's un-fuckin-believable sometimes. *Ibid.* 156: Six o'fuckin' clock. **1973** Layne *Murphy* (unpaged): Do me one more favor, Private. Dis-a-fuckin-pear! **1974** N.Y.U. student: That was out-fuckin-rageous. **1975** C.W. Smith *Country Music* 230: How po-fucking-etic! **1978** R. Price *Ladies' Man* 128: Go away. Go afuckin'way. **1985** in *Maledicta* 8 (1984–85) 244: Of all the cocksucking, cuntlicking, asshole ideas I've ever heard of, this is the most unfuckingbelievable. **1998** T. Junod, in *Esquire* (Nov.) 136: Holy shit! It's Mister Fucking Rodgers!

fucking A *noun* the least bit.

1966 S. Stevens *Go Down Dead* 203: Youth workers. Shit on them. They don't know fucking A about us.

fucking-A *adverb, adjective, interjection, & infix* [FUCK-ING + *a* (origin unknown; perhaps taken from a phrase such as *"you're fucking A-number-one right!"*)]

1.a. Especially *Military.* yes, indeed; absolutely (correct); especially ☞ in phrase: **[you're] fucking-A,** occasionally with elaborations, especially **fucking-A [well] told.**

1947 Mailer *Naked & Dead* 21 [refers to WWII]: "You're fuggin ay," Gallegher snorted. **1961** J. Jones *Thin Red Line* 137 [refers to WWII]: "No, I never." "You fucking A you never." **1961** Peacock *Valhalla* 181 [refers to 1953]: Fucking A. **1967** Crowley *Boys in the Band* 827: Fuckin' A, Mac. **1967** Brelis *Face of South Vietnam* 29: "It can't be the same kid." "You're

129

fuckin' A, it's the same fuckin' kid." **1969** Briley *Traitors* 273: You're fucking A I had to work. **1969** Sidney *Love of Dying* 146: Fucking-eigh. **1970** Wakefield *Going All the Way* 42 [refers to *ca*1950's]: Fuckin-A John Do. **1970** Wexler *Joe* (film): Fuckin' A! **1970** Ponicsan *Last Detail* 171: Fucking-ay-John Ditty-Bagwell-told I don't. **1970** Woods *Killing Zone* 143: Fuckin-A-well-told. *Ibid.:* Fuckin-A-number-one-well-told. **1975** Larsen *Runner* 38: Your fucking A told he is. *Ibid.:* "Fucking A told," Antonino agreed. *a***1982** Berry *Semper Fi* 192 [refers to WWII]: "Hey, Bull, you going on liberty?" "Fuckin' A doodle de doo." **1985** J. Dillinger *Adrenaline* 199: "You were traumatized." "You're fuckin' A we were traumatized." **1985** N. Kazan *At Close Range* (film): "Looks like a nice gun." "Fucking-A-plus it's a nice gun."

b. (used to express astonishment, dismay, or recognition).

1979 Hiler *Monkey Mountain* [refers to 1972] 103: "Three pair and...the deuce of spades."... "Fuckin' A!" **1980** J. Carroll *Land of Laughs* 168: Fuck-ing A!...The guy who walked around the world! **1988** Eble *Campus Slang* 4: *Fuckin' A*—exclamation, either positive or negative. "What? A Quiz today?...Fuckin' A!" **1992** *Vanity Fair* (July) 130: Fookin' A, she looks good. **1997** *New Yorker* (Aug. 18) 51: I jumped out of my chair. Fucking A! I love football!

c. splendid.

1986 Stinson & Carabatsos *Heartbreak* 29: The night had gone from fucking-A to all-fucked-up in record time. **1986** Chapman *New Dictionary of Amer-*

ican Slang: We won? Fucking a! Polfrey & Carabatsos *Hamburger Hill* 51 [refers to Vietnam War]: The ham's fucking A, Ma.

2. Especially *Military.* **a.** FUCKING; goddamned. [The 1955 quotation is euphemistic.]

1955 Sack *Here to Shimbashi* 18: "That was a mighty freaking-A loud sneeze," declared the sergeant major. **1968** Bullins *In the Wine Time* 389: That's right...that's fucken "A" right. **1986** Heinemann *Paco's Story* 20: Guys with their chests squashed flat from fuckin'-A booby-trapped bombs. **1987** B. Raskin *Hot Flashes* 87: "That was too-fucking-A-much," Joanne says tersely. **1998** *Schizo* (#3) [inside front cover]: I can see you cum and cum...and finally DIE, all at the same fuckin-A time!

b. FUCKING WELL; very well; very.

1960 Sire *Deathmakers* 211 [refers to WWII]: You can fucking-aye say that again. *Ibid.* 262: You fucking-aye have spoken, Captain. **1968** Heard *Howard Street* 72: You fuckin'-A-right! **1970** *Evergreen Review* (Apr.) 66: You know fucking-A I deserve it, Krim, now where is it going to be published? **1970** Appleman *Twelfth Year* 89: You hear, I do not fuckin'-aye *intend* it! **1972** Ponicsan *Cinderella Liberty* 8: No one knew who first got carried away...and wound up with the melodious inventive "Fuckin' aye John Ditty Bag," but since then any number of sailors have gilded the lily and produced things like, "Fuckin' well told aye John Ditty Bag I be go to hell on a forklift!" **1973** Hirschfeld *Victors* 38: Now that is fucking-A important. **1973** "J. Godey" *Pelham* 151: He fucking-aye-right *better* be. **1976** C.R. Anderson *Grunts* 78 [refers to 1969]: You know fucking A well you can't ask the man no dumbass question like that. **1978** Truscott *Dress Gray* 443: You could fuckin'-A say that again. **1981** Hathaway *World of Hurt* 209: You're my fuckin'-A favorite ridge-runner. *a***1982** Berry *Semper Fi* 192: *Fuckin' A told* or *Fuckin' A right* were everyday expressions [in the Marine Corps during WWII]. **1985** Frede *Nurses* 237: I am fucking-A *ripped!* **1985** Bodey *F.N.G.* 4: Marines. Fuckin'-A filthy.

fucking Able [FUCKING + former military communications alphabet *Able* 'A'] *Military.* see FUCKING-A.

1966 Newhafer *No More Bugles* 176: That certainly is tough shit, Danang. You are fucking able right I violated air space.

fucking-A well *adverb* see FUCKING WELL.

1976 Crews *Feast of Snakes* 83: He fucking-A-well had the words right.

fuckingly *adverb* damned; extremely.

1927 in Hemingway *Selected Letters* 261: Got a sheet to fill out from Who's Who and my life has been so fuckingly complicated that I was only able to answer two of the questions.

fucking well *adverb* very well; absolutely; (often used for emphasis). Compare similar use of *bloody*. [*Furkin'* in the second 1939 quotation is euphemistic.]

1922 T.E. Lawrence *The Mint* 80: She'll stay as she fuckin' well is. **1931** Brophy & Partridge *Song & Slang* (ed. 3) 17 [refers to WWI]: By adding -ing and -ing-well [to *fuck*] an adjective and adverb were formed and thrown into every sentence. **1939** Bessie *Men in Battle* 177: God send the—day when we'll—fuckin' well march no more! **1939** in *Southern Folklore Quarterly* XL 104: Look at the people, furkin' well cryin';/Isn't it nice to be furkin' well dead. **1945** in Hemingway *Selected Letters* 590: If he doesn't take care of you he better never fucking well run into me. **1952** Kerouac *Visions of Cody* 201: You got the whole thing fuckingwell summed up. **1952** in Russ *Last Parallel* 13: I was behind the wheel of a fuckin' Diesel truck before you ever learned to fuckin' well drive.... **1965** Friedman *Totempole* 267: You better fucking-well believe it! **1971** Selby *Room* 42: You're fucking well right he did. **1973** Maas *Serpico* 200: Get this fucking-well straight. **1974–77** A. Hoffman *Property Of* 166: I fucking well do not know, all right? **1987** College instructor, age 34: You fucking-well *better*.

fuckish *adjective* eager for copulation.

*a***1890–93** Farmer & Henley *Slang & Its Analogues* III 81: *Fuckish*...wanton;...inclined for coition. **1969** "Iceberg Slim" *Mama Black Widow* 246: Dorcas is fuckish as hell. **1992** K. Amis, in *Independent* (London) (Apr. 12) ("Review page") 37: If you wanna make me fuckish/get your ass into some lingerie & smell good.

fuck job *noun* an act of victimization; victimization.

1973 U.S. Air Force Sgt.: Someone's always tryin' to do the old fuck job on me. **1988** Southern attorney, age 36: I tell you, the fuck job never stops.

fuck-juice *noun* semen or vaginal fluid.

1975 *Ribald* (Sydney, Australia) (May 29) 15: My wife began to suck him madley [*sic*], licking all of Brad's and Trudy's mingled fuck juices. **1976** J. Vasco *Three-Hole Girl* 10: Clear fuckjuice oozed from the slit at the tip of the huge member. **1998** *A Fivesome Story*, on Usenet newsgroup alt.sex.stories (July 2): Her fuck-juice covered my face and hands and I smeared it all over her ass.

fuck-knuckle *noun Australian* a stupid or offensive person.

1981 A. Loukakis *For the Patriarch* 155: You stay outa this fucknuckle! **1994** in *Macquarie Dictionary* files: Don't worry about him, he's a fuck knuckle. **1997** *Sick Puppy Comix* (Sydney, Australia) (No. 6) 5: It's been such a long time since I've been to the beach, I've forgotten what an oily, muscle-headed, fuck-knuckle looks like.

fuckload *noun* a large number or amount of.

1993 in Random House files: I've got a fuckload of stuff to move. **1996** "Sublime" *Caress Me Down* (pop. song): I'm a star (with a fuckload of money 'cause you know I'm a star). **1998** *Re: What are the effects,* on Usenet newsgroup alt.drugs (Oct. 1): The effects aren't far less than lsd,...you just have to eat a fuckload of them.

fuck-me *adjective* (especially of an article of clothing) intended to invite sexual advances. Also as noun, a sexually provocative item of clothing, especially a pair of shoes. Compare CFM.

1974 D. Bowie *We Are the Dead* (pop. song): I love you in your fuck-me pumps/And your nimble dress that trails. **1989** P. Munro *U.C.L.A. Slang* 41: *Fuck-me boots*...mid-calf or higher boots worn under a miniskirt. **1990** P. Munro *Slang U.* 86: *Fuck-me eyes*...flirtatious stares or glances/I'm feeling some serious fuck-me eyes from that guy in the corner. **1992** *Letters to Penthouse* III 63: Her legs ended in a pair of "fuck-me" stilettos. **1993** A. Adams & W. Stadiem *Madam* 125: In her garter belt and silk stockings and Blahnik fuck-mes. **1998** N.Y.C. writer, age 70: I remember clearly in the 1960s when the niece of the then-editor of *Vogue,* Diana Vreeland, startled me by referring to her "fuck-me boots." I am prepared to sign an affidavit that this happened in the '60s. High boots were just beginning to be the style.

fucknob *noun* [probably from *nob* 'head'; compare FUCKHEAD] a stupid or contemptible person.

1995 *New Yorker* (May 8) 76: Look who's talking, fucknob....Your whole life is fucked up. **1998** *Re: Crows & Umpiring,* message on Usenet newsgroup aus.sport.aussie-rules (Aug. 9): It's not considered polite to call someone a "fucknob."

fuck-nutty *adjective* obsessed with thoughts of copulation.

1942 H. Miller *Roofs of Paris* 32: Those fuck-nutty kids.

fucko *noun* [probably influenced by *bucko*] see FUCKER, definition 2.

1973 Schiano & Burton *Solo* 76: Hey, fucko, what're you following me for? **1974** Terkel *Working* 582: Hey, fucko, come over here....You fucker. **1976** R. Price *Bloodbrothers* 247: No sweat, fucko. **1988** Gallo *Midnight Run* (film): My name's *Carmine,* fucko!

fuck-off *noun* Especially *Military.* a person who shirks duties or responsibilities; loafer or shirker; an incompetent.

1947 N. Mailer *Naked & Dead* 229 [refers to WWII]: You think I'm just a fug-off, don't you? **1953** Eyster *Customary Skies* 141 [refers to WWII]: How come you fuckoffs waited to now to start this fussing? How come you didn't pray none in calm water? **1961** Hemingway *Islands in the Stream* 356: Where you two fuck-offs been? **1964** in H.S. Thompson *Proud Highway* 436: I have turned into a fuck-off as far as this journalism is concerned—one of those woodsy types who talks a good article but never writes it. **1968** "J. Hudson" *Case of Need* 271: The radiologist for the night is Harrison. He's a fuck-off. **1969** in *Rolling Stone Interviews* 274: I tell you the whole world is a drop-out. I mean, everybody's a fuck-off. **1978** Wharton *Birdy* 176: I hate to think of going into combat with fuck-offs like these. **1984** J.R. Reeves *Mekong* 76: You fuckoff!

fuck off *verb*

    1. to run away; get away; get out; go to hell.—usually as an imperative.

    1929 Manning *Fortune* 20 [refers to WWI]: As soon as a bit o' shrapnel comes their way, [they] fuck off 'ome jildy, toot sweet. **1939** Bessie *Men in Battle* 89: No one ever saw him again. He "fucked off" over the border, as the men expressed it. *Ibid.* 91: "You're talking through your hat." "Fuck off." **1943** in *American Speech* (Apr. 1944) 108: You would say of a man who has absented himself at the approach of some unpleasant job of work, "Oh, he *fucked off.*" **1944** in Bowker *Out of Uniform* 119: Another...use, exclusively intransitive, exists in combination with the preposition "off." In this case, the meaning is "to leave hurriedly." The most frequent usage occurs in connection with a request to stop annoying the speaker. Often it is followed by the words, "—will ya!" added for emphasis. **1948** in Hemingway *Selected Letters* 640: The opposing characters will fuck off once the column shows. *Ibid.* 647: There is no substitute in English for the phrase "Fuck off, Jack," if you mean it and will make it good. **1961** McMurtry *Horseman, Pass By* 58: "Fuck off," he said. "You ain't got no private milkin' rights." **1966** Manus *Mott the Hoople* 23: Fuck off, and quick. **1967** Aaron *About Us* 183: That wasn't brave. I knew they'd fuck off. **1971** M.J. Harrison *Committed Men* 24: Oh, fuck off. **1981** "Dead Kennedys" *Nazi Punks Fuck Off* (rock song title). **1988** Cleese *A Fish Called Wanda* (film): Tell those pigs to fuck off. **1986–91** Hamper *Rivethead* 21: I...told everyone to fuck off. **1995** Philip Roth, in *New Yorker* (June 26) 117: He could have told her to fuck off, of course.

2.a. to loaf or evade duty; shirk. [The 1955 quotation is euphemistic.]

1945 in Shibutani *Company K* 275: What's the use of being on the ball....May as well fuck off. **1945** in D. Levin *From Battlefield* 55: They...fuckoff [*sic*],...quarrel, bellyache, beat their gums. **1951** *American Journal of Sociology* LI 42 [refers to WWII]: There is little stigma to the expression "f— off" applied to...acts, such as when a man gets away with something against the Army by evading a detail...or in some other way avoids an Army requirement. **1955** Klaas *Maybe I'm Dead* 327 [refers to WWII]: Vat are you furkin' off for? **1964** Rhodes *Chosen Few* 65: You missed formation. You fucked off and we don't tolerate fuckoffs. **1968** Maule *Rub-a-Dub* 127: And I personal am gonna see you get logged if you fuck off. **1970** Terkel *Hard Times* 136: If he didn't fuck off those four years in the steel mills, he could've gotten ahead. **1977** Sayles *Union Dues* 57: You let me know he stots fuckin off, right? **1980** College professor, age *ca*58: I first heard *fuck off* in 1939 when I was working in the railroad yards [in N.Y. state]. "Quit fuckin' off," they'd say. **1985** B.E. Ellis *Less Than Zero* 33: Don't fuck off. Don't be a bum. **1987** Zeybel *Gunship* 10: I fucked off in Bangkok a few days.

b. to slack off; fail through inattention.

1954–60 Wentworth & Flexner *Dictionary of American Slang* 204: *Fuck off*...to make a blunder or mistake. **1964** Rhodes *Chosen Few* 225: You were on yo way t'breakin' some kinda record, son, bu'cha fucked off on th' five hundred.

c. to be deprived of through bungling.

1972 Bunker *No Beast* 158: It's too late. We fucked off a score because you weren't here.

3. to disregard; brush aside; put off.

1962 G. Ross *Last Campaign* 431 [refers to 1951]: They been trying to retire him for months...but he keeps fucking them off and turning down his retirement and refusing to leave the division.

4. to idle away.

1966 Braly *On the Yard* 14: The big yard's a cold place to fuck off your life. **1969** *Playboy* (Dec.) 301: You're going to get tired of running around in a pair of dirty Levis, fucking off your time with those other young cats. **1972** in *Journal of American Folklore* LXXXVI (1973) 222: Do you know what an old whore does on her vacation?—She just fucks it off. *a***1979** Pepper & Pepper *Straight Life* 332: I used to get on his case all the time behind his talent, fuckin' off that talent in the pen.

5. to anger; upset; "piss off." Compare FUCKED OFF.

1995 N. Hornby *High Fidelity* 297: "I'm glad you're back to sort him out."...This really fucks me off.

fuck out *verb*

1. to give out; break down.

1978 College student: My car fucked out on me. Motor conked. You can't even jump it anymore.

2. to be sexually unfaithful.

    1984 L. McCorkle *Cheer Leader* 15: "I cannot tell a lie" is important and fucking out on Martha is not.

fuck over *verb* [probably FUCK (UP) + (*work*) *over*] Especially *Black English*.

    1. to treat harshly or with contempt, in any manner whatsoever; mistreat, victimize, cheat, betray, etc.; damage. [The 1961 quotation is euphemistic.]

    1961 J.A. Williams *Night Song* 155: Eagle ain't even cold yet and you cats are effin' over him already. **1965** C. Brown *Manchild in the Promised Land* 98: We couldn't be fucked over but so much. **1966** in Indiana Univ. Folklore Archives *Folk Speech:* Used to mean that someone or something has been used to the point of abuse. *fucked over.* **1967–68** N. von Hoffman *We Are the People Our Parents Warned Us Against* 55: My head's pretty badly fucked over by life in general. **1968** Mares *Marine Machine* 93: You fucked over those weapons so much they probably will never fire again for other privates. **1969** Mitchell *Thumb Tripping* 125: He couldn't let this Brylcreamer fuck over his head. He'd have to keep it together. **1969** E. Willis, in *New American Review 6* (Apr.) 103: Fuck over the city. Do them in. **1970** Ponicsan *Last Detail* 17: Don't it sound like somebody's fucking over Meadows? **1970** Whitmore *Memphis-Nam-Sweden* 134: I was refusing to be a part of that country which was fucking over my own people. **1972–76** Durden *No Bugles, No Drums* 16: It was a weird scene, a noncom fuckin' over an officer in front of grunts. **1976** in Mack *Real Life* (unpaged): Bill, it's a dog eat

dog world. They gonna fuck all over you, man!
1974–77 A. Hoffman *Property Of* 221: Something gets
fucked over in the store, take it out of her wages.
1979 Coleman Young, Mayor of Detroit, in Terkel
American Dreams 357: I was attracted to this...way of
fighting back at the thing that had been fuckin' me
over all my life. **1985** Boyne & Thompson *Wild Blue*
453: We can't let these punks fuck over the whole
goddam Air Force! **1991** C. Fletcher *Pure Cop* 282:
Don't fuck *over* me! **1994** *New Yorker* (Mar. 21) 125: If
Joel Silver fucked me over tomorrow, if he murdered
my family, ruined me financially, I would still have to
say, "But, God, when you add it all up, he was so
great to me."

2. to beat up; work over.

1970 Landy *Underground Dictionary* 84: *Fuck
over*...Beat someone up. **1971** T. Mayer *Weary Falcon*
31: The fourth mission I went on was the time they
really fucked us over. **1986** College instructor, age
35: When I first heard *fuck someone over* in 1966, it
meant specifically to beat them up.

fuck-ox *noun Army in Vietnam.* a water buffalo.

1984 Holland *Let Soldier* 239 [refers to 1967]: Ah,
Wolf Lead, do you have that fuck-ox in sight?

fuck-pig *noun* a contemptible person. Compare PIG-
FUCKER.

*a***1950** E. Partridge *Dictionary of Slang & Unconventional English* (ed. 3) 1054: *F*ck-pig.* A thoroughly
unpleasant man...from ca. 1870. **1981** R. Spears

Slang & Euphemism 150: *Fuck-pig* a very low and worthless person; someone who would copulate with a pig. **1997** *Sick Puppy Comix* (Sydney, Australia) (No. 4) 13: Ahh...what's your name? Hey, ahh...fuck-pig!...Where are you going? **1998** *Schizo* (#3) 5: My co-workers were all loutish...fuck-pigs.

fuckpole *noun* the penis; FUCKSTICK, definition 2.

1965 in B. Jackson *Swim like Me* 159: A fuck-pole longer than mine. **1972** B. Rodgers *Queens' Vernacular* 49: Bone...fuckpole...meat. **1975** *Ribald* (Sydney, Australia) (May 29) 15: My fuck-pole was growing. **1985** "J. Blowdryer" *Modern English* 72: Genitalia... Male...*Fuck pole.* **1989** (quotation at FUCKSTICK, definition 2). **1996** *Into the Lion's Teeth,* on Usenet newsgroup alt.sex.stories: Sliding the throbbing fuckpole into the helpless girl's warm mouth.

fuckrag *noun* a worthless, contemptible, or despicable person.

1996 K. Williamson *Scream* (film): It's called tact, you fuckrag. **1998** D. Gaines, in *Village Voice* (N.Y.C.) (Mar. 10) 135: His gift can be used for something much more than generating chaos, using people like disposable whip- and fuck-rags, and attaining petty ego gains. **1998** *Re: Question to MonkeyMan,* on Usenet newsgroup alt.atheism (Oct. 7): Shit-for-brains...ASSWIPE! What say you now, FUCKRAG?

fuck rubber *noun* a condom. Also **fucking rubber.**

1981 R. Spears *Slang & Euphemism* 150: *Fucking-rubber* a condom. **1984** K. Weaver *Texas Crude* 114: She found that fuckrubber under her pillow.

fucksome *adjective* [probably punning on *buxom*] (of women) sexually desirable.

1879 *Harlequin Prince Cherrytop* 29: Hot, wriggling, moist-lipped, fucksome Columbine. **1890–93** Farmer & Henley *Slang and Its Analogues* III 80: *Fuckable,* adj....Desirable. Also *Fucksome.* **1998** *Deadfuck owl,* on Usenet newsgroup alt.tasteless (July 13): She is a comely young flapper, coiffed and petite and oh, so fucksome!

fuckster *noun* see FUCKER, definition 1.

*ca***1675** in Burford *Bawdy Verse* 170: Fucksters,... Have a care. **1867–92** Capt. E. Sellon *Ups and Downs of Life* 110: I'm a mere fuckster. I like women, and I have them. **1890–93** Farmer & Henley *Dictionary of Slang* III 81: *Fuckster*...A good performer...one specially addicted to the act. **1930** *Lyra Ebriosa* 20: Nearby there lived a fuckster tall.

fuckstick *noun* [perhaps modeled on British English slang *funk stick* 'a coward']

1. a worthless, contemptible, or despicable person.

1958 Talsman *Gaudy Image* 222: There's still the heavenly debasement of the imperturbable fuckstick. Surely that appeals to you. **1968** Baker et al. *Col. Undergrad. Slang Survey* 122: *Fuck-stick.* A person who always fools around. **1967–72** Weesner *Car Thief* 47: Go to sleep, fuckstick. *Ibid.* 67: You dumb fuckstick. **1974** N.Y.C. man, age *ca*28: A *fuckstick* is a really foul, ugly prostitute. This was at Fort Polk and environs in 1969. It's like a *skank*. **1975** College student: That guy at the other end was a real fuckstick, too. **1978** Truscott *Dress Gray* 152: Hey, fuckstick, buck up, man. **1980** Conroy *Lords of Discipline* 145: Get your fucking chin in....Rack it in, fuckstick. *a***1981** in S. King *Bachman* 479: You stupid fuckstick. **1983** S. King *Christine* 362: The fuckstick had parked at the far set. **1993** R. Peters *Flames of Heaven* 190: One...spit at Samsonov's feet, saying: "Fuckstick."

2. the penis.

1976 J. Vasco *Three-Hole Girl* 139: Bob had been filming the whole lewd performance she had been giving Trish's butt and Craig's fuckstick. **1977** Torres *Q & A* 239: My pistol is like my fuck-stick. Don't go nowhere without it. **1981** *Penthouse* (Apr.) 26: I pulled my fuck-stick out of her cunt. **1989** *Maledicta* X 55: Penis...*fuck-stick...fuckpole* [etc.].

fuckstress *noun* a woman who copulates.

1890–93 Farmer & Henley *Dictionary of Slang* III 81: *Fuckster*...A good performer....in feminine *fuckstress*. **1990** *Footlicker* 77: Verushka and I will be waiting for your report on that little psychofuckstress. **1996** *Boarding School Adventures,* on Usenet newsgroup alt.sex.stories (Dec. 18): You are going to be an accomplished fuckstress.

fuck-struck *adjective* obsessed with copulation.

1966 E. Shepard *Doom Pussy* 160: Like a tomcat at a petting party, Alby tried to force two B-girls to sit on his knee. Tors eyed him with distaste. "He's fuck-struck," observed the Swede to no one in particular.

fucktruck *noun*

1. a van or car in which people engage in sexual activity.

1979 in *Australian National Dictionary:* The boys wearing blue singlets in their striped fuck trucks yelled & pressed down on the horns but fifi [*sic*] kept going. **1982** in *Australian National Dictionary:* How did you adapt your fuck-truck style of driving to a foreign car? **1990** T. Thorne *Dictionary of Contemporary Slang: Fuck truck*...another term for *passion wagon*. **1993** *Independent* (London) (June 9) ("Focus") 22: There was this Australian freak who had this van called the Fuck Truck. **1995** *Time Out New York* (Oct. 25) 25: Fucktruck...was common parlance in a certain Tennessee town in the late '70s. **1998** N.Y.C. editor: We used *fuck truck* in the '60s to mean "passion wagon."

2. a bus on which one can meet a prospective sexual partner.

1998 N.Y.C. woman: As a student at Wellesley, I—and most of my classmates—referred to the bus that took us from campus to M.I.T. and Harvard as the "fucktruck."...the M.I.T. and Harvard guys called it the same thing. **1998** N.Y.C. man: The fucktruck was the bus that went from M.I.T. out to Wellesley.

fuck-up *noun* Especially *Military.*

1. a chronic bungler; misfit. [The 1942 quotation, collected from Australian schoolchildren, may

145

have resulted from a misunderstanding of this term.]

[**1942** S.J. Baker *Australian Language* 206: *Fug-up.* A stodgy person, one who prefers a "fuggy" atmosphere to playing out of doors.] [**1944** *Newsweek* (Jan. 24) 68: I am not a messup any more. I like the army.] **1945** in Cheever *Letters* 108: Last night two fuckups were discussing their disatisfactions [*sic*] with the army. **1947** Mailer *Naked & Dead* 224 [refers to WWII]: Bunch of fug-ups, lose a goddam gun, won't even take a drink when it's free. **1946–50** J. Jones *From Here to Eternity* ch. iv: He's such a fuckup I was afraid we'd shoot somebody on a problem. **1951** in Hemingway *Selected Letters* 721: To me he is an enormously skillful fuck-up and his book will do great damage to our country. **1954** F.I. Gwaltney *Heaven & Hell* 194 [refers to WWII]: You're not commanding a fuckup company. This is a regiment, and not every man in it is a fuckup. **1955** T. Anderson *Your Own Beloved* 8: Whenever he screwed up they knew it. He was a fuckup. **1962** Killens *Then We Heard the Thunder* 39 [refers to WWII]: You're nothing but a first-class fuck-up. **1965** C. Brown *Manchild in the Promised Land* 145: The cats who had a little bit of sense but who were just general fuck-ups were sent to the Annex. **1967** Kornbluth *New Underground* 14: What stupid fuck-ups men are! **1971** *Playboy* (May) 207: You mean we're gonna let them fuck-ups play on *our* ball diamond? **1979** in Terkel *American Dreams* 396: I'm not a great believer in failure as a sin. A couple of our writers are fuckups. **1980** Kopp *Mirror, Mask* 81: I become…[an] uncomfortably vulnerable fuck-up whose blunder is now exposed to my eyes and to theirs. **1985** E. Leonard *Glitz* 152: I thought maybe I was a total fuckup. *a***1990** E. Currie *Dope & Trouble* 22: I used to be a real fuck-up, you know?

    2. a blunder; botch; FOUL-UP, definition 1. Compare 1941 quotation at FRIG-UP.

*a***1950** Partridge *Dictionary of Slang & Unconventional English* (ed. 3) 1054: *F*ck-up of, make a.* To fail miserably at; to spoil utterly; low coll.: C.20. **1951** in J. Kerouac *Selected Letters* 321: [Interference] promises fuckups. **1958** J. O'Hara *From the Terrace* 257: Such a Goddam fuck-up. **1964** Allen *High White Forest* 266 [refers to WWII]: Two of our divisions got tangled up there...and the Krauts hit them from the slope. What a fuck-up! **1968–71** Cole & Black *Checking* 105: Not only was that a fuck-up of LEAP's name but why the hell did I accept their stealing? **1972** *Metropolitan Review* (May) 4: No fuck-up should go unridiculed. **1977** Coover *Public Burning* 455: And now it scared them that somebody might catch them in a fuck-up. **1984** "W.T. Tyler" *Shadow Cabinet* 241: A royal bureaucratic fuck-up, take my word. *a***1986** D. Tate *Bravo Burning* 96: A small..., probably perfectly explainable fuck-up.

fuck up *verb* [compare synonym *bugger up;* also influenced by (if not the inspiration for) *muck up.*]

    1. to ruin, spoil, or destroy; (*specifically*) to botch; ☞ in phrase: **fuck up the detail,** *Military.* to bungle. Compare *screw up,* FRIG UP.

    1916–29 in Manning *Fortune* 51 [refers to WWI]: And they'll call up all the women/When they've fucked up all the men. [**1932** Halyburton & Goll *Shoot & Be Damned* 206 [refers to 1918]: That big tub of sour owl milk will jazz up the detail for all of us. You'd better dust off a court martial for him.] **1942** H. Miller *Roofs of Paris* 248: You and Sid are going to fuck up everything before you're through. **1942** in Morriss *South Pacific Diary* 33: If there is any way for a thing to be fucked up, the Army will find it....Sometimes they'll even fuck it up when you'd think it's impossible. **1944** in J. O'Hara *Selected Letters* 184: I know I fucked up your afternoon schedule. **1951** in *International Journal of Psycho-Analysis* XXXV (1954) 35: When a man says: "I got my day all fucked up," he is [yet] fully aware of the primary sexual meaning of the word. **1952** in Perelman *Don't Tread on Me* 123: So many bothersome and ridiculous complications with which you'd managed to fuck up your life here. **1953** M. Harris *Southpaw* 143: Them goddam bastards would as soon f— up my ball club as not. **1956** Chamales *Never So Few* 574: They fucked something up when they moved that piece....They're missing us. **1965** Yurick *Warriors* 71: That fucked everything up, Hector thought. **1966–67** W. Stevens *Gunner* 119 [refers to WWII]: It's not going to do...anybody...any good if you go around fucking up the detail. **1968** Mares *Marine Machine* 29: Mouse, the coffee's cold! You're a Kremlin spy sent here to fuck up my stomach. **1969** Stern *Brood of Eagles* 341: Oh, I would have fucked it up for fair. I know that. **1974** P. Larkin *This Be the Verse:* They fuck you up, your mum and dad./They may not mean to, but they do./They fill you with the faults they had/And add some extra, just for you. **1984** J. Fuller *Fragments* 23: Duds, the drill sergeants would call us....Fuck up a two-car funeral. **1991** "R. Brown" & R. Angus *A.K.A. Narc* 188: They'll fuck this up like they fucked up everything else. **1998** *Starr Report* VIII L: Ms. Lewinsky said she wanted two things from the President. The first was contrition: He needed to "acknowledge...that he helped fuck up my life."

    2.a. to blunder badly; (*hence*) get oneself into trouble of any kind; fail. Compare synonym *screw up*.

    1943 in Morriss *South Pacific Diary* 114: They...fucked up beautifully. **1945** in Shibutani *Company K* 115: We always fuck up when we march. **1953** M. Harris *Southpaw* 201: The first man that f—s up in this respect is going to get hit in the pocketbook, and hit hard. **1944–57** Atwell *Private* 33: He f—ed up there too, so they sent him down to us in C Company. **1957** Simmons *Corner Boy* 73: People will fugg up. **1961** Forbes *Goodbye to Some* 53: I really fucked up. We were going way too fast. **1961** McMurtry *Horseman, Pass By* 48: "You fucked up," Hermy said. **1963** J. Ross *Dead Are Mine* 87: Keep your nose clean and this will all be forgotten. Fuck up and you're dead. **1964–66** R. Stone *Hall of Mirrors* 271: But in my journalistic opinion they're gonna fuck up. **1971** Meggyesy *Out of Their League* 189: I also watched how Ernie and Larry did and I must admit I was pleased when they made mistakes and fucked up. **1972** Halberstam *Best & Brightest* 281 [refers to 1963]: Americans in Vietnam...had come up with a slogan to describe the ARVN promotion system: "Fuck up and move up." **1978** Rascoe & Stone *Who'll Stop the Rain?* (film): "I've been waiting all my life to fuck up like this." "Well, you've finally made the big time." **1972–79** T. Wolfe *Right Stuff* 221: *Falling behind* put you on the threshold of *fucking up.* **1982** Gino *Nurse's Story* 318: Maybe somebody fucked up.

b. to go awry; malfunction; break down.

1976 D. Mamet *American Buffalo* 35: There's the least *chance* something might fuck up. **1980** J. Carroll *Land of Laughs* 90: How many things are going to fuck up before we get this straightened out. **1982** D.J. Williams *Hit Hard* 175 [refers to WWII]: A-17 gun fucked up. **1985** Sawislak *Dwarf* 193: In case you miss a transmission or the radios fuck up.

3.a. to befuddle or confuse; confound; thwart; interfere with.

1945 in Shibutani *Company K* 133: I bet that fuckin' CO stays awake every night tryin' to think up some new way to fuck us up. **1950** in J. Kerouac *Selected Letters* 239: I don't see how these cocksuckers could have done a better job trying to fuck me up as a...novelist. **1968** in E. Knight *Belly Song* 15: Perhaps it was just the brother's definition that fucked me up. **1968–71** Cole & Black *Checking It Out* 223: "It will be six months before they use those rooms again...." "That's cool...I dig fucking up white prejudiced pricks." **1971–72** Giovanitti *Medal* 109: I said what I said because I had nothing else to go on. I ain't changing that story now. And nobody's going to fuck me up. You understand? **1976** Chinn *Dig the Nigger Up* 37: I'd sure like to do it to her!...She fucks me all up! **1978** E. Thompson *Devil to Pay* 156: It was

Milt's idea to cook out. "Really fuck up the neighbors, man. They'll think it's springtime." **1995** *Journal of American Folklore* CVIII 215: Why aren't...voices that would fuck theory up included in this collection?

b. to make intoxicated.

1971 in H.S. Thompson *Shark Hunt* 147: Five reds, enough to fuck *anybody* up. **1980** DiFusco et al. *Tracers* 46 [refers to Vietnam War]: There's enough shit here to fuck up the entire squad for at least a week.

4.a. Especially *Black English.* to injure, especially severely; mangle; wound.

1962 in Wepman, Newman & Binderman *The Life* 23: He romped and stomped, and he fucked up his face. **1965** C. Brown *Manchild in the Promised Land* 144: Man, those bullets can really fuck you up. **1966–67** P. Thomas *Down These Mean Streets* [refers to *ca*1950]: I felt his fist fuck up my shoulder. *Ibid.* 209: Louie, if the motherfucker makes a move, fuck him up good. **1970** Cole *Street Kids* 88: The guy who was on our kid fucked the other guy up. The guy was bleeding from his eye. **1970–71** Rubinstein *City Police* 358: You think it was a gun?...O.K., pal, just relax, at least he didn't fuck you up. **1972** T. O'Brien *Combat Zone* 76: You don't get mangled by a mine, you get fucked up. **1972–74** Howes & Asher *Raise Up* 84: My man from Harlem had overheard the...hassle...and asked if I wanted him to get some cats to fuck up the bass player. **1975** S.P. Smith *American Boys* 162: A few losers who'd been fucked up not quite bad enough to be sent home. **1978** W. Brown *Tragic Magic* 152: "Fuck him up!" "Waste his ass!" **1982** Del Vecchio *13th Valley* 22: Some innocent dudes always get fucked up and blown away. **1997** *New Yorker* (July 21) 38: Or I can wait for you after work and fuck you up.

b. *Military.* to kill. Compare 1916–29 quotation at definition 1, above.

1967 in Edelman *Dear America* 87: The company lost 5 KIA and about 40 wounded. We fucked up at least two times as many Charlies as far as KIA, but we have more wounded. **1987** Whitely *Deadly Green* 201 [refers to Vietnam War]: Fuck them up! Fuck them fuckers up!...Get some!

5. *Black English.* to fool around.

1969 Hannerz *Soulside* 62: I earn good money, you know, with those two jobs, and my old lady earns a lot on her job, so actually I don't have to leave too much money at home 'cause she takes care of much of that. So this means I got a lot to spend just fucking up. **1970** A. Young *Snakes* 125: We both need to get away from this old school grind for awhile. Why don't we go out and fuck up tonight? It's Friday, man....Let's go out and party!

☞ In phrase: **could fuck up a wet dream,** *Military.* is or are exceedingly clumsy or stupid.

1967 Dubus *Lieutenant* 52 [refers to 1956]: Freeman, you are nothing but a skinny turd and would fuck up a wet dream. **1971** Flanagan *Maggot* 242 [refers to *ca*1956]: They fuck-up everything. Some of them would fuck-up a wet dream. **1975** Wambaugh *Choirboys* 185: Roscoe Rules could fuck up a wet dream. **1966–80** McAleer & Dickson *Unit Pride* 391 [refers to *ca*1951]: Billy, I swear you'd fuck up a wet dream. **1984** Caunitz *Police Plaza* 193: That guy could fuck up a wet dream. **1987** D. Sherman *Main Force* 191 [refers to 1966]: Lewis, you'd fuck up a wet dream. Go back to sleep.

fuckwad *noun* a stupid or contemptible person.

   1974 Student slang survey: Motherfucker, fuckwad, sonofabitch, [etc.]. **1986** J. Cain *Suicide Squad* 97: I wanna see ID cards on all these fuckwads. **1987** "J. Hawkins" *Tunnel Warriors* 144: That goofy fuckwad. **1990** Rukuza *West Coast Turnaround* 8: Some fuckwad was shootin' up da scenery wit' a machine gun.

fuckwit *noun* Chiefly *Australian & British* a stupid person. Hence **fuckwitted,** *adjective* stupid; **fuckwittage,** *noun,* stupidity.

   1968 A. Buzo, in *Plays* 89: Well, ta-ta for now, fuckwit. **1970** S. Jarratt *Permissive Australia* 142: Of course they do, you fuckwit. **1971** in J. Hibberd *Stretch of Imagination* 40: You two-timing, fuck-witted mongrel of a slut! **1973** in *Australian National Dictionary:* That fuckwitted agent of yours is really driving me right off my brain. **1979** in *Australian National Dictionary:* It sounded like a load of fuck-wit shit to me. **1986** M. Johnson *Lear* 7: It is not your turn, fuckwits! **1995** Will Self, in *Esquire* (Feb.) 108: Dear Fuckwit. **1997** *N.Y. Press* (Aug. 27) 30: Fuckwit on a wet-bike. **1998** H. Fielding *Bridget Jones's Diary* 18: Sharon started on a long illustrative list of emotional fuckwittage in progress in our friends: one whose boyfriend of thirteen years refuses to even discuss living together [etc.]. *Ibid.* 66: I am not interested in fuckwittage.

fuck with see under FUCK, *verb,* definition 5a.

fucky *adjective* sexually attractive or stimulating.

1973 N. Mailer *Marilyn: A Biography* 102: Never again in her career will she look so sexually perfect as in 1953 making *Gentlemen Prefer Blondes,* no, never—if we are to examine a verb through its adverb [*sic*]—will she appear so fucky again. **1976** in G. Legman *New Limerick* 461: I feel fucky. **1991** "Red Hot Chili Peppers" *If You Have to Ask* (pop. song): A little lust/To the fucky-ass Flea [*sc.,* the band's bass player]. **1994** *Guardian* (London) (June 29) T8: T-shirts with slogans like *Have You Wanked Over Me Yet?* and *I'm So Fucky.* **1998** *Playboy* (Dec.) 86: What was a sweet fucky marriage but the sublimation of orgies never taken?

fuck-you *noun* a statement or expression of contempt, hostility, or the like.

[**1946–51** J.D. Salinger *Catcher in the Rye* 202: I went down by a different staircase, and I saw another "Fuck you" on the wall.] **1964** in H.S. Thompson *Proud Highway* 537: I had a bad wrangle with them on a Tom Wolfe review, and we said a mutual fuck you, with me about $500 ahead. **1992** *Rolling Stone* (Dec. 10) 45: The disc was a relentlessly catchy and fuzz-filled "fuck you." **1993** *Rolling Stone* (Oct. 14) 68: Who else could insult Budweiser, Michael Jackson, Whitney Houston, Calvin Klein, the entire recording industry and MTV all in one video? "This Note's for You" is Neil Young's finest "fuck you." **1994** *Granta* 47 (Spring) 129: She never learned English, even though she had come here at sixteen: a fuck-you to the New World. **1995** *New York* (Mar. 13) 33: When it's as bad as it can be, and people still act like there's nothing wrong, then it's sort of like a fuck-you to the audience—"we don't have to be good, because we're Saturday Night Live!" **1996** *N.Y. Observer* (Apr. 1) 3: The line was a veiled fuck-you to David Letterman,....the symbolic whipping boy for how the East Coast element screwed up the Oscars.

fuck-you *adjective* contemptuous; hostile; confrontational.

1972 *Rolling Stone* (July 20) 8: For clenched fists and gritted teeth and fuckyou rock and roll. **1973** *Rolling Stone* (March 1) 42: See if you can keep your integrity without a flat out fuck-you challenge. **1981** *Times Literary Supplement* (May 15) 548: The Beatles....A pretentious gobbledygook introduction by Leonard Bernstein: "...the Fuck-You coolness of these Four Horsemen of Our Apocalypse." **1993** N. Maclean, in *Harper's* (Feb.) 35: Under the influence of those dreams, some of the finest fuck-you prose in the English language has been composed but, alas, never published. **1994** *Rolling Stone* (Feb. 10) 53: We've endured so much phony Hollywood nobility about disease that Jean's fuck-you rampage against death comes off as horrifically honest. **1996** *Newsweek* (Feb. 19) 39: The bombing...is "the politics of fuck-you rage and resentment rather than political calculation." **1997** *New Yorker* (Oct. 6) 48: Youthful hubris or fuck-you candor. **1998** *New Yorker* (Dec. 1) 64: He has the real fuck-you blood.

fuck-you lizard *noun* [suggested by a resemblance between the English phrase and the gecko's call] *Military in Southeast Asia.* a tokay gecko.

[**1933** Clifford *Boats* 309: A gecko lizard in a nearby papaya tree croaked throatily. "Obscene devils, those," he went on dryly. The colonel laughed.] **1971** *Playboy* (Aug.) 199: From the underground comes the chant of "Fuck you, fuck you" from small lizards, not unexpectedly called fuck-you lizards.

FUCK-YOU LIZARD

1978 Hasford *Short-Timers* 151 [refers to Vietnam War]: The fuck-you lizards greet us. **1984** J. Fuller *Fragments* 78: Did you know that if you grab one of those Fuck You lizards by the tail, he just lets go and walks away? **1986** Thacker *Pawn* 133: That's because of the fuck-you lizard. **1987** Lanning *Only War* 253: FNGs were told that the "fuck-you" lizards were NVA taunting us. **1988** Clodfelter *Mad Minutes* 33 [refers to 1965]: Naturally we labeled these leftovers from the prehistoric past "Fuck You Lizards."

fuck-you money *noun* Especially *Business.* sufficient money, especially from an unexpected source, to give one personal freedom; (*broadly*) a financial windfall.

1975 L. Rust Hills, in *Esquire* (Dec.) 180: "But all that money...."..."Well, it's 'fuck-you' money....It gives me freedom and independence so I won't have to write something that doesn't appeal to me." **1986** *New Republic* (Dec. 8) 11: [Donald] Regan huddled in the Oval Office with the president.... "I've got something that none of those other guys have."... "What is it?" To which Regan, wealthy from his days as boss of Merrill Lynch, replied, "Fuck you money." **1988** *Granta* 23 (Spring) 246: Earning more doesn't make the problem go away unless you're saving for "fuck you" money. A month ago Brian told me about "fuck you" money. "It's the amount of money you need to be able to say 'Fuck you' to anyone." Brian reckoned the current amount to be three million pounds. **1994** N.Y.C. man, age 30: When you win the lottery, you get *fuck-you money.* Anyone you don't want to bother with, you can afford to say "Fuck you!" **1994** N.Y.C. businessman, age 60: When you sell your business for a lot of money, that's called *fuck-you money.* Then, even though you're supposed to stay and work for the company, you can say "Fuck you" and leave. It's very common in business, especially among mergers-and-acquisition types. **1994** *Times Literary Supplement* (Nov. 18) 9: "Fuck-you-money," for having enough money set aside to tell one's boss to screw off, should the impulse to do so arise. **1995** *New York Times Magazine* (Nov. 19) 46: The Number is often used interchangeably with another term, an unprintable one that describes the sum you need to be able to tell your boss you've had enough. Its family-newspaper approximation would be Forget You Money.

fuck-your-buddy week *noun* Especially *Military.* a hypothetical period during which betrayal and exploitation of one's friends is supposedly encouraged. *Jocular.* Also variants. Compare BUDDY-FUCK.

[**1952** Haines & Krims *One Minute to Zero* (film): John, this isn't help-your-buddy week. We might need those guys again.] **1960** MacCuish *Do Not Go Gentle* 342 [refers to WWII]: National American custom of Screw Your Buddy Week. **1962** Crump *Killer* 279: Don't worry about it, weed.... This is Frig Your Buddy Week. *ca***1963** in Schwendinger & Schwendinger *Adolescent Subculture* 296: It's fuck your buddy week, fifty-two weeks of the year....If you have a buddy kind and true, you fuck him before he fucks you. *a***1967** in M.W. Klein *Juvenile Gangs* 98: It's fuck your buddy week, fifty-two weeks of the year. **1971** *Playboy* (Apr.) 182: That old Army expression, "Every week is fuck-your-buddy week!" **1973** W. Crawford *Gunship Commander* 148: The whole army overreacted, filed charges against everybody in sight, good old fuck-your-brother week. **1980** Manchester *Darkness* 156 [refers to WWII]: The school's shabbiest custom [was] known as "fuck-your-buddy night." Every candidate was required to fill out a form rating his fellows. **1984** Partridge *Dictionary of Slang & Unconventional English* (ed. 8) 1323: What *is* this?— International Fuck-Your-Buddy Week?...Prob. adopted from the US forces in Korea, 1950–53.

FUCK-YOUR-BUDDY WEEK

fugly *adjective* [blend of FUCKING + *ugly*] *Students.* very ugly.

[**1962** in H.S. Thompson *Proud Highway* 316: Get these dogs off me! These fucking ugly dogs!] **1970** in *More than Mere Bravo: Fugly*—an extremely ugly woman. A blending of "fucking" and "ugly" to describe the woman. **1984** Mason & Rheingold *Slanguage: Fugly*, adj.... fucking ugly. **1988** Eble *Campus Slang* (Fall) 4: *Fugly*—extremely ugly. **1989** P. Munro *U.C.L.A. Slang* 41: She's so fugly she makes my mother-in-law look cute. **1993** N.Y. man, age 23: This girl asked me out yesterday, but man, she was fugly. **1998** Personal letter to editor (Aug. 25): *Fugly*—I picked up the term from my college roomie, 1974–75.

FUJIGMO *interjection Military.* "*fuck you*, *Jack, I got my orders.*" *Jocular.* Compare FUIGMO under FIGMO.

1950 *Saturday Evening Post* (Aug. 5) 89: With him flew Lt. Col. "Pappy" Hatfield, in his famous bomber

159

the "Fujigmo"—translation unprintable. **1953** in Valant *Aircraft Nose Art* 295: FUJIGMO. **1980** D. Cragg *Lexicon Militaris* 158: *FUJIGMO. Fuck You, Jack, I Got My Orders.*

futhermucker *noun* [intentional spoonerism] see MOTHERFUCKER. *Jocular.*

1965 Walnut Ridge, Ark., high school student: Every one of your Hoxie friends turns out to be a futhermucker, if you ask me. **1972** R. Wilson *Playboy's Forbidden Words* 171: *Mammy-jammer,... futher-mucker.* **1972–76** Durden *No Bugles, No Drums* 41: Thanks, futhermucker. **1982** in G. Tate *Flyboy* 21: Well, goddamn, these furthermuckers [*sic*] must not be bullshitting. **1998** G. Tate, in *Village Voice* (N.Y.C.) (Mar. 10) 124: His peers are those lofty, low-rent, high-concept, swing-baiting furthermuckers [*sic*].

futz *noun*

1. a foolish or unpleasant fellow.

1935 *Bedroom Companion* 79: Some crusty old futz who has had too much drink starts off on this tangent. **1940** W.R. Burnett *High Sierra* 35: He was an old phutz and a has-been. **1959–60** Bloch *Dead Beat* 84: The old futz inside the loan office gave him a cold eye.

2. (used as a euphemism for *the fuck,* under FUCK, *noun*).

1947 Schulberg *Harder They Fall* 104: Nobody knows what the futz you're talkin' about.

futz *verb*

1. [probably an alteration of Yiddish *arumfartsn*] to fool or play.—used with *around* or *with*. [Often regarded as a euphemism for FUCK, *verb,* definition 5, or FUCK AROUND.]

1929–30 J.T. Farrell *Young Lonigan* 63: Studs kept futzing around until Helen Shires came out with her soccer ball. **1932** *American Speech* VII (June) 335: *Phutz around*—to trifle; to interfere; "to horse around." **1936** Levin *Old Bunch* 64: There was a fellow that never wasted time. No fuzzy futzing around. *Ibid.* 249: No more futzing around being a schoolboy. **1941** Brackett & Wilder *Ball of Fire* (film): Why do you think we're futzin' around with these? **1941** in Boucher *Werewolf* 129: Futzing around with the occult. **1944** Liebling *Back to Paris* 113: Have we really started, or are we still futzing around? **1948** Wolfert *Act of Love* 158: What's he futzing around for? **1949** Robbins *Dream Merchants* 14: At least he didn't say a word about my futsing around all those years. **1959–60** Bloch *Dead Beat 3:* "Good crowd," said Eddie, futzing around with his mustache. **1964–66** R. Stone *Hall of Mirrors* 78: To...watch a room full of stooges futz with soap. **1968** P. Roth *Portnoy's Complaint* 263: I am nobody to futz around with. **1970** C. Harrison *No Score* 55: You futz around in the darkroom all the time. **1973** Schiano & Burton *Solo* 106: All that futzing around with bits of paper. **1984** *USA Today* (Nov. 7) 3A: President Reagan...[suggested] it is time to "stop this futzing around." **1998** *New Yorker* (Oct. 5) [inside back cover] [advertisement]: Da Vinci didn't mess with the Mona Lisa. Beethoven didn't futz with his 5th Symphony.

futz *continued*

    2. to treat with contempt.—used with *around.*

    1966 Brunner *Face of Night* 165: Futz me around a little more and find out.

futzer *noun* see FUTZ, *noun,* definition 1.

    1938 H. Miller *Tropic of Capricorn* 30: You poor old futzer, you, just wait.

futz off *verb* to loaf.

    1968 Baker et al. *Col. Undergrad. Slang Survey* 123: *Futz off.* Waste time, not study.

futz out *verb* FUTZ UP.

    1963 Coon *Short End* 254: What happens to you, if you are Halstead...and the whole shooting match futzes out right in your face and lies there?

futz up *verb* to spoil, confound; FUCK UP.

    1947 Willingham *End as a Man* 296: I've got her all futzed up. She does everything I tell her. **1948** Wolfert *Act of Love* 293: If you're futzing it up I want to know. **1965** Hardman *Chaplains* 64: Not while you're futzing up the clergy I won't!

FYFI [initialism punning on standard *FYI*] Especially *Business.* "for your fucking information." *Jocular.*

    1995 N.Y.C. publisher, age 52: *FYFI* means "for your fucking information." I've seen it used on memos for at least ten years—everyone knows what it means. **1996** *Re: 2 10,000 Maniacs Questions,* on Usenet newsgroup alt.music.alternative.female (Feb. 23): This "some guy or something" is called Salman Rushdie, FYFI. **1998** *Re: Truth,* on Usenet newsgroup rec.audio.tubes (July 20): FYFI, it is easy to spot an unsuccessful author. He publishes two books and is gone.

G

Words

gang-fuck *noun* a gangbang: an occasion on which a number of people copulate successively with one person; (*also*) gang rape; (*also*) a sexual orgy. Also **gang-screw.**

> **1941** G. Legman, in G.V. Henry *Sex Vars.* II 1166: *Gang-fuck.* An instance of pedication or irrumation of a single boy or homosexual by two or more men consecutively, and with or without his consent. Also used as a verb, and in both senses heterosexually. **1946–51** Motley *We Fished* 350: The fellows had the girl back behind a stairway. She was willing. It was another gang-screw. *a***1968** in Haines & Taggart *Fort Lauderdale* 60: Gang fucks. **1972** D. Jenkins *Semi-Tough* 58: Less fun than being next-to-last on a high school gang-fuck.

gang-fuck *verb* to copulate with (someone) in a GANG–FUCK.

> **1916** Cary *Slang of Venery* I 103: *Gang Fucked*—Said of a woman who, willingly or unwillingly, submits to the embraces of the individuals in a crowd of men in succession. **1938** "Justinian" *Americana Sexualis* 24: A *gang* of boys or young men escorts a girl or young woman to its rendezvous and proceeds to *gang-fuck*

164

her. U.S. vulgarism, C. 20. **1940** *Tale of a Twist* 77: I guess I've been gang-fucked a few times. **1959** W. Burroughs *Naked Lunch* 125: I been gang fucked. **1975** C.W. Smith *Country Music* 84: They'd just as soon gang-fuck you as look at you! **1984** Ehrhart *Marking Time* 66: What kind of person could gang-fuck some poor starving refugee in the middle of a war?

genderfuck *noun* an instance of reversal of normal gender roles; (*specifically*) transvestism.

1973 *Rolling Stone* (Aug. 30): The new "macho" transvestitism, called vulgarly "gender-fuck," a curious satire of female impersonation—dresses, pumps, full make-up and beards—is represented by, among others, three men in WAC uniforms and big moustaches. **1979** Robert Christgau, in Greil Marcus *Stranded: Rock and Roll for a Desert Island* 133: Ordinarily, their [*sc.* the New York Dolls'] gender-fuck was a lot subtler. **1985** *Village Voice* (N.Y.C.) (Sept. 10) 74: Part of Phranc's appeal is the genderfuck of her sweet feminine voice coming from such a masculine frame. *a***1988** *Maledicta* IX (1987–88) 173: Real transvestites and transsexuals are...embarrassed...[by] the gender-fuck Cockettes and such (in dresses and beards). **1995** E. Weisbard *Spin Alternative Record Guide* 135: Gender-fuck goddess Annie Lennox and wacky rock professor Dave Stewart were a match made in video-pop heaven. **1995** in *Village Voice* (N.Y.C.) (Jan. 2, 1996) 6: The hot-off-the-press Gender Fuck issue of Porn Free—"the Porn 'Zine Dedicated to Getting You Off for Nothin'." **1996** *N.Y. Press* (Nov. 6) 36: "The boys wanna be girls and the girls wanna be boys." He was right—the crowd was pure third-sexer genderfuck. **1997** *Village Voice* (N.Y.C.) (Sept. 16) 35: That led me to a realm of gender fuck that's beyond category.

GFO *noun* [general *fuck-off*] *Military.* a lazy individual. *Jocular.*

1948 *N.Y. Folklore Quarterly* 20 [refers to WWII]. **1957** Myrer *Big War* 213 [refers to WWII]: Snap-to, you pitiful gutless GFO!

GFU *noun* [general *fuck-up*] *Military.* an incompetent individual. *Jocular.*

1942 *Yank* (Nov. 25) 21: G.I. Jones...was the GFU of Bat. B 66th CA (AA). **1944** in *American Speech* XX 148: *G.F.U.* General foul up; a soldier who does not do the work he is supposed to do. **1945** *Saturday Review of Literature* (Nov. 3) 7: He had better learn. Otherwise he will be known as a GFU... and that would be just TS. **1945** *American Speech* (Dec.) 262: *G.F.U.,* "a soldier who never does anything correctly." **1948** *N.Y. Folklore Quarterly* (Spring) 21. **1962** Killens *Then We Heard the Thunder* 208 [refers to WWII]: Sad sacks and GFUs and...goldbricks. **1991** Reinberg *In the Field* 93 [refers to Vietnam War]: *G F U* abbr. for General Fuck-Up, usually referring to specific persons.

give-a-shit *noun* one's sense of motivation, enthusiasm, or concern. Also **give-a-fuck.**

1976 College student: That's not a question of talent; it's a question of *give-a-shit.* *ca***1985** in K. Walker

Piece of My Heart 127 [refers to 1970–71]: The frontal
lobe—what one of the corpsmen, and shortly after
that everybody, called the "give a shit" lobe, because
once you lose it you don't give a shit about anything.
1985 Dye *Between the Raindrops* 235 [refers to Vietnam War]: Feel like all my give-a-fuck drained out.
Ibid. 237: I can't seem to work up a good give-a-shit
about it. *ca***1987** in K. Marshall *Combat Zone* 140
[refers to *ca*1970]: Like that kid I told you about; he
lost his frontal lobe—it was what the corpsmen used
to call the "give a shit" lobe because in an adult if
you took out the frontal lobe, they didn't give a shit
about anything.

goat *noun* ☞ In phrase: **been to three county
fairs and a goat-fucking** [or (*euphemistically*)
goat-roping] *Southern.* seen many astounding
sights. *Jocular.*

    1974 College student: I been to three county fairs
and a goat-fuckin' and I ain't never seen the like of
that. **1981** B. Bowman *If I Tell You* 98: "I've been to
three county fairs, two goat-ropings and a "'tater
digging." I know what's going on; I've been around.
1984 K. Weaver *Texas Crude* 30: I've seen a goat-roping, a fat stock show and a duck fart under water,
but if that don't beat any damn thing I've *ever* seen,
I'll put in with you!! **1988** Dye *Outrage* 16: Colonel,
you and me been to three county fairs and a goat-
fuckin' contest and I ain't seen you hit by nothin'
heavier than shrapnel.

goat fuck *noun* Especially *Military.* a fiasco; mess.
Also (*euphemistically*) **goat dance, goat screw,
goat rope.**

goat fuck *continued*

1965 in H.S. Thompson *Proud Highway* 481: Kentucky was a Wolfean nightmare and New York was a goatdance. **1971** T. Mayer *Weary Falcon* 15: "What a goatfuck," I said. **1986** Chapman *New Dictionary of American Slang.* **1990** Ruggero *38 N. Yankee* 80: There seemed to be some order creeping into Barrow's "goat screw." **1991** Marcinko & Weisman *Rogue Warrior* 199: It had been one humongous goatfuck. *a***1991** Kross *Splash One* 34 [refers to Vietnam War]: What's a guy like you doing in a goat rope like this? **1995** *Guardian* (London) (Sept. 2) 1: Britain now has what the Americans call "goat-fucks," those swaying edifices of cameramen, snappers, sound recorders and hacks which lurch perilously round press conferences.

green motherfucker *noun Army & U.S. Marine Corps.* the U.S. Army or U.S. Marine Corps.—usually used with *this.*—used opprobriously. Also variants. [Quotations refer to Vietnam War. The 1968 quotation is a euphemism.]

1968 Stuart *Typescript* (unpaged): I'll be out of this "green thing" in another year. **1973** Karlin et al. *Free Fire Zone* 137: Plan on getting out of this green amphibious motherfucker. **1976** C.R. Anderson *Grunts* 146: How did you ever get in this green mother anyway? **1978** J. Webb *Fields of Fire* 210: The Corps...I *love* this green motherfucker. **1982** R.A. Anderson *Cooks & Bakers* 116: They talked about how much they hated Vietnam and the Marine Corps—the "Crotch," the "Green Motherfucker." **1983** Ehrhart *Vietnam to Perkasie* 54: The Army buys...jeeps that work. But the Green Mother spend money for good equipment? **1985** Dye *Between the Raindrops* 144: Could have gotten *out* of this green motherfucker and been set, man.

GRF *noun* see under RATFUCK, *noun,* definition 2a.

guaranfuckingtee *verb* to guarantee absolutely. Also **guarandamntee.** Compare -FUCKING-. [The 1948 quotation is a euphemism.]

   1948 Manone & Vandervoort *Trumpet* 180: I guaran-(fussin')-tee you, when we got the place fixed up it was real pretty. **1954** LeMay *Searchers* 122: Not the Texas legislature, I guarandamtee. **1961** J. Jones *Thin Red Line* 42 [refers to WWII]: I guaran-fucking-tee you! **1973, 1975** *American Speech* 55 (1980) 173: Guarandamntee. **1986** Stinson & Carabatsos *Heartbreak* 14: I'll guaranfuckintee you. **1988** *New Yorker* (Dec. 5) 61: They say they never do it, but I guaranfuckintee you someone fooled with the ball this year.

H

Words

ham and motherfuckers [or **mothers**], see under MOTHERFUCKER.

handfuck *verb* to masturbate with the fingers or hands. Also (as in 1989 quotation) figurative. Also as noun. Also **hand frig.**

    1879 *Harlequin Prince Cherrytop* 4: Hand frig, stand frig,/That's the sport for him. *a***1989** C.S. Crawford *Four Deuces* 48 [refers to Korean War]: To find the break they wrap their hands around the telephone line...and let it run between their fists. That's what they call "hand-fucking" the line....They were out hand-fuckin' a line lookin' for a break in it. **1992** A. McGahan *Praise* 44: I set to with three fingers and finally she came...."Hand fucking is wonderful." **1996** *Ploughshares* (Sept. 1) [short story by Leslie McKenzie Bienen]: You want hand fuck...How much you give me? **1997** *Making the Bride's Maid*, pornographic story on USENET newsgroup alt.sex.stories (Sept. 5): He had his fingers greased with oil....[He] began to hand-fuck her, opening her up.

hate-fuck *noun* an act of intercourse motivated by animosity towards one's partner.

1968 P. Newman, in *Playboy* (July) 69: There was the hate fuck, the prestige fuck—and the medicinal fuck, which is, "Feel better now, sweetie?" *a***1976** J. Nicholson, in A.W. Read *An Obscenity Symbol After Four Decades* 3: People that I don't like are not sexually attractive to me at all. I remember in my early 20s I had a few hate-fucks and they were groovy. But not now. **1987** "Pussy Galore" *Groovy Hate Fuck* [rock album title]. **1995** R. Athey, in *Village Voice* (N.Y.C.) (Feb. 14) 32: When he comes home fucked up, I'm sure to give him a good hate fuck.

headfuck *verb* to confuse, mislead, or the like, especially deliberately; MINDFUCK.

1978 R. Price *Ladies' Man* 211: I feel like you're fucking with my head....I feel head-fucked. **1985** Frede *Nurses* 287: I told you, Trina. Don't pull that headfucking with me.

headfucker *noun Narcotics.* a powerful hallucinogenic or psychotropic drug; mindbender.

1975 in Spears *Drugs & Drink* 254: Headfucker ["a potent head drug"]. *a***1989** Spears *NTC Slang Dictionary* 176: This stuff is a real headfucker. Stay away from it.

honeyfuck *noun* a sexy girl.

1970 E. Thompson *Garden of Sand* 295: Come on,... honeyfuck. **1979** L. Heinemann, in *Tri-Quarterly* (Spring) 184: The snazziest hot-to-trot honey fuck to hit the mainland since the first French settlers.

honeyfuck *verb* [probably an alteration of earlier *honeyfuggle* in its sense 'to engage in kissing and hugging'] to engage in unusually gratifying copulation.

1954–60 Wentworth & Flexner *Dictionary of American Slang: Honey-fuck*...v.i., v.t. To have sexual intercourse in a romantic, idyllic way; to have intercourse with a very young girl...*honeyfucking*...extremely gratifying and slow intercourse. **1980** L. Heinemann, in *Harper's* (June) 64: She's honey-fucking the everlasting daylights out of some guy. **1986** Merkin *Zombie Jamboree* 121: We were honey-fuckin', real slow and low, takin' our time.

horsefuck *verb* to copulate with (someone) from behind; DOGFUCK.

1972 Wambaugh *Blue Knight* 114: Sexy little twist....I'd like to break her open like a shotgun and horsefuck her. **1977** College student: Horsefuckin' is the best position.

horse-fucking *adjective* huge.

*a***1968** in Legman *Rationale* 549: Two great horse-fucking volumes.

hot *adjective* ☞ In phrase: **hot enough to fuck,** furiously angry.

1966 Braly *On the Yard* 201: The doc was hot enough to fuck. **1966–80** McAleer & Dickson *Unit Pride* 358: Miller's gonna be hot enough to fuck before this mess is over.

J

Words

JANFU *noun* [*j*oint *a*rmy-*n*avy *f*uck-*u*p; suggested by SNAFU] *Military.* a bungled military operation involving the Army and Navy. *Jocular.* [The 1944 quotations are euphemistic.]

    1944 *Newsweek* (Feb. 7) 61: *Janfu:* Joint Army-Navy foul-up... *Jaafu:* Joint Anglo-American foul-up. **1944** in *American Speech* XX 148: *JANFU.* Joint army-navy foulup. **1945** in *Verbatim* XVI (Autumn 1989) 6: *Janfu...*"joint army-navy fxxx up." A failed amphibious military operation considered badly planned and/or executed. **1946** *American Speech* (Feb.) 72: JANFU (Joint Army-Navy FU)...became fairly common in [the Pacific] theater, especially around the time of the Saipan operation.

jug-fuck *noun Military.*

    1. a drinking bout.

    1980 Retired Army sergeant: I first ran across this in a list of Pro Signs given to me after April, 1977. "Let's go have us a jug fuck!"

    2. a confused or frustrating situation; mess; CLUS-TERFUCK, *noun*, definition 2.

    *a***1987** Coyle *Team Yankee* 116: Not until, and only if, we get this jug fuck unscrewed. **1988** Dye *Outrage*

10: Until we get out of this Ethiopian jug-fuck, I don't want to see you any more than six feet away from...your squad.

jumble-fuck *noun* CLUSTERFUCK, *noun*, definition 1.

1938 "Justinian" *Americana Sexualis* 27: *Jumble-Fuck,* n. U.S., low coll., *ca*20 for *Daisy-Chain.*

Words

LBFM *noun* [*little brown fucking machine*] *Military.* a Southeast Asian woman who is sexually promiscuous, especially a bar girl or a prostitute. [Quotations refer to the Vietnam War.]

1971 *Playboy* (Aug.) 203: LBFM's never come. What's an LBFM? A little brown fucking machine. **1974** J. Platt *Laotian Fragments* 12: *Remember:* The Golden Palace LBFMs in their spangled padded bras saying "Melly Clistmas, GI." **1985** Heywood *Taxi Dancer* 61: The…Thais—what the airmen called Little Brown Fucking Machines, LBFMs for short. *Ibid.* 225: Where's my LBFM?…Colonel loves LBFMs. **1991** Marcinko & Weisman *Rogue Warrior* 165: No LBFM's today. *a***1992** T. Wilson *Termite Hill* 377: Swede probably thought she was just another LBFM.

Words

mammy-dodger *noun Black English.* (a partial euphemism for) MOTHERFUCKER.

   1939 in A. Banks *First-Person* 256: Hell yes, mammydodger.

mammy-jammer *noun* Especially *Black English.* (a partial euphemism for) MOTHERFUCKER, in any sense. Also variants.

   1948 Webb *Four Steps* 100: I sure nuff show ol' white boy mammy-dugger how's feel. **1956** Resko *Reprieve* 48: The mammy-jammer...puts the rope aroun mah neck. **1962** Killens *Then We Heard the Thunder* [refers to 1942]: *Ibid.* 31 [refers to WWII]: I just don't like the goddamn mama-jabbing Army, that's all. *Ibid.* 32: Now ain't that a mama-jabber? *Ibid.* 195: You fat-ass mother-huncher. *Ibid.* 266: We gonna step higher than a mama-jabber. **1963** Braly *Shake Him* 97: You know what that dirty mammy-jammer did to me? **1963** Cameron *Black Camp* 12: Grab your socks, mammyjammers. **1967** Baraka *Tales* 18: You talking about a lightweight mammy-tapper. *Ibid.* 20: Yeh, mammy-rammer. **1969** Brown *Die, Nigger* 109: I'd bought a rifle, which...was a sweet mama-jammer, too. **1969** Gordone *No Place* 413: I rassle with light'nin', put a cap on thunder. Set every mammy-jammer in the graveyard on a wonder. **1971** Keith *Long Line Rider* 75: Hey, Max, this mammyjammer don't like my cookin'. Y'all oughta have his butt busted. **1972** R. Wilson *Playboy's Forbidden Words* 165: *Mammy-Sucker* In black slang, an insult that is felt to be even more offensive than motherfucker. **1974** College student: You mama-sticker. **1980** McAleer & Dickson *Unit Pride* 31: You...dirty Yankee mammie-jammer. **1982** Downey *Losing the War* 59 [refers to WWII]: What the fuck do we do with three of these mammy-jabbers? **1985** Dye *Between the Raindrops* 279: I'd been outa this mammy-jammer like a fuckin' shot. *Ibid.* 291: We...a lucky bunch of mammy-jammers. **1987** J. Waters *Hairspray* (film) [refers to 1962]: Just to see me, the big mammy-jammer. **1991** *In Living Color* (Fox-TV): This is one bad mammy-jammer. **1992** *Jerry Springer Show* (syndicated TV series): I'm a bad mammy-jammer...I'm Wonder Woman!

mammy-jamming *adjective* (a partial euphemism for) MOTHERFUCKING. Also variants.

1946 Mezzrow & Wolfe *Really Blues* 105: Those Jim Crow mammyjamming whites. **1958** Talsman *Gaudy Image* 30: Yeah, some real mammy-lovin' goddamn cheap tinhorn place. **1969** Jessup *Sailor* 268: Who! The mammy-rammy *law!* That's who! **1974** Carter *16th Round* 55: You must be out of your mammy-jammy mind! **1974** Murray *Train Whistle Guitar* 117: That ain't no goddamn mammy-hunching patent leather walk. **1977** Bunker *Animal Factory* 59: I ain' no mammyfuckin' *dawg!* **1977** Langone *Life* *at Bottom* 76: Pour the stuff in the trench and it packs hard as a mammy-jammin' cement load.

maw-dicker *noun Southwest.* see MOTHERFUCKER. Hence **maw-dicking,** *adjective.*

1984 Sample *Racehoss* 145 [refers to 1950s]: Why you Gotdam impudent shit-colored mawdicker. *Ibid.* 202 [refers to *ca*1960]: I oughta throw yore mawdickin ass in the pisser.

mercy fuck *noun* an act of intercourse engaged in out of pity. Also as verb.

1968 Paul Newman, in *Playboy* (July) 69: Mercy fucking...would be reserved for spinsters and librarians. **1978** Alibrandi *Killshot* 174: Consider your work here a mercy fuck. **1981** in *National Lampoon* (Jan. '82) 22: But let's not consider this a mercy fuck. There's no joy in that. **1996** "Soul Coughing" *4 out of 5* (pop. song): Quantify my luck I need a mercy fuck.

m.f. or **em-eff** *noun* (a partial euphemism for) MOTHERFUCKER.

1959 in R.S. Gold *Jazz Lexicon* 209: You go and buy me a tenor saxophone and I'll play the m-f. **1964** Howe *Valley of Fire* 190: Being able to call a gook an emm-eff in pig Latin and get away with it. **1965** Ward & Kassebaum *Women's Pris.* 158: And please let me touch you just once you M.F. **1965** Cleaver *Soul on Ice* 58: Why'n't they kill some of the Uncle-Tomming m.f.s? **1965** in Sanchez *Word Sorcerers* 193: I'm a lucky M.F. to have found you. **1965** in W. King *Black Anthology* 304: So I stole the m—f [*sic*]. **1966–67** P. Thomas *Down These Mean Streets* 236: You poor m.f. **1968** B. Caldwell, in G.M. Simmons et al. *Black Culture* 213: Let's get these m.f.'s now! **1969** Rodgers *Black Bird* 38: None of us can relax until the last m.f.'s / been done in. **1970** Terkel *Hard Times* 407: Today you get a guy in court, [he] don't like what the judge says, he calls him a *m f,* you know what I mean? **1970** Cain *Blueschild Baby* 77: A bunch of dirty white M.F.'s. **1970** Quammen *Walk the Line* 222: Cause you ain't having too much left yourself, M-F. **1971** in Matthews & Amdur *My Race* 246: There'd be a lot of dead "M.F.'s" around. **1971** Wells & Dance *Night People* 116: Most of the time I was "Mr. M.F.," and the last straw was upside my head. Then I had to split. **1971–73** Sheehy *Hustling* 89: Then in comes this m.f. from Midtown North, *our* precinct. **1974** Blount *3 Bricks Shy* 159: They say "m-f" worse than a colored person. **1976** G. Kirkham *Signal Zero* 63: *Adios,* MF! **1986** Clayton & Elliott *Jazz World* 101: I did provoke the fight by calling him an MF. *Ibid.* [refers to 1930s]: Billie [Holiday] called all of her close friends MF. **1987** *Newsweek* (Mar. 23) 61: He could stand out on the corner looking sharp as a MF in his Stacy-Adams wingtips and a $100 hat. **1992** *Donahue* (NBC-TV): I'm gonna take all you m.f.s with me.

m.f. or **em-eff** *adjective* (a partial euphemism for) MOTHERFUCKING. Also **emeffing**.

1958 Motley *Epitaph* 120: Them emeffing guards is bringing it in in fountain pens. *Ibid.* 149: You emeffing right. *a***1972** in G.M. Simmons et al. *Black*

Culture 219: That M-F-in' jive. **1973** Childress *Hero*
34: All over the emm-eff community. **1990** *New
Yorker* (Apr. 2) 46: Graffiti...on the... training ship of
the Maine Maritime Academy..."Only 13 more
MFD's, Only 12 more MFD's, Only 11 more MFD's,"
and so on down a toilet stall. The "D" stood for "day."

☞ In phrase: **MFWIC,** *motherfucker what's in charge.*

> **1980** D. Cragg *Lexicon Militaris* 285: *MFWIC.* Moth-
> erfucker What's In Charge.

mindfuck *noun*

1. imaginary copulation with someone as a substitute for actual copulation. *Jocular.*

1964 Faust *Steagle* 265: We could lie down side by
side and think. Oh, a mind fuck? That's nowhere.
1968 *Zap Comix* (No. 3) (unpaged): A mind-fuck.
*a***1977** M. French *Women's Room* 574: They masturbate to it....It's a mind-fuck *a***1991** J. Phillips *You'll
Never Eat Lunch in This Town Again* 163: He rarely
gets a hard-on, but the mind-fuck is really irre-
sistible.

2. a sensational or overwhelming experience;
mindblower.

1971 in L. Bangs *Psychotic Reactions* 7: That elec-
tro-distort stuff...a real earthquake mindfuck. **1972** R.
Barrett *Lovomaniacs* 385: Dolly's eyes said she was
stoned....I...know when someone's full of the...origi-
nal superfreak mindfuck. **1977** *National Lampoon*
(Aug.) 33: His Pressed Wang on Stained Glass is a
religious mind-fuck. **1980** M. Baker *Nam* 40: When

you weren't going through that, you had your recruit regs held up in front of your face memorizing your eleven general orders. It was a real mind fuck. **1993** K. Scott *Monster* 164: You simply prepared ahead of time for the mind-fuck of being a prisoner.

3. *Espionage.* a counterintelligence deception.

1974 Bernstein & Woodward *All the President's Men* 119: Somewhere, Bernstein had been told that the CIA did that kind of thing abroad. He had heard it called Mindfuck but the agency called it Black Operation.

4. a psychotic.

1977 Sayles *Union Dues* 312: Comes back such a mindfuck he can't remember. Fuckin space cowboy. *Ibid.* 176: He was a certifiable mindfuck and you had to keep him on a tight leash.

5. confusion; bafflement.

1986 J. Cain *Suicide Squad* 85: Mindfuck would be terminal this time. **1987** "J. Hawkins" *Tunnel Warriors* 37: Despite the obvious game of mindfuck. **1988–90** M. Hunter *Abused Boys* 279: The mind-fuck you did on me. **1997** *Village Voice* (N.Y.C.) (Sept. 30) 88: Fincher's new movie...is a cynical mindfuck thriller that builds, with increasing pointlessness, to a deflating punchline.

mindfuck *verb* to confuse or outwit, especially by playing on (someone's) emotions.

1966 (quotation at *fuck (someone's) mind* under FUCK, verb). **1967** Wolf *Love Generation* 17: Their

consciousness has been permanently altered. Forever altered. They've been mind-fucked. *Ibid.* 281:
Mind-fucked. Profoundly influenced by something.
1970 J. Howard *Please Touch* 235: Some [encounter]
groups dismiss all abstractions as "headshit" and
"mindfucking." **1971** S. Miller *Hot Springs* 66: They
have nothing to teach you—they mind-fucked you.
1972 Gover *Mr. Big* 11: She mindfucks me again.
1976 J.W. Thomas *Heavy Number* 105: He's really
mind-fucked you. **1987** R. Miller *Slob* 156: They both
felt giddy, hysterical, a little confused, mindfucked,
spent. **1991** Marcinko & Weisman *Rogue Warrior* 165:
I was a veteran of mind-fucking the Vietnamese.

MINDFUCK

mindfucker *noun* something or someone that is
extremely baffling or astounding.

1969 *Woodstock* (film): This thing is a real mind-
fucker! **1970** Landy *Underground Dictionary* 133:
Mind fucker...Thing or situation that upsets or dis-

turbs one. *Ibid.*: *Mind fucker n.* 1. Individual who asserts personal pressure to persuade people to believe his way without regard for the feelings of the people he influences; person who attempts to manipulate another's thinking without regard for the other. **1972** Pelfrey *Big V* 24: Wow man, that's a mind-fucker. **1980** *National Lampoon* (Aug.) 67: You're some kind of mindfucker. You're a witch.

mind-fucking *adjective* baffling or astounding.

    1971 Kopp *Guru* 145: Away from intellectual "mind-fucking" words. **1986** Atlanta, Ga., man, age *ca*30: [Hands Across America] was mindfucking, man! Such a great thing!

mo dicker *noun* (a partial euphemism for) MOTHER-FUCKER.

    1968–70 *Current Slang Cumulation* III & IV 84: *Mo dicker,* n. A lazy, irresponsible person.—New Mexico State. **1989** D. Sherman *There I Was* 129: It started raining like a mo-dicker....I...said "mo-dicker"... 'cause your momma don't like me saying "mother-fucker," but it's really the same word.

mofo *noun* (a partial euphemism for) MOTHERFUCKER. *Jocular.*

    [**1962** H. Simmons *On Eggshells* 143: Get out the way, moa-fugg.] **1965** in H.S. Thompson *Hell's Angels* 33: The "Mofo" club from San Francisco. **1966** Reynolds & McClure *Freewheelin Frank* 116: The Mofos (a motorcycle club that isn't in existence now). **1972** R. Wilson *Playboy's Forbidden Words* 171: *Mother-jumper, mother-ferrier, mo'-fo', mammy-jammer,...futher-mucker.* **1973** *Oui* (Mar.) 69: And now you, too (you jive mofo) can control the minds of women! **1977** College student: I'm sincerely beginning to believe that mofo is a goddamn female impersonator. **1979** L. Blum, D. Goldberg, J. Allen & H. Ramis *Meatballs* (film): I will twist that mofo. **1982** Heat Moon *Blue Highways* 124: He's one useless black mofo. **1983** Leeson *Survivors* (film): Hey, you honky mofo, get the lead out of your ass! *Ibid.:* Your gun jammed, Mr. Honky Mofo? **1987** *National Lampoon* (June) 79: It hurt like a mofo. **1989** W.E. Merritt *Rivers Ran Backward* 20: Get your white ass in the truck, mofo.

mofo *adjective & adverb* see MOTHERFUCKING. *Jocular.*

1989 W.E. Merritt *Rivers Ran Backward* 20: You mofo lucky they sent me along.

mofuck *noun* see MOTHERFUCKER.

1982 Del Vecchio *13th Valley* 477: This mofuck division fucked up. **1983** R.C. Mason *Chickenhawk* 105 [refers to 1965]: [The mongoose] was young and tame, and he named it Mo'fuck.

monkey *noun* ☞ In phrase: **a monkey fucking a football,** a ridiculous figure.

1968 Tauber *Sunshine Soldiers* 117: You know what you look like, Pea-zer, stupid? You look like a monkey trying to fuck a football. **1977** in Lyle & Golenbock *Bronx Zoo* 17: Jesus Christ! You looked like a monkey trying to fuck a football out there! **1981** Hathaway *World of Hurt* 47: You look like a monkey fucking a football. **1984** K. Weaver *Texas Crude* 34: That guy tryin' to change a tire looks like a monkey tryin' to fuck a football. **1988** Poyer *The Med* 422: You people cry like fifteen monkeys fuckin' a football.

MONKEY FUCKING A FOOTBALL

mother *noun* (a partial euphemism for) MOTHER-FUCKER (in any sense).

    1935 in Oliver *Blues Tradition* 232: Dirty Mother For You. **1936** in Leadbitter & Slaven *Blues Records* 297: She's A Mellow Mother For You. **1944** in Himes *Black on Black* 209: That old mother, cotton, is gonna kill me yet. **1958** Gilbert *Vice Trap* 110: Jive and lush don't use together, you mother. **1959** A. Anderson *Lover Man* 52: There's a *bad* mother-hubber/Down the road a way. **1960** in T.C. Bambara

Gorilla 49: Now this jive mother who is my boss thinks he can make some bread by recording some of the old-timers. **1961** Brosnan *Pennant Race* 74: Malone pulls that ball on a line and Willie is a dead mother. **1961** Forbes *Goodbye to Some* 82 [refers to WWII]: That mother Stevens dropped a crab in the beer. **1961** L.G. Richards *TAC* 138: Boy, was I glad to see that mother. **1961** Ellison *Gentleman Junkie* 144: He just grabbed that muthuh by the neck and...beat the crap outta him. **1962** Kesey *One Flew Over the Cuckoo's Nest* 175: Drive, you puny mothers, *drive!*...Practice, you mothers, get that ball and let's get a little sweat rollin'! **1961–64** Barthelme *Come Back, Dr. Caligari* 142: You brought the darkness, you black mother. **1964** Newhafer *Tallyho* 182: If ever...I get out of this mother of a thunderstorm. *Ibid.* 302: There's nothing wrong with these mothers at all. **1965** Herlihy *Midnight Cowboy* 101: It's a powerful mothah, ain't it? **1967** Moorse *Duck* 139: Jeez, Doc,...you're about the smartest muther in the whole world. **1971** Sloan *War Games* 125: There sits a man who is going to go home and tell his wife a mother of a story. **1972** D. Jenkins *Semi-Tough* 188: Some wives is gonna read that mother you writin', you dig what I'm sayin'? **1972** C. Gaines *Stay Hungry* 34: He had worked [his calves] so hard he thought they would pop off, but the mothers wouldn't grow. **1973** Karlin, Paquet & Rottmann *Free Fire Zone* 164: I can take work!...I can work like a mother! **1976** C.R. Anderson *Grunts* 47 [refers to 1969]: You mean it's that hill over there, the bald mother? **1978** Selby *Requiem* 247: Yeah, he be a cool mutha jim. **1980** Hillstrom *Coal* 427: Burn the mother. **1984** Holland

Let Soldier 156: Deal those mothers! **1985** D. Killerman *Hellrider* 9: You muvva. **1986** B. Breathed *Bloom County* (syndicated comic strip) (Dec. 3): Just wing that mother. **1987** *N.Y. Daily News* (July 2) M3: Here comes that evil mother; we can't win now. **1988** *Living Dangerously* (A&E-TV): The river is one tough mother [to cross]. **1992** *New York* (Mar. 30) 61: He has never tried a case before, but he's a tough little mother.

☞ In phrases:

☞ **ham and mothers,** see *ham and motherfuckers* under MOTHERFUCKER.

1973 (quotation at *ham and motherfuckers* under MOTHERFUCKER). **1978** Hasford *Short-Timers* 86 [refers to Vietnam War]: Ham and mothers....I hate... ham and lima beans. **1990** G.R. Clark *Words of Vietnam War* 52: Ham and lima beans..."ham-and-mothers."

☞ **your mother!** Especially *Juvenile.* (used as a derisive retort). [It is widely perceived that the phrase abbreviates *go fuck your mother* and is therefore especially provoking; it is also reminiscent of the "dozens," a game of ritually exchanging insults.]

[**1891** in Dobie *Rainbow in the Morning* 172: Talk about one thing, talk about another;/But ef you talk about me, I'm gwain to talk about your mother.] [**1929** Hemingway *Selected Letters* 298: In a purely conversational way in a latin language in an argument one man says to another "Cogar su madre!"] **1937** Odets *Golden Boy* 243: [On telephone:] I'll bring him right over...you can take my word—the kid's a cock-eyed wonder...*your* mother too! **1939** in Dundes *Mother Wit* 288: An upper-class Negro woman [in a northern city] said...[that] in her high school group...a simple reference to "your ma" or "your mother" was a fighting challenge. The woman herself did not know why one had to fight when she heard this but did know that fight one must. **1953** Paley *Rumble* 86: "Your mother!" Pooch murmured with thick lips. **1957** H. Simmons *Corner Boy* 79: *Your mother, your mother.* **1968** K. Hunter *Soul Brothers* 39: If a Southside boy wanted to start a fight, all he had to say...was, "Your mother—." He didn't even have to finish the sentence. The other boy would tear into him...in a blind fury. **1972** in W. King *Black Anthology* 145: "Your motha'!" she yelled. **1973** Lucas, Katz & Huyck *America Graffiti* 23: "What happened to you, flathead?" "Ah, your mother!" **1974** Strasburger *Rounding Third* 159: Carter turned around. "Your mother," he said to the guy who had just finished talking. **1977** Bunker *Animal Factory* 29: "I'm gonna bust you someday." "You'll bust your mother." "Your mother wears combat boots!" **1978** Schrader *Hardcore* 65: "You're thinking about your father."..."Keep him out of this or I'll break your balls." "Who?" "Your mother, smart-ass." **1985** *Cheers* (NBC-TV): Ya mother!

mother *adjective* (a partial euphemism for) MOTHER-FUCKING.

1958 Meltzer & Blees *High School Confidential* (film): You're the swingin'est chick in the whole mother kingdom. **1962** Reiter *Night in Sodom* 134:

You a fool, Chollie. A rotten muvva fool. **1966–67** P. Thomas *Down These Mean Streets* 201: What a sick mudder scene! **1968** Vidal *Myra Breckinridge* 98: I am going to sell the whole mother score. *ca***1969** Rabe *Hummel* 23: Jesus God Almighty I hate this mother army stickin' me in with weird people! **1970** La Motta, Carter, & Savage *Raging Bull* (film) 25: Everybody down on his knees, you mothers, down on your fuckin' mother knees! **1971** *Go Ask Alice* 102: The fuzz has clamped down till the town is mother dry. **1976** J.W. Thomas *Heavy Number* 44: Wait a motherminute! *Ibid.* 115: I...can't use them...in the middle of the mother desert!

motherfouler *noun* (a partial euphemism for) MOTHER-FUCKER.

1947–52 R. Ellison *Invisible Man* 422: Coolcrack the motherfouler! **1962** L. Hughes *Tambourines to Glory* 238: Sister Laura's going to crack-up and all over Buddy Lomax—who everybody knows is a motherfouler.

motherfuck *noun* see under MOTHERFUCKER.

motherfuck *adverb* (used for emphasis). See MOTHERFUCKER for additional senses.

1970 E. Sanders, in Padgett & Shapiro *New York Poets* 386: And don't you motherfuck forget it!!!

motherfuck *verb*

1. (used to express rejection, dismissal, hatred, etc.); God damn; FUCK, *verb*, definition 4a; curse; to hell with.

189

1965 in *Social Problems* XIII 351: Mother Fuck the Police! **1969** *Black Panther* (Oakland, Calif.): Well, motherfuck the police. **1972** Davidson *Cut Off* 29 [refers to 1944]: Mother-fuck this fuckin' war. **1968–73** Agar *Ripping & Running* 137: Aw man, motherfuck it. **1975** S.P. Smith *American Boys* 37: "Three tears in the bucket," he yelled. "They don't flow, mother fuck it!" **1977** Torres *Q & A* 16: Motha fuck you, ain't tellin' you shit. Who the hell're *you!* **1994** J. Berendt *Midnight in the Garden of Good and Evil* 114: If I offended anyone, two tears in a bucket, honey. Motherfuck it.

2. to destroy, confuse; FUCK UP.

1975 in *Urban Life* IV (1976) 489: We'll motherfuck the bastard's mind!

motherfuck *interjection* see MOTHERFUCKER.

motherfucker or **motherfuck** *noun*

1.a. a man who commits incest with his mother; (*hence*) a despicable or contemptible man or woman. [The 1928, 1935, 1939, and 1946 quotations are euphemistic.]

[**1918** in H. De Witt *Bawdy Barrack-Room Ballads:* The little red runt he grew and grew/****ed his mother and sister too.] **1928** C. McKay *Banjo* 229: I've been made a fool of by many a skirt, but it's the first time a mother-plugger done got me like this. **1935** G.W. Henderson *Ollie Miss* 82: The man from Swanson had passed the ugly word then, and the Hannon boy had flung it back... neatly compounded, with the word "mother" preceding it. The Swanson boy... whipped out his razor. *ca*1935 in Logsdon *Whorehouse Bells* 95: Motherfucker, I'll slice off your prick. **1935** in Oliver *Blues Tradition* 232: He's a dirty mother fuyer, he don't mean no good. [**1936** Little *Harlem to Rhine* 5 [refers to 1917]: And so I saiz ter him, Cap'n Suh, "Ever-ting you saiz Ah am—yoo is double— even de part against yoo mudder....Ef yoo saiz anyt'ing mo' ter me Ah'll cut yoo heart out."] **1938** "Justinian" *Americana Sexualis* 29: *Mother-Fucker.* n. An incestuous male. The most intense term of opprobrium among the U.S. lower classes. Probable Sicilian origin. C. 20. Urban communities only. No sexual connotation; used merely as an epithet. **1939** in A. Banks *First-Person* 255: Why you poor Brooklyn motherfrigger, I'll wreck this goddamn place with you. **1946** Mezzrow & Wolfe *Really the Blues* 14: A motherferyer that would cut your throat for looking. **1946** Del Torto *Graffiti Transcript:* Susie is a mother fucker. **1947** Mailer *Naked & Dead* 152: I was gonna shoot the mother-fugger but you were in the way. **1950** *Commentary* X 62: When asked what his chief duties were in a Negro settlement house for boys, a social worker answered, "Teaching them euphemisms for mother— (unprintable word)." **1954** Lindner *50-Minute Hour* 152 [refers to *ca*1938]: During my years in prison work I had observed that one expletive, that referring to intercourse between son and mother (m-f), was at once the most dangerous and the most frequent on the lips of the psychopath. I had actually seen men killed for using it. **1954** Wepman, Newman & Binderman *The Life* 110: Cocksuckers by the dozens, motherfuckers and their cousins.

1956 in Oliver *Blues Tradition* 240: Your mama...she's a runnin' motherfucker, cheap cocksucker. **1957** H. Simmons *Corner Boy* 79: Kill that mother fug— . **1958** *Stack A Lee* 1: I'm that bad motherfucker they call Stack A Lee. **1958** Gilbert *Vice Trap* 44: "You mother—" she said to me, crying. **1959** W. Burroughs *Naked Lunch* 40: I'll cut your throat you white mother fucker. **1962** Killens *Then We Heard the Thunder* 284: Every time I walk up the company street I hear somebody calling somebody else a mother-fucker or a sonofabitch. **1963–64** Kesey *Sometimes a Great Notion* 71: My brother is a motherfucker. **1964** in Gover *Trilogy* 341: That puts this...lily-white moth-ahfug on like mad. **1965** C. Brown *Manchild in the Promised Land* 137: Don't explain your self to that mother-fucker. **1965** Conot *Rivers of Blood* 222: Even the word *motherfucker* takes on different connotation. For the white it is the image of incest; for the Negro it is the picture of a white man lying with a black woman who is his, the Negro's, mother. *ca***1966** Tamony *Mother Fucker* 9: *Motherfucker*...an ex-con...told me in the 1930's that he had heard the vocable in Dirty Dozen displays through the 1920's [in San Quentin prison]. **1967** Mailer *Why We Are in Vietnam* 54: Don't come near, motherfuck. **1968** A. Montagu, letter to P. Tamony (June 24): Mr. Donald C. Greason has written to me that he heard the epithet [*motherfucker*] often from a friend of his at the front during late 1917. **1968** Van Dyke *Strawberries* 177: If you even touch it, motherfucker, you die. **1968** Gover *JC* 34: Sonny you nacheral sack a twenty diffrent mothahfuggahs. **1971** Guffy & Ledner *Ossie* 46 [refers to *ca*1940]: "You're a motherfucker." "Your mama's one." **1972** *N.Y.U. Cold Duck* (Apr. 17): Fuck you, motherfuck, you're trying to censor my work! **1974** V.E. Smith *Jones Men* 18: Look at that bitch. Nasty motherfucker. **1978** Schrader *Hardcore* 99: You muthafuck! **1986** D. Tate *Bravo Burning* 96: Hey, motherfucks, you don't have to treat him like that. *a***1990** E. Currie *Dope & Trouble* 14: She a grown motherfuck. **1992** Hosansky & Sparling *Working Vice* 197: People called her motherfucker...[and] bitch. **1995** *Jerry Springer Show* (syndicated TV series): Come on, motherf-cker! [vowel bleeped out].

b. Especially *Black English & Military.* (with reduced force) fellow; person; (*often*) a formidable person.

1958 *Stack A Lee* 1: He...said who put the hole in this motherfucker's head?/Who could the murderer of this poor man be? **1970** Landy *Underground Dictionary* 135: *Mother fuck*...Greeting to another person. It has a positive connotation....*Mother fucker*... Positive, complimentary name for a friend—e.g., *Hey, mother fucker, what's happening?* **1971** in Horwitt *Call Me Rebel* 4 [refers to 1930s]: Pretty soon word of the incident spread throughout the gang. "That Alinsky, he's an all-right motherfucker," the kids would say, and... they began to trust me. **1971** in Cheever *Letters* 284: A puertorican drug-pusher...exclaimed: "Oh what a cool motherfucker was that Machiavelli." **1972** in W. King *Black Anthology* 101: Joe was a motherfucker. A revolutionary motherfucker. A black man made of steel iron. **1973** J.R. Coleman *Blue-Collar* 62: A word like "motherfucker" here is often just a synonym for man, no more and no less. ("Who's that new motherfucker over there?" or "I told the motherfucker we'd pick up him and his bitch at eight.") **1973** R. Roth *Sand in Wind* 154: Hey, motherfuckers, look at this. *Ibid.* 438: I've met some of the best motherfuckers I've ever known in the [Marine Corps]. **1972–74** Hawes & Asher *Raise Up* 3 [refers to 1930s]: Anybody who *looked* good was automatically a motherfucker. *Ibid.* 98: We...talked about Debussy and Bach and what bad motherfuckers those cats were hundreds of years ago. **1974** Lacy *Native Daughter* 108: fine...nice legs...tall...would be a motherfucker if she didn't talk so much. **1974** V.E. Smith *Jones Men* 156: I'm just as cool as the next motherfucker. **1977** L. Jordan *Hype* 44: "C'mere, you little motherfucker," he said tenderly, reaching for her. **1978** B. Johnson *What's Happenin'?* 57: Once I figured out that a "bad mother-fucker" was an all-right dude, I at least had a shot at communicating. **1978** Strieber *Wolfen* 127: You the scared-est motherfucker I've seen in a good long while. **1980** High school teacher, age 27: Man, I *love* that motherfucker! *a***1983** Baugh *Black Street Speech* 24: See, like if a brother gets on my case I can tell blood, "Hey motherfucker, you can kiss my ass," and the brother can...take it in stride—cause he know where I'm comin from. But you can't be tellin no white dude that. **1987** D. Sherman *Main Force* 96 [refers to 1966]: "That bad out there, huh?" "Worse, except we're the baddest mother-fuckers in the valley." **1984–88** Hackworth & Sherman *About Face* 510 [refers to Vietnam War]: In the Airborne, the term "motherfucker," unless spoken harshly, was among the highest terms of endearment.

2.a. an infuriating, hateful, or oppressive thing, difficult task, etc.; (*broadly*) a thing.

1947 Mailer *Naked & Dead* 345: You know what the mother-fugger'll be like?...We'll be lucky to get out of there with our goddam heads on. **1960** Peacock *Valhalla* ch. iv: "I'll get the motherfuckers [beer cans]," Dallas offered. **1962** B. Jackson *In the Life* 156: Oh, life's a motherfucker, Bruce. **1962** T. Berger *Reinhart* 386: Let me run that big motherfu—. **1967** Mailer *Why We Are in Vietnam* 82: How'd you get this motherfuck? **1967–68** N. von Hoffman *We Are the People Our Parents Warned Us Against* 98: The street is a rough motherfucker. **1969** *Playboy* (Dec.) 290: Let's burn this motherfucker down. **1973** Jong *Fear of Flying* 4: So I keep concentrating very hard, helping the pilot...fly the 250-passenger motherfucker. **1975** De Mille *Smack Man* 108: What a motherfucker that's going to be, given the rules of evidence in this state. **1978** S. King *Stand* 84: Eight milkshakes (why...had he bought eight of the mother-fuckers?) **1981** L. Heinemann, in *Harper's* (Aug.) 58: The whole company... caught some mean kind of shit and every swinging dick *but* him bought the motherfucker. **1981** *National Lampoon* (July) 16: Being 7′4″ is a motherfucker. **1981** *Penthouse* (Mar.) 174: Heroin is...an insidious motherfucker. **1982** Downey *Losing the War* 23 [refers to WWII]: Some of them... cussed their native state for being a "prejudiced mother-fucker." **1991** J. Lamar *Bourgeois Blues* 32: I knew how to make those motherfuckers gleam. **1993** K. Scott *Monster* 163: The threat of being in prison for life was a muthafucka.

b. an infuriating or surprising state of affairs.

195

1968 in B. Edelman *Dear America* 81: Sometimes it gets pretty hairy in this motherfucker. **1970** Landy *Underground Dictionary* 135: *Mother fucker...* Hard-to-solve problem; rough situation. **1976** Chinn *Dig the Nigger Up* 61: Now ain't this a muthafucker! **1981** Hathaway *World of Hurt* 14: This is the dumbest motherfucker I ever been in. **1982** Del Vecchio *13th Valley* 271: How they gonna get a bird inta the middle a dis mothafuck? **1984–87** Ferrandino *Firefight* 98: I don't want to die in this miserable motherfucker. **1989** Chafets *Devil's Night* 44: We'll probably never solve the motherfucker. **1989** S. Robinson & D. Ritz *Smokey* 78: We're going to remember this motherfucker...'cause I don't intend to let it happen again.

c. a large or outstanding example; hum-dinger.

1972 R. Barrett *Lovomaniacs* 366: I stepped back, to get a better view of the watch...."*Motherfucker!*" I said. **1977** *National Lampoon* (Aug.) 33: Have I got a motherfucker of a stunt for you!

3.a. a damn.

1967 "Iceberg Slim" *Pimp* 277: I wouldn't give a mother-fuck. **1972** Pelfrey *Big V* 106: And I don't *give* a motherfuck. **1985** Attorney, age 32: Who gives a motherfuck anyway?

b. (used as an emphatic expletive); hell; FUCK.—used with *the*.

1975 De Mille *Smack Man* 70: How the motherfuck do a pimp's girl get jealous, man? **1973–76** J. Allen *Assault* 188: You better get the motherfuck out of my place. **1982** Del Vecchio *13th Valley* 309: Where the motherfuck is the C-4? **1986** Philbin *Under Cover* 120: Who the motherfuck are you? **1988** Norst *Colors* 22: What the motherfuck was that you just did.

4. (used as an indefinite standard of comparison).

1962 Wepman, Newman & Binderman *The Life* 139: I just come back....Mad as a motherfucker. **1962** Riccio & Slocum *All the Way Down* 149: Something new has been added...the letters LAMF under a personal name or a gang name....It means "Like A Mother Fucker," and it's supposed to suggest to all who read it that the person or the gang...is rough and tough and hell-bent for war or what may come. **1966–67** P. Thomas *Down These Mean Streets* 160: He went limper'n a motherfucker. **1973** Wideman *Lynchers* 39: It be dark as a muthafucka. **1975** S.P. Smith *American Boys* 100: LaMont was [running] like fifty motherfuckers. **1990** Rukuza *West Coast Turnaround* 39: It was raining like six motherfuckers. **1991** J. Singleton *Boyz N the Hood* (film): This fool got more comics than a motherfucker.

☞ In phrases:

☞ **beans and motherfuckers,** *Military.* a C-ration portion of lima beans and ham.

1980 M. Baker *Nam* 11: I'm not going to say he had cold beans and motherfuckers for breakfast. *Ibid.* 320: Beans and motherfuckers—C-ration delicacy composed of lima beans and ham. **1990** G.R. Clark *Words of Vietnam War* 52: *Beans-and-Motherfuckers* (Ham and Lima Beans). **1991** Reinberg *In the Field: Beans and motherfuckers*, slang for unpopular C-ration lima beans and ham.

☞ **bends and motherfuckers,** *Military.* calisthenic squats and thrusts.

1980 M. Baker *Nam* 39 [refers to *ca*1970]: You look like shit, so we're going to do a little PT now. Bends and motherfuckers. Many, many, many of them. *Ibid.* 320: Bends and motherfuckers: the squat-thrust exercise. **1990** G.R. Clark *Words of Vietnam War* 55: *Bends-and-Motherfuckers*...squat-thrust exercises.

☞ **ham and motherfuckers,** *Military.* a C-ration portion of canned ham and lima beans.

1973 Layne *Murphy* (unpaged): Packaged into the 1942 C-ration case....Ham & little muther fahckers, / Affectionately called, / Ham / & / Mutha's. **1980** DiFusco et al. *Tracers* 41 [refers to Vietnam War]: I haven't got anything left except some ham and motherfuckers, man. **1982** E. Leonard *Cat Chaser* 76: Ham and lima beans: ham and motherfuckers. **1987** "J. Hawkins" *Tunnel Warriors* 332 [refers to Vietnam War]: *Ham & Motherfuckers.* C-rations serving of ham and lima beans. **1988** Clodfelter *Mad Minutes* 258 [refers to 1966]: Cans of "ham and mother fuckers" (ham and lima beans). *a***1989** C.S. Crawford *Four Deuces* 107 [refers to Korean War]: Ham and lima beans... was considered to be one of the good rations even though we called them "ham and motherfuckers."

motherfucker or **motherfuck** *interjection* (used to express astonishment, anger, etc.).

1968 *Nation* (Dec. 2) 595: I said how come you din'

sing the National Anthem?...Motherfucker!...You a bunch of jive motherfuckers. **1970** Woods *Killing Zone* 143: Mother*fuck*—what happened to you? **1974** L.D. Miller *Valiant* 21 [refers to WWII]: Mudderfucker!...I'm hit! **1976** R. Price *Bloodbrothers* 20: Mother-*fuck!* **1979** Gutcheon *New Girls* 249: Motherfuck, guess who that is? **1985** Bodey *F.N.G.* 144: Muthafucker, *can this be?* **1998** *GQ* (Nov.) 172: He spins around, kicks the ground, stares down the offending patch of wood. "Mother*fuck*," he mutters.

motherfucking *interjection & infix* (used for emphasis). [The 1962–63 quotation is euphemistic.]

    1962–63 Kesey *Sometimes a Great Notion* 7: How do you expect *any-motherkilling-one* to know Hank Stamper's reasons? **1967** Ragni & Rado *Hair* 154: Yeah! Emanci-motherfuckin'-pator of the slave. **1977** Torres *Q & A* 54: Motherfuckin'-A right. **1984–87** Ferrandino *Firefight* 124: Just hats up and dismotherfuckinappears.

motherfucking *adjective & adverb*

    1. goddamned; FUCKING.

    1933 O'Hara *Samarra* 154: Why, you small-time chiseling bastard, you. You dirty mother—bastard. [**1933** J. Conroy *Disinherited* 30: Scab! Scab! O, you bloody mother-killin' bastards! O, you lowdown sons of bitches!] **1936** Levin *Old Bunch* 122: Listen, you mother-f— little runt, if you don't—. **1947** Mailer *Naked & Dead* 12: Of all the mother-fuggin luck, that sonofabitch takes it all. *Ibid.* 400: That's the motherfuggin' truth. [**1948** Manone & Vandervoort *Trumpet*

131: If I hurt your beat-out feelings, I beg your mother-robbin' pardon.] **1951** J. Jones *Face of War* 62: Mother fuggin' bastards. **1951** Kerouac *Visions of Cody* 119: I read every WORD of that motherfuckin thing. **1953–55** Kantor *Andersonville* 524: Mother-fucking old Yankee mudsills. [**1957** T.H. White *Mountain Road* 21: The next guy doesn't know a mother-frigging thing about it.] **1958** Berger *Crazy in Berlin* 168 [refers to WWII]: A Southerner or a Negro, passing on the sidewalk out front, described to a mute companion a succession of events that were invariably *mothafuhn*. **1961** in Himes *Black on Black* 69: I'll cut your motherfucking throat. **1961** Forbes *Goodbye to Some* 128 [refers to WWII]: You ain't home with you mother-fuckin' mother! [**1963–64** Kesey *Sometimes a Great Notion* 7: The whole motherkilling agreement.] **1965** Linakis *In Spring* 75: He's a mother-fuckin' liar. **1962–65** Giallombardo *Society of Women* 49: She said…"I'm not showing you a mother—' thing." **1965** C. Brown *Manchild in the Promised Land* 140: I'm gon bust your mother-fuckin' ass. **1966–67** P. Thomas *Down These Mean Streets* 129: They don't come no motherfuckin' better. **1967** Crawford *Gresham's War* 161: You motherhunching son of a hounddog whore. **1967** W. Stevens *Gunner* 231: It was that motherfucking *Ploesti* that reached up and tore his ass apart. **1964–69** in Calt *Rather Be Devil* 57 [refers to *ca*1919]: The guys…wouldn't say: "Pass me such and such a thing, if they wanted a big pan of meat or biscuits or rice….They said, "Let such-and-such a thing *walk* up that motherfuckin' table." **1970** Neary *J. Bond* 174: Mayor Richard J. Daley yelled "Get that motherfucking Jew out of here!" at United States Senator Abraham Ribicoff of Connecticut. **1977** T. Jones *Incredible Voyage* 284: But you tell that mother-fucking chief, Manco Quispe, I want a clan meeting right now. **1986** N.Y.C. man, age *ca*35: You don't sound very motherfuckin' worried. **1986** P. Welsh *Tales Out of School* 64: [The pupils] lapse into street dialect, saying "be" for "are," "mines" for "mine" and of course the ubiquitous adjective "mother-f—." **1989** S. Robinson & D. Ritz *Smokey* 42: This is my motherfucking house and I'm gonna live here and no one's gonna stop me. **1993** *New Yorker* (Feb. 8) 35: Motherfucking cockroach.

2. (used occasionally to emphasize the positive qualities of a following noun).

1954 Wepman, Newman & Binderman *The Life* 42: I love him madly, he's my motherfucking man. **1961** Gover *$100 Misunderstanding* 95: Tee vee man talkin up a mothahfuggin storm! **1973** Flaherty *Fogarty* 157: What a motherfucking man he was, Shamus! *a***1990** in Costello & Wallace *Signifying Rappers* 79: I shoulda kicked your ass/My-motherfuckin-self. **1991** Nelson & Gonzales *Bring Noise* 97: Dizzy Gillespie plays the trumpet, *not the mo'fugging sax.*

mothergrabber *noun* (a partial euphemism for) MOTHERFUCKER.

1963 in J. Blake *Joint* 357: You set me up, mothergrabber. **1966** I. Reed *Pall-Bearers* 34: Goofy mothergrabber!

mother-grabbing *adjective* (a partial euphemism for) MOTHERFUCKING.

1953–58 J.C. Holmes *Horn* 68: Those mother-grabbin' *slacks*...were full of *seeds!* **1961** J. Jones *Thin Red Line* 60: He's a jerkoff. A goddam mothergrabbing jerkoff. **1962** Serling *New Stories* 67: Are you out of your mothergrabbing mind? **1971** *Playboy* (Mar.) 92: "Out of your mother-grabbing mind," Joanne said.

motherhumper *noun* (a partial euphemism for) MOTHERFUCKER.

1963 Doulis *Path* 81: Death, I think, you mother-humper. **1967** Ford *Muc Wa* 133: "C'mon, you mother-humpers!" Ski yelled at his Raiders. **1970** Grissim *Country Music* 281: Anybody that can follow me is a motha-humper. And they ain't many that can do it....I'm a violent motha-humper today. Don't nobody fool with me or *I'll kill!* **1972** *National Lampoon* (Sept.) 6: There are fourteen *fuck you's,* nine *cocksucker's,* and six *motherhumper's* left over. **1986** Stinson & Carabatsos *Heartbreak* 77: Let's smoke this motherhumper's ass.

mother-humping *adjective* (a partial euphemism for) MOTHERFUCKING.

1961 Gover *$100 Misunderstanding* 19: He kin hardly git his mothahhumpin hands roun that wad! **1963** Doulis *Path* 80: Why, that no-good, sneaky, mother-humpin' rebel. **1964** Rhodes *Chosen Few* 99 [refers to *ca*1950]: That mother-humpin' fuckoff wanted *satisfaction!* **1964** in Gover *Trilogy* 215: Right inta this mothahhumpin lounge. **1968** W. Crawford *Gresham's War* 197: Motherhumping cowards. **1969**

202

C. Brown *Mr. Jiveass* 20: Like, it's none of their motherhumping business, right? **1970** Quammen *Walk the Line* 86: I thought we been fittin' to make it to a gray jam, not do a suicide mission with some motherhumping cage-case. **1986** Stinson & Carabatsos *Heartbreak* 163: Friggin' motherhumpin' Highway. **1990** J.E. Wideman *Philadelphia Fire* 122: This mother-humping play can't end no oder way.

mothering *adjective & adverb* (a partial euphemism for) MOTHERFUCKING.

1951 in J. Blake *Joint* 27: He said if the motherin' screw ever caught up to us, he'd wish he hadn't. **1956** Algren *A Walk on the Wild Side* 160: His whole life he ain't worked one single mothering day! **1957** E. Brown *Locust Fire* 95 [refers to 1944]: No more mothering flying. Well, hucklety buck. I don't give a one. **1959** Miller *Cool World* 15: Why shitman them Colts is the same motheren piece they was usen at Cussers Last Stan. *Ibid* 37: Them headbreakers. Motheren headbreakers. **1959** in H. Ellison *Sex Misspelled* 103: You try my mutherin' patience. **1961** Russell *Sound* 31: You're too motherin' much, man. **1962** Riccio & Slocum *All the Way Down* 43: We'll show these mothern bastards. **1963–64** Kesey *Sometimes a Great Notion* 210: I feel...pretty motherin' good. **1965** Matthiessen *At Play in the Fields of the Lord* 37: Them poor mothering Indians. **1966–67** W. Stevens *Gunner* 56: They got some motherin big idea. **1968** *Saturday Evening Post* (Sept. 16) 27: I hope you have four motherin' flat tires. *ca***1969** Rabe *Hummel* 26: You ain't no motherin' exception to that whistle! **1975** *Black World* (June) 75: Not that motherin day.

mother-jumper *noun* (a partial euphemism for) MOTHERFUCKER.

1949 Ellson *Tomboy* 5: It was that no good mother-jumper that owns the store. **1952** Ellson *Golden Spike* 22: What mother-jumpers you been listening to? *Ibid.* 40: Let's kill that mother-jumper! **1955** Ellson *Rock* 121: I hit for the candy store then, mad as a mother-jumper. **1957** Margulies *Punks* 43: But this mother-jumper is a white stud. **1963–64** Kesey *Sometimes a Great Notion* 334: I thought...the motherjumper wasn't even gonna. **1965** Borowik *Lions* 155: Yessir, you motherjumper, you'll be laughing outa the other side of your mouth when the cops come for you. **1966** Fariña *Been Down So Long* 120: You old benevolent motherjumper, I love you! **1966–67** P. Thomas *Down These Mean Streets* 91: I hate all you white mother-jumps. **1970** Woods *Killing Zone* 88: He used to be a sad mother jumper. **1977** J. Wylie *Homestead Grays* 242: He was as quick as a motherjumper. **1977** Butler & Shryack *Gauntlet* 130: All right, you mother-jumpers.

mother-jumping *adjective* (a partial euphemism for) MOTHERFUCKING.

1952 Ellson *Golden Spike* 19: You mother-jumping thief! **1961** Gover *$100 Misunderstanding* 35: He sit up like a mothah jumpin jack-in-a-box. **1962** Crump *Killer* 163: You're a mother-jumping coward. **1963–64** Kesey *Sometimes a Great Notion* 209: And good motherjumpin' riddance. **1969** in Romm *Conspiracy* 138: Fucking sonofabitch Fascist mother jumping cops! **1980** McDowell *Our Honor* 156:

Sanders, you seem to think you're running this mother-jumping platoon, only it's about time you learned differently.

motherlover *noun* (a partial euphemism for) MOTHER-FUCKER.

1950 L. Brown *Iron City* 69: And as for *that* mother-lover—. **1954** E. Hunter *Runaway Black* 18: You broke the mother-lover. **1955** Graziano & Barber *Somebody Up There Likes Me* 215: "Stand straight, you little mother-lover," he says. **1963** Cameron *Black Camp* 63 [refers to WWII]: On your *feet*, motherlover!

motherloving *adjective* (a partial euphemism for) MOTHERFUCKING.

1951 "W. Williams" *Enemy* 149: Oh, those foggers. Those mother-loving foggers. **1954** Schulberg *On the Waterfront* 308: You're a cheap, lousy, dirty, stinkin', mother-lovin' bastard. **1955** Klaas *Maybe I'm Dead* 36: The dirty mother-loving bastards. **1955** Hunter *Jungle Kids* 103: He didn't get out of that mother-lovin' cellar. **1957** Laurents & Sondheim *West Side Story* 145: On the whole! Ever—! Mother—! Lovin'—! Street! **1959** Morrill *Dark Sea* 88: Don't be so mother-lovin' nosy. **1962** Killens *Then We Heard the Thunder* 16: That's a smooth mother-loving curve you throwing. **1968** Spooner *War in General* 53: We got ourselves a mother lovin' home. **1972** *N.Y. Times* (Feb. 6) 19: His one indulgence: a St. Bernard weighing 260 mother-lovin' pounds. **1975** *Atlantic* (May) 43: I'm the Paul mother-lovin Bunyan of the Interstate system.

mother-raper *noun* (a partial euphemism for) MOTH-ERFUCKER.

1959 Himes *Crazy Kill* 33: Turn me loose, you mother-rapers! He's my brother and some mother-raper's going to pay—. *Ibid.* 57: I ain't given Dulcy any mother-raping knife. **1965** Himes *Imabelle* 92: Mother-raper, step on it! *Ibid.* 127: I bled that mother-raper like a boar hog.

mother-raping *adjective* (a partial euphemism for) MOTHERFUCKING.

1932 Halyburton & Goll *Shoot & Be Damned* 306 [refers to 1918]: When I talked to you mother-raping sewer rats at roll call I thought you were Americans. **1960** MacCuish *Do Not Go Gentle* 191 [refers to WWII]: An' that queer's *really* a first-class A-1 mother-rapin' gutless wonder of a horse's ass! **1965** Himes *Imabelle* 67: Leave me see that mother-rapin' roll. *Ibid.* 122: Let's take the mother-raping hearse, too. **1972** C. Gaines *Stay Hungry* 213: The last moth-arapin straw, Newton called it.

motorcycle *noun* (a jocular euphemism for) MOTHERFUCKER.—usually used with *bad*.

1938 in Oliver *Blues Tradition* 235: Ridin' Dirty Motorsickle...He's a dirty motor-cycle. **1967** Lit *Dictionary* 2: *Bad motorcycle*—One who is very sharp, cool, hip, and gets what he wants but, this type of cat is also a little sneaky tricky. **1973** *Oui* (Feb.) 38: She's a bad motorcycle. **1985** Heywood *Taxi Dancer* 92: We got us a bad *motor-cycle* this mornin', gents.

206

motor flicker *noun* (a partial euphemism for) MOTH-ERFUCKER.

> **1967** in *Trans-action* VI (Feb. 1969) 33: This black slick head motor flicker. **1974** Stevens *Rat Pack* 39: Lookit what says black, you funky motorflikker nigger. **1975** B. Silverstein & R. Krate *Dark Ghetto* 107 [refers to *ca*1965]: This black slick head motor flicker got nerve 'nough to call somebody "fat head."

mouth fuck *noun* an act of fellatio.

> *ca***1866** *Romance of Lust* 447: Finishing off with a mouth fuck.

mouth-fuck *verb* to thrust the penis into (a person's) mouth; (*also*) to vigorously perform fellatio on.

> **1972** B. Rodgers *Queens' Vernacular* 89: [*Fuck*] *in the face*...mouth fucking...as opposed to cocksuck-ing. **1976** "Studs" *Creative Head* 39: He mouthfucked her in earnest, slapping his hairy crotch against her face. **1979** C. Keller *Subway Orgy* 78: She concentrated on the stiff rod in her mouth and kept on suck-ing and mouth-fucking the kidnapper. **1981** *Penthouse* (Apr.) 196: She popped my purple glans into her mouth....Then she began mouth-fucking me rapidly. **1998** *Taxi!*, pornographic story on Usenet newsgroup alt.sex.stories (Oct. 26): I take his glans in my mouth....Covering my teeth with my lips, I mouth-fuck him vindictively. Tender isn't what's required.

muck *verb* (used as a euphemism for FUCK in various figurative senses). See also MUCK UP. [Perhaps origi-

nally suggested by *mess (around)*, but the rhyme with
FUCK has ultimately given the word the euphemistic
quality with which it is now used.]

*a***1890—96** Farmer & Henley *Slang & Its Analogues*
VI 372: *To muck about.*...To fondle; to mess about.
1896 R. Kipling, in *Oxford English Dictionary:* Our
Colonel...mucks about in 'orspital. **1928** in *Oxford
English Dictionary Supplement:* His art...[is] the one
thing a genuine artist won't muck about with. **1929**
R. Aldington *Death of a Hero:* Spree be mucked—one
of you **fired his rifle and muckin' near copped me.
1936 E. Partridge *Dictionary of Slang & Unconventional English: Muck!, mucker, mucking,* have from
ca. 1915 represented *f**k!,* etc. **1940** E. Hemingway
For Whom the Bell Tolls 369: You're just
mucked....Muck this whole treacherous muck-faced
mucking country. **1950** E. Hemingway *Across River*
58: Now muck off. **1950** in Wentworth & Flexner *Dictionary of American Slang:* Too many bones mucking
about. **1958** T. Capote *Breakfast at Tiffany's* 8: You got
to be rich to go mucking around in Africa. **1961** *Time*
(Jan. 27) 57: There is one in every outfit—the snivel-
ing, creepy little muckup who not only fails to pull
his weight but manages to add it to the load carried
by others. **1982** *N.Y. Times* IV E19: Muck around with
us and you'll reap the typhoon—unless you have H-
bombs, rockets [etc.]. **1990** *Future Watch* (CNN-TV)
(Aug. 18): I want to muck with real astrophysics.

muck up *verb* to botch; spoil; ruin; *fuck up.* [Perhaps
originally suggested by *mess up,* but now always
regarded as a euphemism for FUCK UP.]

1886 (cited in E. Partridge *Dictionary of Slang & Unconventional English*). **1922** in *Oxford English Dictionary Supplement:* You seem to have pretty well mucked it up. **1949** *Saturday Evening Post* (Oct. 8) 125 :That does make it bad, doesn't it? Makes a pair of us mucking things up. **1951** *N.Y. Times* (July 22) I 11: The Iranians had always done something to "muck things up." **1954–60** Wentworth & Flexner *Dictionary of American Slang: Muck up...= fuck up,* a euphem. **1967–68** N. von Hoffman *We Are the People Our Parents Warned Us Against* 91: We need the tourists even if they may have mucked up the Haight. **1968** C. Victor *Sky Burned* 44: The squad would probably muck up the mission on top of it. **1982** *N.Y. Times* (Mar. 25) D2: You mucked it all up, gang. **1987** D. Mamet *House of Games* (film): You're mucking up my timing. **1988** *Newsday* (N.Y.) (June 20) II 6: By the mid-70's, Thompson...had already mucked up nicely. **1994** *New Republic* (Nov. 28) 56: Francis Ford Coppola... has been mucking up his own career lately. **1996** *Dr. Katz* (Comedy Central TV): Dad, please. Don't muck it up with conversation!

muh fuh *noun* (a partial euphemism for) MOTHER-FUCKER.

1969 B. Beckham *Main Mother* 148: Where you muh fuhs from? **1972** Beckham *Runner Mack* 186: We're taking over, muhfuh. **1975** *Black World* (Jan.) 57: Get *out* of here, you muh-fuh! **1980** Gould *Fort Apache* 81: Hey, muh fuh, I ain't no junkie.

muscle-fuck *noun* an act of rubbing the penis between a woman's breasts; (*also*) see 1977 quotation.

1974 (quotation at FRENCH FUCK). **1977** Vermont student: A muscle-fuck is one where the Jane can contract the muscles in her vagina. It can drive you up the wall. I heard about muscle-fucks in the marines. **1992** *Playboy* (July) 37: Sex quiz...Been involved in breast fucking (a.k.a. the Hawaiian muscle fuck)?

N

Words

NFG *adjective* **1.** [elaboration of earlier *N.G.* 'no good'; compare earlier *N.B.G.* 'no bloody good'] no fucking good. Also as interjection.

1945 in *Verbatim* (Autumn, 1989) 6: *NFG*...Abbrev. for *no fxxx'n good*....An individual, situation or state without any redeeming features; hopeless, incompetent, utterly worthless: *I'm NFG before my coffee in the morning.* **1977** Torres *Q&A* 162: He's...N.F.G., with the oak leaf cluster. **1988** T. Logan *Harder They Fall* 106: N.F.G.! Start grouping your shots....Like this. **1990** G.R. Clark *Words of Vietnam War* 356: NFG...no-fuckin'-good.

2. *Army.* see under FNG.

1992 Rodrique *Heading Home* 152 [refers to Vietnam War]: "You're just one more N.F.G." "An N.F.G." "New Fucking Guy; a cherry."

NFW *interjection.* no fucking way.

1974 J. Mills *One Just Man* 125: Just NFW. No fuckin' *way.* **1987** *Wall St. Journal* (Oct. 26): "N.F.W." Loosely translated: "No Feasible Way."

P

Words

Philadelphia rat fuck see under RAT-FUCK, *noun*, definition 4.

pig-fucker *noun* a worthless, disgusting person.

1938 "Justinian" *Americana Sexualis* 31: *Pig-Fucker*, n. A concupiscent man whose sensibilities are so atrophied that he would even "fuck a pig."...Obsolete Br., U.S., C. 19–20. Obsolescent. **1965** in H.S. Thompson *Proud Highway* 509: Ah, this fucking rotten machine. One more strike against those pigfuckers. **1970** in H.S. Thompson *Shark Hunt* 40: Bug off, you worthless faggot! You twisted pigfucker! **1973** College student: A *pig-fucker* is a name you call somebody you really hate. **1972–76** Durden *No Bugles, No Drums* 263: Five fuckin' people against five thousand pissed-off pig fuckers. **1976** Rosen *Above Rim* 82: Wayne Smalley was a racist white pigfucker and Jeremy hated him. **1982** D.A. Harper *Good Company* 70: Why I'd be a lyin' pigfucker if I told you that! **1983** R. Thomas *Missionary* 145: Just call him a pig fucker and let him deny it. **1987** Robbins *Ravens* 69: "Pig Fucker."... The name hails from the early days of Vietnam when fighter pilots called each other by it as a form of affectionate...abuse. *a***1989** R. Herman, Jr. *Warbirds* 97: All *right*, you pig-fuckers. I do *not* like

212

surprises. **1990** R. Herman, Jr. *Force of Eagles* 451: Yes, it was, you pigfucker. **1990** "My Life with the Thrill Kill Kult" *Days of Swine & Roses* (pop. song): Fuck you, pig fucker!

pig-fucking *adjective* worthless; disgusting.

1948 Wolfert *Act of Love* 503: Frig you, you pig-frigging turd. **1972** Bertolucci *Last Tango in Paris* (film): You goddam pig-fucking liar! **1972–76** Durden *No Bugles, No Drums* 175: I knew the pig-fuckin' cocksucker was settin' me up. **1977** T. Jones *Incredible Voyage* 371: The fair-haired bastard of a pig-fucking detective... kicked out the boy's eye! **1978** E. Thompson *Devil to Pay* 103: They'll hang your ass in this pigfucking country and look for justification later.

pity-fuck *noun* see under MERCY FUCK.

1994 B. Maher *True Story* 107: "Need some loving," she had said—what was this, a pity fuck? **1996** *Frontiers* (Sept. 1): We have a horror of the pity fuck. We cannot face the charity of the mercy orgasm. **1997** *Re: Daniel Mocsny's writing style,* on Usenet newsgroup soc.singles: Why are you banging a woman so repulsive she wouldn't rate a pity-fuck from me on my worst day?

R

Words

rat-fuck *noun*

1. (used as a term of abuse).

1922 in E. Wilson *Twenties* 116 [undefined list of terms]: Dumbbell upstage lousy highhat rat-fuck to crab someone or someone's act. **1955** Wepman, Newman & Binderman *The Life* 171: That dirty rat fuck—/He thought he was slick. **1970** Southern *Blue Movie* 173: Yes, you rat fuck! What heinous deception! **1970** Sorrentino *Steelwork* 16: He stood in front of them and kicked their balls off! The rat fucks. **1973** Breslin *World Without End* 109: Is that where the rat-fuck...is going? **1976** in L. Bangs *Psychotic Reactions* 199: Those ratfucks in Chicago can suck my asshole. **1990** Rukuza *West Coast Turnaround* 230: He was watching..., the ratfuck! **1991** *Southern Atlantic Quarterly* XC 836: The ratfuck FCC....The...fuckwad station manager. **1996** D. McCumber *Playing off the Rail* 95: That's right, you ratfuck bastard.

2.a. *Army.* a confused or bungled situation, especially an assault. [The 1930 examples are euphemistic.]

1930 Nason *Corporal* 139 [refers to WWI]: This here gigantic rat-copulation they call a war. *Ibid.* 171: This isn't going to be the same kind of a

214

damned disgusting...rat-copulation such as we've been going through on the Border. *Ibid.* 260: This will be just the same old rat dinging all over again. **1971** Vaughan & Lynch *Brandywine's War* 57: A GRF...means Giant Rat Fuck....It's a nickname the men have for an aerial assault mission. **1983** Groen & Groen *Huey* 217: Every insertion was a Romeo Foxtrot (RF), translated rat fuck, the name given by flyers to doomed missions. *Ibid.* 272: He was mad as hell about that rat fuck already. **1984** Holland *Let Soldier* 184 [refers to 1967]: I was on this rat fuck down south...and on short final the whole world went up. **1987** Chinnery *Life on Line* 35 [refers to 1965]: The next day was my first combat assault or GRF (Grand Rat F***) as they were called.

b. an unimportant task or mission.

1987 Chinnery *Life on Line* 227 [refers to 1970]: As a new scout pilot they send you out on...rat-f*** missions, in areas where you don't expect to see much....They generally sent him on the rat-f***s so that no one would have to depend on him in a bad situation.

3. a damn.

1971 Dahlskog *Dictionary* 48: *Ratfuck, R.F.*...a damn, as: I don't give a *rat-fuck* what you do! **1980** D. Hamill *Stomping Ground* 245: Me, I couldn't give a hairy rat fuck.

4. a frenetic party, especially one marked by fashionable socializing.—often in phrase **Philadelphia rat fuck.**

1995 in *Vanity Fair* (Jan. 1996) 118: The only thing I went to was that Michael Fuchs HBO thing in Sag

Harbor arranged by Peggy Siegal, and I'd never go again. It was a real rat fuck. **1997** *Guardian* (London) (June 3) ("Feature") 18: The luxe preview of the Harriman goods...was "the ratfuck to end all ratfucks," attracting about as repellent a collection of people as can be imagined. **1997** *N.Y. Observer* (Oct. 6) 42: Glenn Bernbaum...throws a Philadelphia rat-f*#k for Joan Collins and her new autobiography. **1997** S. Quinn *The Party* 42: A huge cocktail party where you've invited everyone you've ever known and everyone you've ever owed....This sort of event has a name, coined by the late Marie Harriman, the dazzling second wife of statesman Averell Harriman. It is called a "Philadelphia rat fuck"—"P.R.F." or "rat fuck" for short.

rat-fuck *verb*

1. to botch; FUCK UP.

1966 Indiana Univ. Folklore Archives *Folk Speech:* Used as a verb meaning to botch in the worst possible way. *Rat-fuck.*

2. to outwit; trick.

1989 Chapple & Talbot *Burning Desires* 290: Gotta rat-fuck those guys, Missy! It's the only way. **1989** Leib *Fire Dream* 400: Poor rat-fucked back-stabbed...bastard.

rat fucker *noun* a hated or offensive person.—used as a term of abuse. [The 1914 quotation may be a chance coincidence.]

[**1914** J. London *Jacket* 19: It is so absurd, my dear Warden, to think that your rat-throttlers of guards can shake out of my brain the things that are clear and definite in my brain.] **1967** P. Welles *Babyhip* 61: "Scum," John mumbled. "Ratfucker, prick," George said. **1974** Bernstein & Woodward *All the President's Men* 135: For the first time, he considered the possibility that the President of the United States was the head ratfucker. **1987** Zeybel *Gunship* 138: Them dirty... Commie ratfuckers.

rat-fucking *noun* destructive activity; (*also*) a confusing situation. [The early examples are probably euphemisms; the 1930 euphemistic quotation at RAT-FUCK, definition 2a, may belong here instead.]

1928 Nason *Sgt. Eadie* 110 [refers to 1918]: This time to-morrow, Jake, I'll be with my own outfit and that's the only ray of sun in my black sky at present. All other troubles fade when I think of that. No more of this rat-kissing. **1928–29** Nason *White Slicker* 88: You know, I had a sergeancy clinched if we hadn't run into all this rat-kissing! **1944** in P. Smith *Letters from Father* 391: Rat fucking...at Hanover [New Hampshire] means the raiding of the students rooms on one floor by the students from another floor—the boys go in groups of eight or ten—turn everything upside down...even fire buckets of water are employed to make the wreck complete. **1972** in Bernstein & Woodward *All the President's Men* 132: Yes, political sabotage is associated with Segretti. I've heard a term for it, "ratfucking." *Ibid.* 138: Ratfucking? He had heard the term. It meant double-cross and, as used by the Nixon forces, it referred to infiltration of the Democrats.

RTFM *interjection Computers.* "read the fucking manual."

1988 *MacUser* (Mar.) 73: <RTFM> [heading of query and response column]. **1991** E. Raymond *New Hacker's Dictionary: RTFM*...Used by gurus to brush off questions they consider trivial or annoying. **1993** S. Lambert & W. Howe *Internet Basics* 472: *RTFM* (Read The Fine Manual) This acronym is often used when someone asks a simple question for the 100th time. The word "fine" is only one way to translate the acronym.

S

Words

skull fuck *verb* see MOUTH FUCK. Also as noun, an act of skull fucking.

[**1972** B. Rodgers *Queens' Vernacular* 34: BJ...knob job...skull job.] **1993** B. Moore *Lexicon of Cadet Language* 345: *Skull fuck*...the act of fucking a woman in the mouth. **1996** *Skull-fuck Me,* title of advertisement on Usenet newsgroup alt.sex.telephone (Aug. 23). **1997** *L.A. Weekly* (Oct. 24) 27: A woman advertising over the CB that she would "skullfuck" anyone listening for $50. **1998** *Review: "Sex Lies,"* review of pornographic movie on Usenet newsgroup rec.arts. movies.erotica (Apr. 27): Both ladies take turns sucking him off when he says he wants to skull-fuck them. **1998** N.Y. man: You ever hear the term *skull fuck* for a blowjob?

snafu *noun* [*s*ituation *n*ormal: *a*ll *f*ucked *u*p] Originally *Army.* a botched or confused situation, especially a military operation botched by incompetent planning or execution of orders.

1941 *American Notes & Queries* I (Sept. 4) 94: *Snafu*—situation normal [*sic*]. **1942** *Time* (June 15): The Army has a laconic term for chronic befuddlement: *snafu*, situation normal; all fouled up. **1943** in

219

Best from Yank 33: They worked hard and steadily, with a minimum of snafu. **1946** Haines *Command Decision* 11: But yesterday they [*sic*] was a SNAFU at the Quartermaster's and he run clean out of Spam. **1948** Cozzens *Guard of Honor* 184: It's a stupid damn snafu. **1953** Dibner *Deep Six* 23: He's chasing down another of your snafus. **1958** Hailey & Castle *Runway* 9: It would have to be a big show in Vancouver to justify this snafu. **1962** Shepard *Press Passes* 60: On the housing snafu, he displayed the statement of a leading Soviet lawyer [etc.]. **1963** Doulis *Path* 223: There's gonna be a big snafu....It means situation normal, all...fucked up. **1982** Del Vecchio *13th Valley* 1: It was one more snafu in a series of snafus. **1983** Groen & Groen *Huey* 105: John, your orders won't be coming in for two or three weeks. Some kind of a snafu. **1984** *N.Y. Post* (Aug. 2) 60: Bettors furious over Big A snafus.

snafu *adjective Army.*

1. hopelessly botched or confused. [Quotations refer to WWII.]

1942 in C.R. Bond & T. Anderson *Flying T. Diary* 183: What a SNAFU operation. **1943** Twist *Bombardier* (film): You'll be plenty snafu if Captain Oliver hears about this. **1943** Scott *God Is My Co-Pilot* 22: And so we began our airmail flying—slightly SNAFU, as we have learned to say from the gremlins in World War II. **1944** *Collier's* (Apr. 1) 21: This all sounds snafu. **1945** Chase *This Man's Navy* (film): This place is all mixed up, snafu. **1945** Scowley & Friel *513th Retrospect* (unpaged): Once on shore things began to go SNAFU. **1948** Murphy *To Hell and Back* 1: If the landing schedule had not gone snafu, we would have come ashore with the assault waves. **1953** Dodson *Away All Boats* 285: This is the most snafu beach I ever did see. **1959** Cochrell *Barren Beaches* 84: "Jesus," Willy said. "Sounds sort of snafu." **1970** Corrington *Bombardier* 53: The coffee splashed out, and the sugar fell into the eggs, and it was snafu.

2. mentally confused; crazy.

1975 Stanley *WWIII* 87: He's snafu, Sarge, snafu. I'm on your side. I swear it.

snafu *verb* Originally *Army*.

1. to bring into a state of great confusion; ruin through incompetence; botch; confuse; FUCK UP. Usually **snafued**, *adjective*.

1943 Wakeman *Shore Leave* 66: "There you go," the P-Boat pilot said. "Letting a lot of big sloppy words get you all snafued." **1944** Stiles *Big Bird* 74: It can snafu the works. **1948** Lay & Bartlett *Twelve O'Clock High!* 45: The warning order just came down....Snafu'd as usual. It says we're low group at *nine* thousand feet. **1970** Lincke *Jenny Was No Lady* 20: St. Jude, the patron saint of snafued ventures. **1979** in Raban *Old Glory* 348: He ain't going to allow some dumbhead bargeman to snafu the whole rest of his life for a can of Bud.

2. to blunder elaborately; FUCK UP.

1946 J.H. Burns *Gallery* 317: I snafu'd just like the rest of them. **1951** Leveridge *Walk on Water* 179 [refers to WWII]: Maybe the Army Post Office snafued again!

221

snafu *continued*

3. *Military.* to go wrong, especially to become botched or confused.

1957 McGivern *Against Tomorrow* 175: But when things snafu they start acting like a bunch of crazy women.

snefu *adjective* [situation *n*ormal: *e*verything *f*ucked *u*p; variant of SNAFU] *Military.* see SNAFU, *adjective.*

1942 in P. Jordan *Tunis Diary* 38: SNEFU, as an American officer said at dinner....Snefu means Situation Normal: Everything F—d Up.

sportfuck *verb* to engage in casual, indiscriminate copulation [with]. Also as noun.

1968 Paul Newman, in *Playboy* (July) 69: There was sport fucking. There was mercy fucking. **1989** Chapple & Talbot *Burning Desires* 124: I still sportfish. I no longer sportfuck. **1991** University professor, age 60: You'd think he'd have some better form of recreation than sportfucking some groupie on the lawn.... *Sportfuck* is a word I remember from Chicago, about 1959. **1991** Jenkins *Gotta Play Hurt* 43: Even enjoying a sport-fuck occasionally.

starfucker *noun* see CELEBRITY-FUCKER. Hence **star-fucking**.

1970 Grissim *Country Music* 259: In the rock and roll fifties they were called star-fuckers. In the acid rock world of the Sixties (and now Seventies) they were called groupies. **1972** *Playboy* (Aug.) 70: Groupies and star-fuckers abound and you certainly don't have to marry them, though a lot of poor fools do. **1978** C. Crawford *Mommie Dearest* 277: They were the "starfuckers," people who...would go to any lengths to have their own names associated with anyone famous. These people were not just fans, they had professions and services to sell. **1981** C. Nelson *Picked Bullets Up* 181: Because of his notoriety as a bisexual star-fucker. **1990** *Nation* (June 4) 796: Wenner,...inveterate starfucker (he once claimed to have started the magazine [*Rolling Stone*] in order to meet John Lennon). **1992** *Vanity Fair* (Nov.) 283: Some people might say he's starfucking. **1993** *New Republic* (Nov. 15) 34: The '60s turned even serious people into starfuckers.

T

Words

tarfu *noun & adjective* [*things are really fucked up*; suggested by SNAFU] Especially *U.S. Air Force*. see SNAFU.

   1944 Pyle *Brave Men* 212: The colonel had a coal-black Labrador retriever named Tarfu. That's one of those mystic military names which you'll have to get somebody else to explain to you. *ca***1944** in Valant *Aircraft Nose Art* 295: Tarfu. **1945** in *California Folklore Quarterly* V (1946) 387: TARFU. fouled up. **1948** Cozzens *Guard* 409: On the side of the plane's black nose, spiritedly sketched in dark red paint, was a cavorting skeleton who danced with a nude woman. Under it, in fancy letters, were the words: *Tarfu Tessie.* **1972** Davidson *Cut Off* 30: Tarfu, a word coined around the time of the Battle of the Bulge, was...the acronym for Things Are *Really* Fucked Up. *Ibid.:* In a Tarfu like this, nothing surprises me. **1995** Linguist, age 65: *Tarfu* is very common in E-mail messages.

tit-fuck *noun* an act of rubbing the penis between a woman's breasts; FRENCH FUCK. Also as verb. Also **titty-fuck**.

   [**1879** *Harlequin Prince Cherrytop* 4: Breast fuck, best fuck, Cherry's prick shall ne'er be in it.] **1972**

R.A. Wilson *Playboy's Book of Forbidden Words* 285: *Tit fuck* Insertion of the penis between a lady's breasts. **1975** *Ribald* (Sydney, Australia) (Sept. 18) 2: "Down in the valley something stirred." English-speaking people called it a tit-fuck. **1976** J. Vasco *Three-Hole Girl* 20: Lisa's jugs looked like they'd feel great if she pressed them down around his dick and let him tit-fuck her. **1984** R. Coover, in *Playboy* (Jan. 1985) 122: Safely closeted off in his rooms over the town saloon, tit-fucking the hero's wife. **1986** *Penthouse Letters* (Mar.) 89: In the soft version of Annie's flick, we lose a great tit-fucking scene. **1987** *Penthouse Letters* (Oct.) 27: Her scene...ends quite rightly with a tit-fuck. **1995** *Jennie's Happy Days,* on Usenet newsgroup alt.sex.stories: Moving his hips forward, he began to tit-fuck her. **1998** *Schizo* (#3) [back cover]: I heard Gary Coleman titty-fucked your DAD!

U
Words

unfuck *verb* to correct (a fault); fix (a problem); etc. Sometimes used with *up*.

1997 2nd Lieutenant, USMC: "Unfuck it, Corporal!"...That means "fix it," "make it not fucked up." Almost any kind of screw-up. **1998** *Re: How well do you know your "C" or "C++"?*, on Usenet newsgroup comp.lang.c (Oct. 28): You need to seriously unfuck up your testing interface.

un-fucking-believable *adjective* see under
-FUCKING-, *infix*.

W

Words

windfucker *noun* a type of kestrel; (*hence*) (used as a vague term of opprobrium).

1599 T. Nashe, in *Oxford English Dictionary:* The Kistrilles or windfuckers that filling themselues with winde, fly against the winde euermore. **1602** in *Oxford English Dictionary:* I tell you, my little windfuckers, had not a certaine melancholye ingendred with a nippinge dolour overshadowed the sunne shine of my mirthe, I had been I pre, sequor, one of your consorte. **1609** Ben Jonson *Epicene, or the Silent Woman* I.iv: Did you euer heare such a Wind-fucker, as this? *ca***1611** Chapman *Iliad* (preface): There is a certaine enuious Windfucker, that houers vp and downe, laboriously ingrossing al the air with his luxurious ambition. **1614** Beaumont & Fletcher *Wit Without Money* IV.i: Husbands for Whores and Bawdes, away you wind-suckers [*sic*].

Z

Words

zipless fuck *noun* an act of intercourse without an emotional connection; (*hence*) a person with whom one has such an act of intercourse.

1973 E. Jong *Fear of Flying* 11: My fantasy of the Zipless Fuck....Zipless because when you came together zippers fell away like petals. **1978** G. Vidal *Kalki* 79: Girls who feared flying tended to race blindly through zipless fucks. **1982** in *Playboy* (1983) 108: The zipless fuck is alive and well. Thirty percent of our female respondents say that they have asked strangers to have sex. **1992** in *Esquire* (Jan. 1993) 109: I stumbled through the early '80s and an address book filled with zipless fucks. **1994** *Village Voice* (N.Y.C.) (Aug. 2) 38: Ever dedicated to the zipless fuck, Patsy, the predator, exhibits the kind of natural cleavage that renders the Wonderbra irrelevant.